LIVING FAITH

YEARBOOK & HOME JOURNAL

Living Faith

Copyright © 2006 by Faith Inkubators, 423 South Main Street, Stillwater, MN, 55082

Toll Free Phone: 1-888-55FAITH, In Minnesota (651) 430-0762, Fax (651) 430-2377

Written and Compiled by Rich Melheim,
Nancy Gauche & the Faith Inkubators Writing Guild
Original Paintings and Theme Art by Dr. He Qi (*www.heqiarts.com*)
Verbatim Bible Songs for all of the quoted verses by the Faith Inkubators Music Guild
Book Design by Lookout Design (*www.lookoutdesign.com*) and Faith Inkubators
Ten Commandment Woodcuts by Tom Maakestad (*maak@winternet.com*)
Lord's Prayer Inks by James Reid (No, not that James Reid. The other one.)
Little People found and retreived from Rich's Toy Closet (circa 1966)
Cartoons by the Occasionally Most Reverend Rich Melheim
Cartoon Inking by the Sometimes Reverent Erin DeBoer-Moran
International Director of H2H Ministries Monty Lysne
Production Direction by Jedi Master Ben Dolmar
Quotations from the FINK Quotelopedia

90 lessons corresponding to the themes
from the Living Journals, PowerPoint™ presentations supporting
each lesson, music for each Bible verse, and a myriad of additional resources
are included in a membership to the Head to the Heart confirmation system.
Learn more about this adolescent ministry system at *www.faithink.com*

CIP

ISBN 0-9785621-1-9

TABLE OF CONTENTS

神 God

愛 love

家庭

family

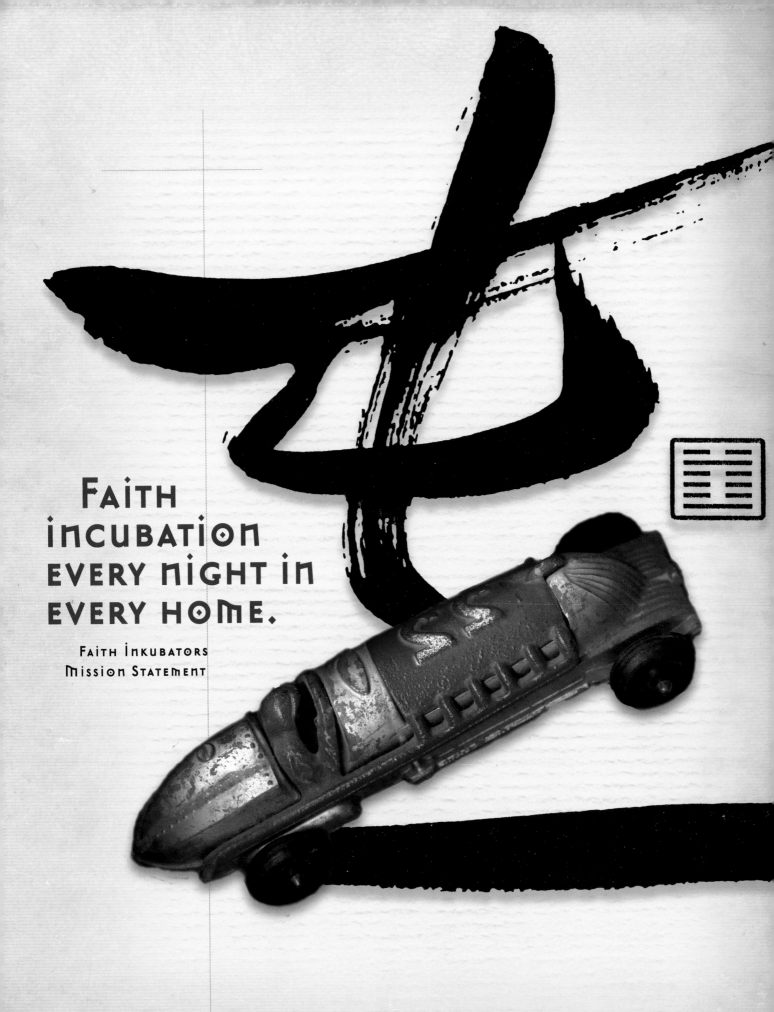

Faith incubation every night in every home.

Faith Inkubators
Mission Statement

Wouldn't it be fun to be able to look back on every single day of your adolescent journey and know what you were thinking?

THIS LIVING JOURNAL IS DESIGNED TO DO JUST THAT. IT CAN'T DO THE WORK FOR YOU, BUT IF YOU TAKE A FEW MINUTES TONIGHT AND EVERY NIGHT, YOU HOLD IN YOUR HANDS A TOOL THAT WILL HELP YOU SEE WHAT YOU WERE GOING THROUGH, WHAT YOU WERE THINKING, WHAT YOUR FRIENDS WERE UP TO, AND HOW GOD HELPED YOU ALONG THE WAY—EVERY DAY—ON YOUR JOURNEY TO BECOMING AN ADULT.

THE LIVING JOURNAL

IT MAY NOT SEEM LIKE A BIG DEAL RIGHT NOW, BUT THE NEXT FEW YEARS ARE GOING TO BE FILLED WITH LIFE-ALTERING CHANGES. YOUR FRIENDS, YOUR BODY, YOUR SCHOOL, YOUR FAMILY, YOUR SHOE SIZE AND YOUR BRAINS—ALL OF THESE ARE IN TRANSITION. AND TRANSITIONS CAN CAUSE CHAOS.

THE SYMBOL FOR CHAOS (LEFT) MEANS BOTH CHALLENGE AND OPPORTUNITY. THE YEARS AHEAD ARE GOING TO BE FILLED WITH BOTH. THAT'S A GUARANTEE. WOULDN'T IT BE FUN—AND VALUABLE—TO HAVE A RECORD OF IT ALL? YOU CAN IF YOU WANT TO. IT'S IN YOUR HANDS.

RIGHT NOW.

DURING EACH WEEK OF YOUR FAITH JOURNEY, WE ARE HONORED TO FEATURE THE ARTWORK OF DR. HE QI.

WWW.HEQIARTS.COM

FAITH INKUBATORS

THE NIGHTLY JOURNAL

If you really want to have fun, keep your family communicating, and grow in your understanding of life, yourself, and God, journaling can be a powerful tool. This living yearbook—designed around the big themes of your teen years—will help you clarify thoughts, gain insight into problems, and train yourself to see how and where God is active in your life. Simply record a sentence or two each night on the lines provided. If you use this tool regularly, you will one day be able to look back on your adolescent faith journey and see where you have been, who you have become, and where God has taken you.

THE HOME HUDDLE

The most important part of all this happens at home in a simple, five-step process which the good folks at Faith Inkubators like to call a Home Huddle (or the "FINK Five"). Here's how it works: Whoever is going to bed first in your house calls "Huddle Up!" Everyone must drop what they're doing, turn off the television and computer, put down their homework, and gather in a room of the convener's choice. Then take turns going through these five simple steps:

THE FINK FIVE

FIVE STEPS TO KEEPING YOUR FAMILY TOGETHER IN A WORLD THAT CAN TEAR YOU APART

TRY THESE HAND MOTIONS
TO HELP YOU REMEMBER THE

THE FINK FIVE STEPS

1. THUMBS UP/THUMBS DOWN *(HIGHS & LOWS)*; 2. POINT TO THE SKY *(READ THE ASSIGNED BIBLE VERSE)*; 3. CROSS YOUR FINGERS *(T FOR TALK)*; 4. THUMB TO RING *(PRAYER HAS A PROMISE, TOO!)*; 5. LITTLE FINGER UP *(SOMETIMES THE BIGGEST BLESSINGS COME FROM THE SMALLEST PLACES)*.

1. **SHARE** HIGHS & LOWS OF THE DAY

2. **READ** AND HIGHLIGHT THE VERSE OF THE NIGHT IN YOUR BIBLES

3. **TALK** ABOUT HOW TODAY'S VERSE RELATES TO YOUR HIGHS & LOWS

4. **PRAY** FOR YOUR HIGHS & LOWS, FOR YOUR FAMILY, AND FOR THE WORLD

5. **BLESS** ONE ANOTHER USING THE WEEKLY BLESSING PROVIDED

FINK (fîngk)-n. 1.*Slang* term for Faith Inkubators (circa 1993), a fun-loving Christian education systems think tank and international learning organization committed to creating family-centered ministry models, training, and resources that help parents incubate faith every night in every home and have a blast while doing it.

New FINKlinks Online

There are a pile of surprises and fun new theme-related resources awaiting you online each night to enrich your Home Huddle experience. You can play the FINK*mania* Quiz Bowl live with family and friends. Listen to and learn the week's key Bible verse in song (NRSV verbatim) and purchase it if you wish to carry it along with you all week. Nightly devotions are online free for those wishing to dig deeper into each verse. You can also view and purchase signed artist proofs of each theme's artwork by China's most amazing contemporary Christian artist, He Qi. Simply go to *www.faithink.com* and enter the FINK*link* code listed for each specific theme.

At Church

For churches using Faith Inkubators' Head to the Heart confirmation system, each theme in this book is designed to connect what you're learning at church with your nightly family conversations. You will unveil a key Bible concept in art, song, cartoons, skits, and Bible Time at church. Small groups will then use the first six pages of each lesson in this book to review all they have covered and do their own HIGHS & LOWS. Once the church has helped kick off the theme, youth will bring it on home using this book to share with their families what they've learned. The theme then continues every night for the next one or two weeks in Home Huddles with the other Bible verses provided.

Beginning of the Year

Use the next few pages for pictures of each member of your small group, along with a geeky photo of your small group Guide when they were your age. Record and share the information requested as a way to get to know your new friends. Then hop to the last page of this book and play OPERATION SPYGLASS to get to know the journal. Add photos of small group events on the last pages of the book as the year goes by. At the end of the year, take one last picture of your small group and use the final pages to summarize where you've been. You may look back on this book one day and see just how much fun it was to go through the CHAOS with such awesome friends and your awesome God!

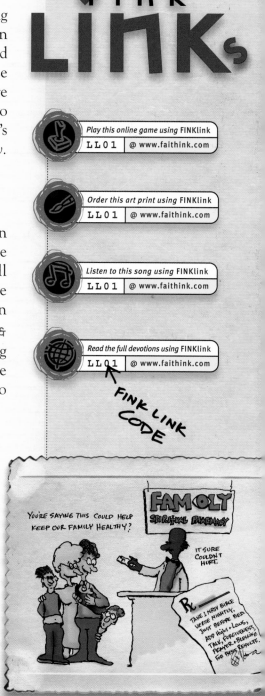

Play this online game using FINKlink
LL01 @ www.faithink.com

Order this art print using FINKlink
LL01 @ www.faithink.com

Listen to this song using FINKlink
LL01 @ www.faithink.com

Read the full devotions using FINKlink
LL01 @ www.faithink.com

FINK LINK CODE

YOU'RE SAYING THIS COULD HELP KEEP OUR FAMILY HEALTHY?

FAMILY SPIRITUAL PHARMACY

IT SURE COULDN'T HURT.

RX
TAKE 1 NRSV BIBLE VERSE NIGHTLY, JUST BEFORE BED. ADD HIGHS + LOWS, TALK, FORGIVENESS, PRAYER + BLESSING FOR BEST RESULTS.

A Moment in TIME

This Book Belongs To:

Take a moment to personalize this book. Include information about your family, friends and small group at church.

Name

Age & Grade   Today's Date

Phone   Email/IM

Birthdate   Baptism Day

My family includes (names and ages)

My three best friends are...

My favorite food is,,,

My favorite band is...

My favorite activities are...

Looking Ahead

Confirmation Day

Drivers' Licence Day

Graduation Day

When I grow up, I can hardly wait to...

One great thing I'd like to do with my life for the world is...

This is Me

This is My Family

PASTE
ANCIENT
SCHOOL PHOTO
OF YOUR SMALL
GROUP
GUIDE
WHEN
THEY WERE
YOUR AGE
HERE

Name

Phone

Email/IM

Birthday

One thing about me...

My Small Group Guide

PASTE

SCHOOL

PHOTO

HERE

Name

Phone

Email/IM

Birthday

One thing about me...

My Small Group Friend

PASTE

SCHOOL

PHOTO

HERE

Name

Phone

Email/IM

Birthday

One thing about me...

Another Friend

PASTE

SCHOOL

PHOTO

HERE

Name

Phone

Email/IM

Birthday

One thing about me...

One More Friend

PASTE

SCHOOL

PHOTO

HERE

Name

Phone

Email/IM

Birthday

One thing about me...

Yet Another Friend

PASTE

SCHOOL

PHOTO

HERE

Name

Phone

Email/IM

Birthday

One thing about me...

Even One More Friend

The Ten Commandments

1. Gods and Idols
2. Name in Vain
3. Remember the Sabbath
4. Honoring Parents
5. Killing
6. Adultery
7. Stealing
8. False Witness
9. Coveting
10. Ten Commandments Review

"The Ten Commandments"   Dr. He Qi. Order prints at www.heqiarts.com

"I am the Lord your God, who brought you out of the

land of Egypt, out of the house of slavery; you shall

have no other gods before me. You shall not make for

yourself an idol, whether in the form of anything that

is in heaven above, or that is on the earth beneath,

or that is in the water under the earth.

— Exodus 20:2-4

Listen to this song using FINKlink
LF01 | @ www.faithink.com

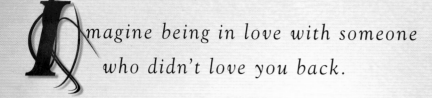

Imagine being in love with someone who didn't love you back.

Imagine giving your time, affection, gifts, and total attention to someone who took them all without returning the love or even saying thanks. How long could a one-sided relationship like that last? How long would you keep giving, loving, and living in the hope that your love might one day be returned?

Now imagine watching the person you love more than anyone in the world fall in love with someone else. Imagine seeing them running around with their new love and a bad crowd, doing foolish and dangerous things that could lead to their harm or death. Wouldn't you just want to shake them and tell them to straighten up?

Maybe that's how God feels, lavishing love on us and not getting much in return. Giving gracious gifts and miracle moments, brilliant sunrises and beautiful sunsets to people who don't even acknowledge the giver. Watching us mess around with earthly idols. Watching us do destructive things to the planet. Watching us use people and value things, rather than using things and valuing people.

In Old Testament times, God's prophets often warned Israel that the God who created them was like a jealous lover. This lover didn't want them chasing around with any other loves—any other gods. In the First Commandment, God made it perfectly clear: We are to fear, love, and trust the one true God above everything else.

Why? Maybe God knows something we don't know. All other gods are false and will lead us only to emptiness and frustration. The idols of our day promise life but deliver death. The lover of our souls only wants the best for us, and knows the best will only come when we surrender our idols and focus our love, attention, and lives on the giver of all gifts.

IDOLS TODAY?

Are there idols today? You bet! Idols aren't just made of wood and stone. An idol can be anything that pushes God out of first place in your life—anything that gets more time and attention than your creator.

The First Commandment doesn't say you can't value sports, grades, relationships, or your iPod. These can all be good in their place. But God does say "you shall have no other gods before me." Nothing is to be in front of God.

Take a look at your calendar. Is there anything crowding out God right now? What will you do about it?

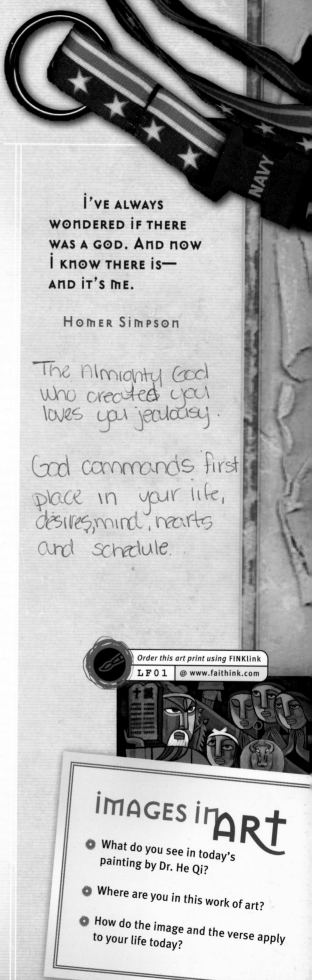

I'VE ALWAYS WONDERED IF THERE WAS A GOD. AND NOW I KNOW THERE IS— AND IT'S ME.

HOMER SIMPSON

The Almighty God who created you loves you jealousy.

God commands first place in your life, desires, mind, hearts and schedule.

Order this art print using FINKlink
LF01 @ www.faithink.com

IMAGES IN ART

- What do you see in today's painting by Dr. He Qi?
- Where are you in this work of art?
- How do the image and the verse apply to your life today?

So What Does This Mean?

So God says "There's a difference between being God's and being gods" and then he tells me to take a hike and think about it.

YOU SHALL HAVE NO OTHER GODS

Prayer

TRUE GOD, YOU LOVE ME MORE THAN I CAN EVER KNOW. YOU LISTEN. YOU PROVIDE. YOU PROTECT. I SEEM TO SPEND MUCH OF MY TIME APART FROM YOU. I SEEM TO SPEND MY ENERGY RUNNING IN EVERY DIRECTION BUT TO YOU. I SEEM TO GIVE YOU LEFTOVERS. WHAT CAN I SAY?

I DON'T WANT TO PUT ANYTHING IN FRONT OF YOU. CAN YOU HELP ME?

AMEN.

So What?

Here's a way to help you recognize idols in your life. Ask yourself:

- Where do you spend most of your free time?

- Where do you spend most of your money?

- Where do you go for comfort when you have problems?

- What can't you live without?

Most things in life are neutral. They don't start out to be gods to us. Relationships, work, popularity, entertainment, sports, food - all of these are actually gifts from God. However, if we find our security in them and give them our time, energy, and attention above God, they become the objects of our worship. Life gets out of line. If they crowd out God, even good things become idols.

Bible Time

Read and highlight the following, writing "No Other Gods" in the margin.

Exodus 20:2-4	Isaiah 44:6
Matthew 6:19-21	Mark 12:28-31
John 10:30	I John 5:21

Role Play

A teen spends five hours a night on the internet chatting, playing games, and instant messaging. Her homework, chores, family time, and sleep suffer. Her grades slip because she isn't handing in her assignments. She doesn't even have five minutes a night to do *Highs & Lows* with her family. Sunday morning arrives and she is too tired to go to church. You are her parent. What do you say?

Questions to Ponder

1. Where do you spend most of your extra:

   Time   Money   Energy

2. When do good things (like sports, relationships, grades) become gods? How can you keep this from happening?

3. Why do you think God gave the "no other gods" command first?

   I He thinks its the most important

Small Group
SHARE, READ, TALK, PRAY, BLESS

1. SHARE your highs and lows of the week one-on-one with another person. Listen carefully and record your friend's thoughts in the space below. Then return to small group and share your friend's highs and lows.

MY HIGHS + LOWS THIS WEEK WERE:

....

MY FRIEND'S HIGHS + LOWS THIS WEEK WERE:

....

2. READ and highlight the theme verse in your Bibles. Circle key words and learn the verse in song if time permits.

3. TALK about how today's verse relates to your highs and lows. Review the art for today, the Quiz Bowl questions, the terms, and the cartoons. Then write a sentence on each of the following:

ONE NEW THING I LEARNED TODAY:

....

ONE THING I ALREADY KNEW THAT IS WORTH REPEATING:

....

ONE THING I WOULD LIKE TO KNOW MORE ABOUT:

....

4. PRAY for one another, praising and thanking God for your highs, and asking God to be with you in your lows. Include your friend's highs and lows in your prayers.

A PRAISING PRAYER: ....

A THANKING PRAYER: ....

AN ASKING PRAYER: ....

5. BLESS one another using the blessing of the week. (right) Mark each person with the sign of the cross as you bless them.

THIS WEEK'S BLESSING
(NAME), CHILD OF
GOD, MAY THE LORD BE
FIRST IN YOUR HEART AND
MIND THIS DAY.

THE HOME HUDDLE JOURNAL
SHARE, READ, TALK, PRAY, BLESS

Read the full devotions using FINKlink
LF01 | @ www.faithink.com

DAY #1

TODAY'S BIBLE VERSE:

EXODUS 20:2-3

I am the Lord your God, who brought you out of the land of Egypt, out of the house of slavery; you shall have no other gods before me.

MY HIGH TODAY WAS:

MY LOW TODAY WAS:

MY PRAYER TODAY IS:

DAY #2

TODAY'S BIBLE VERSE:

EXODUS 20:4

You shall not make for yourself an idol, whether in the form of anything that is in heaven above, or that is on the earth beneath, or that is in the water under the earth.

MY HIGH TODAY WAS:

MY LOW TODAY WAS:

MY PRAYER TODAY IS:

DAY #3

TODAY'S BIBLE VERSE:

EXODUS 20:5A

You shall not bow down to them or worship them...

MY HIGH TODAY WAS:

MY LOW TODAY WAS:

MY PRAYER TODAY IS:

my HIGH today was: _____

my LOW today was: _____

my PRAYER today is: _____

_____

_____

DAY #4

TODAY'S BIBLE VERSE:

Matthew 6:21

For where your treasure is, there your heart will be also.

---

my HIGH today was: _____

my LOW today was: _____

my PRAYER today is: _____

_____

DAY #5

TODAY'S BIBLE VERSE:

i john 5:21

Little children, keep yourselves from idols.

---

my HIGH today was: _____

my LOW today was: _____

my PRAYER today is: _____

_____

DAY #6

TODAY'S BIBLE VERSE:

Isaiah 44:6

I am the first and I am the last; besides me there is no god.

---

my HIGHEST HIGH this week was: _____

my LOWEST LOW this week was: _____

my PRAYER for next week is: _____

_____

DAY #7

THIS WEEK'S BLESSING

(NAME), CHILD OF GOD, MAY THE LORD BE FIRST IN YOUR HEART AND MIND THIS DAY.

THE HOME HUDDLE JOURNAL
SHARE, READ, TALK, PRAY, BLESS

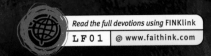

Read the full devotions using FINKlink
LF01 @ www.faithink.com

DAY #1

TODAY'S BIBLE VERSE:

ROMANS 11:33

O the depth of the riches and wisdom and knowledge of God! How unsearchable are his judgements and how inscrutable his ways!

MY **HIGH** TODAY WAS:

MY **LOW** TODAY WAS:

MY **PRAYER** TODAY IS:

DAY #2

TODAY'S BIBLE VERSE:

EXODUS 32:1

The people gathered around Aaron, and said to him, "Come, make gods for us, who shall go before us; as for this Moses, the man who brought us up out of the land of Egypt, we do not know what has become of him."

MY **HIGH** TODAY WAS:

MY **LOW** TODAY WAS:

MY **PRAYER** TODAY IS:

DAY #3

TODAY'S BIBLE VERSE:

PROVERBS 1:7

The fear of the Lord is the beginning of knowledge.

MY **HIGH** TODAY WAS:

MY **LOW** TODAY WAS:

MY **PRAYER** TODAY IS:

1. **SHARE** HIGHS & LOWS OF THE DAY.

2. **READ** AND HIGHLIGHT THE VERSE OF THE DAY IN YOUR BIBLES.

3. **TALK** ABOUT HOW TODAY'S VERSE RELATES TO YOUR HIGHS & LOWS.

4. **PRAY** FOR YOUR HIGHS & LOWS, FOR YOUR FAMILY AND FOR THE WORLD.

5. **BLESS** ONE ANOTHER USING THIS WEEK'S BLESSING (ON THE PREVIOUS PAGE).

MY HIGH TODAY WAS:

MY LOW TODAY WAS:

MY PRAYER TODAY IS:

DAY #4

TODAY'S BIBLE VERSE:

MARK 12:30

You shall love the Lord your God with all your heart, and with all your soul, and with all your mind, and with all your strength.

MY HIGH TODAY WAS:

MY LOW TODAY WAS:

MY PRAYER TODAY IS:

DAY #5

TODAY'S BIBLE VERSE:

PROVERBS 3:5-6

Trust in the Lord with all your heart, and do not rely on your own insight. In all your ways acknowledge him, and he will make straight your paths.

MY HIGH TODAY WAS:

MY LOW TODAY WAS:

MY PRAYER TODAY IS:

DAY #6

TODAY'S BIBLE VERSE:

ISAIAH 40:28

The Lord is the everlasting God, the Creator of the ends of the earth. He does not faint or grow weary; his understanding is unsearchable.

THEME IN REVIEW

And the people
bowed and prayed

to the neon god
they'd made.

Paul Simon

DAY #7

MY FAVORITE VERSE
FROM THE THEME WAS:

LOOKING BACK ON THESE TWO WEEKS, MY HIGHEST HIGH WAS:

MY LOWEST LOW THESE PAST WEEKS WAS:

ONE WAY GOD ANSWERED MY PRAYERS WAS:

ONE WAY GOD MIGHT USE ME AS A SACRED AGENT
TO ANSWER THESE PRAYERS:

FAMILY COVENANT

We have shared *Highs & Lows* this week, read and highlighted the verses assigned in our Bibles, talked about our lives, prayed for one another's highs and lows, and blessed one another.

....

Parent's Signature   Teen's Signature   Date

THE FINKMANIA QUIZBOWL

QUESTION 1:

The First Commandments is

(A) "I am the Lord, your God, you shall have no other gods before me,"

(B) "Do unto others as you would have them do unto you,"

(C) "Love your neighbor as yourself,"

(D) "Get more"

QUESTION 2:

God gave the Ten Commandments to:

(A) Moses in Egypt,

(B) Moses on Mt. Sinai after Israel's escape from Egypt,

(C) Joshua in Jerusalem,

(D) Ashton Kutcher in a dream

QUESTION 3:

What "gods" do people worship above the one true God today?:

(A) Movie stars and sports stars,

(B) Money and power,

(C) Sex and fashion,

(D) All of the above

QUESTION 4:

Why is the Zodiac a poor place to put your trust?:

(A) The Zodiac is based on stars, which are only hot balls of gas,

(B) It would be wiser to place your trust in the Creator of the stars rather than to rely on the intelligence of hot balls of gas,

(C) Stars can't forgive your sins,

(D) All of the above

QUESTION 5:

Why is God sometimes called "jealous" in the Bible?:

(A) God is like a jealous lover who can't stand it when we flirt around with other gods,

(B) God's jealous love is like a devouring fire,

(C) The Bible says God's name is jealous,

(D) All of the above and then some

QUESTION 6:

After the First Commandment, God said, "You shall not make for yourself...":

(A) An American Idol,

(B) An idol,

(C) A graven image,

(D) B or C, depending on your Bible translation

QUESTION 7:

What makes something a true "god" or idol?

(A) A diploma from God School,

(B) A recording contract from Arista Records,

(C) People trust it and turn to it in time of need,

(D) The paparazzi

QUESTION 8:

What name did God reveal to Moses on the mountain?:

(A) Allah (the God),

(B) Yahweh (I Am),

(C) Yahwuz (I wuz),

(D) Ya Sure (You Betcha)

QUESTION 9:

Money becomes a "god" when:

(A) We try to hoard it,

(B) It becomes our life's goal,

(C) We look to it in times of trouble,

(D) All of the above

FINKMANIA FINAL QUESTION:

Exodus 20:2-3, the First Commandment, tells us:

(A) "I am the Lord, your God,"

(B) "I brought you out of the land of Egypt, out of the house of slavery,"

(C) "You shall have no other gods before me,"

(D) All of the above

 Play this online game using FINKlink
LF01 | @ www.faithink.com

THE WEAKEST FINK

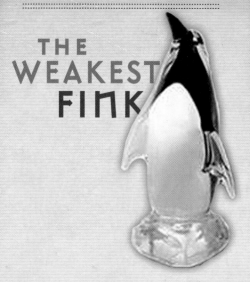

THERE ARE TWO CENTRAL FACTS IN LIFE ONE MUST COME TO TERMS WITH: 1) THERE IS A GOD; AND 2) IT AIN'T YOU.

RICH MELHEIM

TERMS
WRITE A DEFINITION BELOW.

GOD

IDOL

LOVE

PRIORITIES

TEN COMMANDMENTS

 **FAITH** INKUBATORS

Name In Vain

"Balaam and His Donkey" Dr. He Qi: Order prints at www.heqiarts.com

"YOU SHALL NOT MAKE WRONGFUL USE OF THE NAME OF THE

LORD YOUR GOD, FOR THE LORD WILL NOT ACQUIT ANYONE

WHO MISUSES HIS NAME..."

— EXODUS 20:7

 Listen to this song using FINKlink
LF02 @ www.faithink.com

"**O**h, my God," said Carol as she noticed the jacket sale in the newspaper. Her mother looked up and smiled, "Go ahead and finish that prayer."

"What?" asked the girl.

"I just heard you call God," said her mom. "Go ahead and finish the prayer."

"I didn't mean anything by it," said Carol. "It's just a word."

"That's the problem," continued her mother. "God's name is special. When we use God's name, we are entering into sacred space. God's name shouldn't be just a word. Isn't there a commandment about something like that?"

"Don't you think you are overreacting just a little?" asked Carol.

Her mother left the room. About a half hour later, Carol smelled fresh cookies baking and heard her mother call her name.

"Yes, mom?" No reply. Again she heard her mother speak her name. "What do you want?" Again, no reply. A third time Carol heard her name. She followed the aroma of the cookies down the stairs and into the kitchen. Her mother sat with a cup of coffee next to a plate of huge oatmeal raisen cookies.

"What's up?" Carol asked. "What do you want?"

"Nothing."

"You called my name three times."

"Oh, I didn't mean anything by it," her mother smiled. "It's just a word."

What's in a Name?

Plenty. Names matter. Imagine how you would feel if your friends called you "Dog Poop" every time they saw you. How would you react? How would it shape what other people thought of you and how you saw yourself over time?

Imagine winning a contest for a small speaking part in a movie to be shot in your town. You have the opportunity to meet a number of famous film stars. What will you call them when you meet them? Will you use their first names? Will you add a Mr. or Miss when addressing them? Why might you add a title of reverence or respect? You do it because names and titles matter.

Now imagine being invited to dinner at Buckingham Palace. You are told you will have an opportunity to meet the Queen of England. "Please address her as 'Your Majesty,'" says an aide. Will you disregard the instructions and call her "queenie?" Will you call her by her first name? No. Why? Whether you like her politics or not, you would use the proper, dignified title out of respect for the office. How you address someone says something about them—and about you.

Names are serious business. Names matter.

GARBAGE IN,
GARBAGE OUT.

COMPUTER LOGIC

Order this art print using FINKlink
LF02 @ www.faithink.com

IMAGES IN ART

- What do you see in today's painting by Dr. He Qi?

- Where are you in this work of art?

- How do the image and the verse apply to your life today?

So What Does This Mean?

You Shall Not Take God's Name in Vain

Prayer

Dear God, your name is holy. I don't always treat it that way, but I want my language to please you. Words are powerful. May the words of my mouth and the meditation of my heart always be pleasing to you.

Amen.

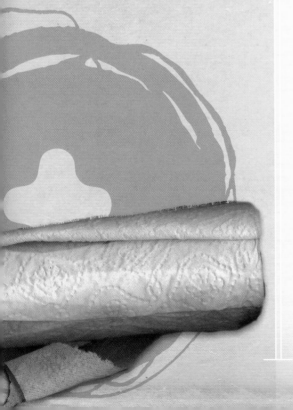

So What?

The almighty, amazing, awesome God of the universe is worthy of much more respect than any movie star or queen. God's name certainly deserves honor, yet God's name has come to mean next to nothing in our society. Most people don't think twice about using God's name as a fill word. It's "God this" and "God that" and "Oh, my God!" When confronted with it, they say it doesn't matter. It is just a phrase. The name is just a word. But that is precisely the point! God's name does mean something. God's name does matter. For the holy name of God to be lowered to the status of a common fill word just isn't right. Using God's name in vain dishonors God, disrespects who God is, and says something about you. God commands that you don't misuse the holiest name of all.

So, what are you going to do about it?

Bible Time

Read and highlight Exodus 20:7, writing "Honor God's Name" in the margin. Next, read the following verses. What do each say about proper and improper uses of God's name?

Psalm 141:2

Hosea 4:2-3

Malachi 4:2

Matthew 5:34-37

Role Play

A friend swears a lot. She says it's no big deal. What might you say or do to show how her language offends you and disrespects God without looking judgmental?

Questions to Ponder

1. In Bible times, people didn't even dare whisper the name of God out loud for fear of breaking this commandment. Today "God" is simply a fill word in our conversations. Do you think God cares how we use God's name? Why or why not?

2. How do cursing and swearing relate to respect and disrespect?

3. Where and with whom are you most likely to use "garbage" language? How can you start to change this situation?

Small Group
SHARE, READ, TALK, PRAY, BLESS

1. **S H A R E** your highs and lows of the week one-on-one with another person. Listen carefully and record your friend's thoughts in the space below. Then return to small group and share your friend's highs and lows.

> **MY HIGHS + LOWS THIS WEEK WERE:**
>
> ....
>
> **MY FRIEND'S HIGHS + LOWS THIS WEEK WERE:**
>
> ....

2. **R E A D** and highlight the theme verse in your Bibles. Circle key words and learn the verse in song if time permits.

3. **T A L K** about how today's verse relates to your highs and lows. Review the art for today, the Quiz Bowl questions, the terms, and the cartoons. Then write a sentence on each of the following:

> **ONE NEW THING I LEARNED TODAY:**
>
> ....
>
> **ONE THING I ALREADY KNEW THAT IS WORTH REPEATING:**
>
> ....
>
> **ONE THING I WOULD LIKE TO KNOW MORE ABOUT:**
>
> ....

4. **P R A Y** for one another, praising and thanking God for your highs, and asking God to be with you in your lows. Include your friend's highs and lows in your prayers.

> **A PRAISING PRAYER:** ....
>
> **A THANKING PRAYER:** ....
>
> **AN ASKING PRAYER:** ....

5. **B L E S S** one another using the blessing of the week. (right) Mark each person with the sign of the cross as you bless them.

THIS WEEK'S BLESSING
(NAME), CHILD OF GOD,
MAY THE BEAUTY AND GRACE
OF GOD'S SPIRIT BE REFLECT-
ED IN YOUR HEART AND ON
YOUR LIPS THIS DAY. AMEN.

THE HOME HUDDLE jOURNAL

SHARE, READ, tALK, PRAY, BLESS

Read the full devotions using FINKlink

LF02 | @ www.faithink.com

DAY #1

tODAY'S BiBLE VERSE:

EXODUS 20:7

You shall not make wrongful use of the name of the Lord your God, for the Lord will not acquit anyone who misuses his name.

MY **HiGH** tODAY WAS:

MY **LOW** tODAY WAS:

MY **PRAYER** tODAY iS:

DAY #2

tODAY'S BiBLE VERSE:

PSALM 102:8

All day long my enemies taunt me; those who deride me use my name for a curse.

MY **HiGH** tODAY WAS:

MY **LOW** tODAY WAS:

MY **PRAYER** tODAY iS:

DAY #3

tODAY'S BiBLE VERSE:

MALACHi 4:2A

But for you who revere my name the sun of righteousness shall rise; with healing in its wings.

MY **HiGH** tODAY WAS:

MY **LOW** tODAY WAS:

MY **PRAYER** tODAY iS:

my HIGH today was: ....

my LOW today was: ....

my PRAYER today is: ....

....

today's bible verse:

job 2:9

Then his (Job's) wife said to him, "Do you still persist in your integrity? Curse God, and die."

---

my HIGH today was: ....

my LOW today was: ....

my PRAYER today is: ....

....

DAY #5

today's bible verse:

Matthew 5:34-35

Do not swear at all, either by heaven, for it is the throne of God, or by the earth, for it is his footstool, or by Jerusalem, for it is the city of the great King.

---

my HIGH today was: ....

my LOW today was: ....

my PRAYER today is: ....

....

DAY #6

today's bible verse:

Matthew 5:36-37

And do not swear by your head, for you cannot make one hair white or black. Let your word be 'Yes, Yes' or 'No, No'; anything more than this comes from the evil one.

---

my HIGHEST HIGH this week was: ....

my LOWEST LOW this week was: ....

my PRAYER for next week is: ....

....

DAY #7

this week's blessing

(NAME), child of God, may the beauty and grace of God's Spirit be reflected in your heart and on your lips this day. Amen.

THE HOME HUDDLE JOURNAL
SHARE, READ, TALK, PRAY, BLESS

Read the full devotions using FINKlink
LF02 | @ www.faithink.com

DAY #1

TODAY'S BIBLE VERSE:

Psalm 104:33

I will sing to the Lord as long as I live; I will sing praise to my God while I have being.

MY HIGH TODAY WAS:

MY LOW TODAY WAS:

MY PRAYER TODAY IS:

DAY #2

TODAY'S BIBLE VERSE:

Psalm 141:2

Let my prayers be counted as incense before you, and the lifting up of my hands as an evening sacrifice.

MY HIGH TODAY WAS:

MY LOW TODAY WAS:

MY PRAYER TODAY IS:

DAY #3

TODAY'S BIBLE VERSE:

Proverbs 15:2

The tongue of the wise dispenses knowledge, but the mouths of fools pour out folly.

MY HIGH TODAY WAS:

MY LOW TODAY WAS:

MY PRAYER TODAY IS:

PLEASE REMOVE STAIN ↓

1. SHARE HIGHS & LOWS OF THE DAY.

2. READ AND HIGHLIGHT THE VERSE OF THE DAY IN YOUR BIBLES.

3. TALK ABOUT HOW TODAY'S VERSE RELATES TO YOUR HIGHS & LOWS.

4. PRAY FOR YOUR HIGHS & LOWS, FOR YOUR FAMILY AND FOR THE WORLD.

5. BLESS ONE ANOTHER USING THIS WEEK'S BLESSING (ON THE PREVIOUS PAGE).

MY HIGH TODAY WAS:

MY LOW TODAY WAS:

MY PRAYER TODAY IS:

DAY #4

TODAY'S BIBLE VERSE:

PROVERBS 26:2

Like a sparrow in its flitting, like a swallow in its flying, an undeserved curse goes nowhere.

MY HIGH TODAY WAS:

MY LOW TODAY WAS:

MY PRAYER TODAY IS:

DAY #5

TODAY'S BIBLE VERSE:

HOSEA 4:2-3

Swearing, lying, and murder, and stealing and adultery break out; bloodshed follows bloodshed. Therefore the land mourns, and all who live in it languish; together with the wild animals and the birds of the air, even the fish of the sea are perishing.

MY HIGH TODAY WAS:

MY LOW TODAY WAS:

MY PRAYER TODAY IS:

DAY #6

TODAY'S BIBLE VERSE:

PSALM 113:3

From the rising of the sun to its setting the name of the Lord is to be praised.

S|M|T|W|TH|F|S
THEME iN REViEW

Cursing is a sign
of either an uneducated
person with a limited
vocabulary, an educated
person with limited intelligence, or an intelligent
person with limited class.

Rich Melheim

DAY #7

MY FAVORITE VERSE
FROM THE THEME WAS:

....
....
....
....
....
....

First Class

LOOKING BACK ON THESE TWO WEEKS, MY HIGHEST **HIGH** WAS:

....

MY LOWEST **LOW** THESE PAST WEEKS WAS:

....

ONE WAY GOD ANSWERED MY **PRAYERS** WAS:

....

ONE WAY GOD MIGHT USE ME AS A **SACRED AGENT**
TO ANSWER THESE PRAYERS:

....

....

FAMILY COVENANT

We have shared *Highs & Lows* this week, read and highlighted the verses assigned in our Bibles,
talked about our lives, prayed for one another's highs and lows, and blessed one another.

....
Parent's Signature   Teen's Signature   Date

THE FINKMANIA QUIZBOWL

THE WEAKEST FINK

QUESTION 1:

The Second Commandment is

(A) "You shall not make for yourself an idol,"

(B) "You shall not make wrongful use of the name of the Lord your God,"

(C) "You shall not kill,"

(D) A or B, depending on whether you order them like a Catholic and Lutheran or like most other Protestants

QUESTION 2:

Wrongful use of God's name includes:

(A) Cursing,

(B) Cursing and swearing,

(C) Cursing, swearing, lying and deceiving,

(D) Blessing

QUESTION 3:

Another way of saying this commandment is:

(A) "You shall not take the name of the Lord your God in vain,"

(B) "You shall not take the name of the Lord your God in vain,"

(C) "You shall not take the name of the Lord your God in vain,"

(D) All of the above and then some

QUESTION 4:

The word "vain" can mean:

(A) Having no value,

(B) Useless,

(C) Blasphemous,

(D) All of the above

QUESTION 5:

Using God's holy name as a meaningless swear word is like:

(A) Telling the world God means nothing to you,

(B) Showing the world you have a limited vocabulary,

(C) A & B,

(D) No big deal to God

QUESTION 6:

Proper use of God's name includes:

(A) Prayer,

(B) Praise,

(C) Thanksgiving,

(D) All of the above and then some

QUESTION 7:

The word "respect" literally means:

(A) To get your vision checked,

(B) To look out,

(C) To look again,

(D) Spectacles are useful

QUESTION 8:

What name did the ancient Hebrews substitute for "Yahweh" (I Am) for fear of breaking this commandment?

(A) Adonai (Lord),

(B) Elohim (God),

(C) Jehovah (Yahweh),

(D) El Shut Eye (Sleep)

QUESTION 9:

Jesus said we can call God:

(A) Abba (Daddy),

(B) Father,

(C) Frequently,

(D) All of the above

FINKMANIA FINAL QUESTION:

Exodus 20:7 tells us:

(A) Don't curse with God's name,

(B) Don't use God's name to make a false oath,

(C) Don't use God's name as a "filler" word,

(D) All of the above

Play this online game using FINKlink
LF02 @ www.faithink.com

TERMS
WRITE A DEFINITION BELOW.

CURSE

NAME IN VAIN

PRAISE

SWEAR

THANKSGIVING

FAITH INKUBATORS

REMEMBER THE SABBATH

"Flight into Egypt" Dr. He Qi. Order prints at www.heqiarts.com

"REMEMBER THE SABBATH DAY, AND KEEP IT HOLY."

— EXODUS 20:8A

Listen to this song using FINKlink
LF03 | @ www.faithink.com

Do you want to dramatically change your life, reduce stress, and burn off pounds of ugly, unwanted, unhealthy fat?

How about a tighter tummy and a firmer rear end? Flip around late night television and you will come across a number of infomercials trying to sell you a new body. If only you will only buy this ab-roller or that tummy tucker, you are guaranteed noticeable results in only a few weeks. Some products promise your life will change dramatically if you merely use them three times a week for 20 minutes per session. That's quite a claim. Think of it: just 60 minutes a week and you will be on your way to health, vitality, and a whole new you!

But what's the catch? Millions buy and try these miracle solutions. Most fail. The machines turn up in attics, on curbsides, and in garage sales. Why? The machines don't do the work for you. Results are only guaranteed if you use the product and the program together. You have to make a commitment to a disciplined habit of exercising at least three times a week and eating moderately. If you don't follow the instructions, you won't get the results. That's guaranteed.

GOD'S SABBATH INSTRUCTIONS

God gave some interesting instructions to us about getting into spiritual shape and staying strong. In the Genesis 1 creation story, God made the whole world in six days and rested on the seventh. God called this seventh day (*sabbath* in Hebrew) holy, and instructed Israel not to do any work on that day. No physical labor. No commerce. Nada! To the ancient world, this was quite a command! Why would you give up 1/7 of your productivity? Why wouldn't you work all day every day? Further, why wouldn't you work your slaves, animals, and fields around the clock, year-in, year-out? What good is rest? It doesn't accomplish anything, does it?

People who study sleep will tell you something different. You can live a lot longer without food than you can without sleep. Sleep and rest are essential for health.

People who study muscles know that rest between workouts is extremely important. Muscles are made up of millions of tiny fibers. The strain of a good workout tears these fibers. It is not until torn muscles rest and bond over onto themselves with a little muscular glue that they become toned. It is not simply the hard workout that builds muscles up. It is the rest between working times that creates muscle tone and new strength.

This is true for physical muscles. Is it also true for spiritual muscles? Do our spirits need to be "exercised" frequently, and then rest in order for us to gain spiritual strength? Is that what Sabbath rest is really about?

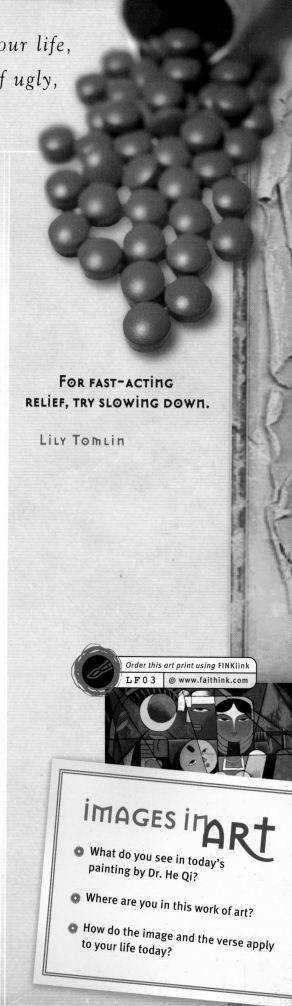

FOR FAST-ACTING RELIEF, TRY SLOWING DOWN.

LILY TOMLIN

Order this art print using FINKlink
LF03 | @ www.faithink.com

IMAGES IN ART

- What do you see in today's painting by Dr. He Qi?
- Where are you in this work of art?
- How do the image and the verse apply to your life today?

So What Does This Mean?

Going to church doesn't make you a Christian any more than going to the garage makes you an automobile.

Billy Sunday

Recreation or Wreck Creation?

In a world that is constantly on the go, Sabbath is a tough lesson to learn and an even tougher practice to keep. We cram so much into our weekends that we are often exhausted by Sunday night. We pack vacations so full of activities that we sometimes need vacations from our vacations. In a wireless world, some people take work home with them and never unplug. In our media-bombarded society, we are constantly surrounded by noise. There is rarely a moment for us to stop, unplug, relax, turn off, and tune in to the still, small voice of God.

But without Sabbath, we may find ourselves living full schedules and empty lives with full houses and empty homes.

God set the Sabbath apart as a marvelous gift. It is meant for rest, worship, refocus, replenishment, and re-creation. (Not wreck creation!) Maybe God knows us better than we know ourselves. Maybe we need Sabbath more than we know. Maybe the Sabbath "machine" is waiting to help us improve and strengthen our lives. Maybe we need to listen to God and follow the instructions.

Bible Time

Read and highlight Exodus 20:8, writing "Sabbath Rest" in the margin. Next, highlight the following. What do they teach you about keeping Sabbath?

Matthew 12:7-8

Mark 2:27-28

Exodus 20:11

Proverbs 30:5

Role Play

Respond to friends who tell you the following:

1. "I don't need to go to church. I can worship God in the woods."

2. "Sunday is the only day I can sleep in."

3. "I have to work on Sunday mornings because I need the money."

Questions to Ponder

1. What are some spiritual exercises that keep people strong?

2. Working out once a week is better than nothing, but doing a little every day is a much healthier way to live. Which of the spiritual exercises listed above can you do every day? Why would you do them? Will you do them?

3. What is the difference between recreation and wreck creation?

SMALL GROUP
SHARE, READ, TALK, PRAY, BLESS

1. **SHARE** your highs and lows of the week one-on-one with another person. Listen carefully and record your friend's thoughts in the space below. Then return to small group and share your friend's highs and lows.

   MY HIGHS + LOWS THIS WEEK WERE:

   ....

   MY FRIEND'S HIGHS + LOWS THIS WEEK WERE:

   ....

2. **READ** and highlight the theme verse in your Bibles. Circle key words and learn the verse in song if time permits.

3. **TALK** about how today's verse relates to your highs and lows. Review the art for today, the Quiz Bowl questions, the terms, and the cartoons. Then write a sentence on each of the following:

   ONE NEW THING I LEARNED TODAY:

   ....

   ONE THING I ALREADY KNEW THAT IS WORTH REPEATING:

   ....

   ONE THING I WOULD LIKE TO KNOW MORE ABOUT:

   ....

4. **PRAY** for one another, praising and thanking God for your highs, and asking God to be with you in your lows. Include your friend's highs and lows in your prayers.

   A PRAISING PRAYER: ....

   A THANKING PRAYER: ....

   AN ASKING PRAYER: ....

5. **BLESS** one another using the blessing of the week. (right) Mark each person with the sign of the cross as you bless them.

THE FINE 5

THIS WEEK'S BLESSING

(NAME), CHILD OF GOD, MAY YOU REST IN THE ARMS OF THE GOD WHO LOVES YOU.

THE HOME HUDDLE jOURNAL
SHARE, READ, tALK, PRAY, BLESS

Read the full devotions using FINKlink
LF03 | @ www.faithink.com

DAY #1

TODAY'S BIBLE VERSE:

EXODUS 20:8

Remember the Sabbath day, and keep it holy.

MY HIGH TODAY WAS:

MY LOW TODAY WAS:

MY PRAYER TODAY IS:

DAY #2

TODAY'S BIBLE VERSE:

EXODUS 20:9-10

Six days you shall labor and do all your work. But the seventh day is a sabbath to the Lord your God; you shall not do any work—you, your son or your daughter, your male or female slave, your livestock, or the alien resident in your towns.

MY HIGH TODAY WAS:

MY LOW TODAY WAS:

MY PRAYER TODAY IS:

DAY #3

TODAY'S BIBLE VERSE:

EXODUS 20:11

For in six days the Lord made heaven and earth, the sea, and all that is in them, but rested the seventh day; therefore the Lord blessed the sabbath day and consecrated it.

MY HIGH TODAY WAS:

MY LOW TODAY WAS:

MY PRAYER TODAY IS:

MY HIGH TODAY WAS:

MY LOW TODAY WAS:

MY PRAYER TODAY IS:

TODAY'S BIBLE VERSE:
EXODUS 16:23A

This is what the Lord has commanded: "Tomorrow is a day of solemn rest, a holy sabbath to the Lord."

MY HIGH TODAY WAS:

MY LOW TODAY WAS:

MY PRAYER TODAY IS:

DAY #5

TODAY'S BIBLE VERSE:
1 SAMUEL 3:10

Now the Lord came and stood there, calling as before, "Samuel! Samuel!" And Samuel said, "Speak, for your servant is listening."

MY HIGH TODAY WAS:

MY LOW TODAY WAS:

MY PRAYER TODAY IS:

DAY #6

TODAY'S BIBLE VERSE:
PSALM 122:1

I was glad when they said to me "Let us go to the house of the Lord!"

RE-CREATION NOT WRECK CREATION

MY HIGHEST HIGH THIS WEEK WAS:

MY LOWEST LOW THIS WEEK WAS:

MY PRAYER FOR NEXT WEEK IS:

DAY #7

THIS WEEK'S BLESSING
(NAME), CHILD OF GOD, MAY YOU REST IN THE ARMS OF THE GOD WHO LOVES YOU.

THE
SHA

DAY #1

today's bible verse:

Luke 2:49b

Did you not know that I must be in my Father's house?

my **HIGH** today was:

my **LOW** today was:

my **PRAYER** today is:

DAY #2

today's bible verse:

Proverbs 30:5

Every word of God proves true; he is a shield to those who take refuge in him.

my **HIGH** today was:

my **LOW** today was:

my **PRAYER** today is:

DAY #3

today's bible verse:

2 Kings 17:39

You shall worship the Lord your God; he will deliver you out of the hand of all your enemies.?

my **HIGH** today was:

my **LOW** today was:

my **PRAYER** today is:

1. S H A R E HIGHS & LOWS OF THE DAY.

2. R E A D AND HIGHLIGHT THE VERSE OF THE DAY IN YOUR BIBLES.

3. T A L K ABOUT HOW TODAY'S VERSE RELATES TO YOUR HIGHS & LOWS.

4. P R A Y FOR YOUR HIGHS & LOWS, FOR YOUR FAMILY AND FOR THE WORLD.

5. B L E S S ONE ANOTHER USING THIS WEEK'S BLESSING (ON THE PREVIOUS PAGE).

MY HIGH TODAY WAS:

MY LOW TODAY WAS:

MY PRAYER TODAY IS:

DAY #4

TODAY'S BIBLE VERSE:

LUKE 4:8

Jesus answered him, "It is written, 'Worship the Lord your God, and serve only him.'"

MY HIGH TODAY WAS:

MY LOW TODAY WAS:

MY PRAYER TODAY IS:

DAY #5

TODAY'S BIBLE VERSE:

MATTHEW 18:20

For where two or three are gathered in my name, I am there among of them.

MY HIGH TODAY WAS:

MY LOW TODAY WAS:

MY PRAYER TODAY IS:

DAY #6

TODAY'S BIBLE VERSE:

ROMANS 10:17

So faith comes from what is heard, and what is heard comes through the word of Christ.

s | m | t | w | th | f | s

THEME iN REViEW

If you listen to Jesus carefully, you worship not by going through the liturgy and jumping through hoops. How do you worship? "When did I see you hungry and poor and feed you..."

Bill Easum

DAY #7

my favorite VERSE from the theme was:

....

....

....

....

....

....

....

LOOKING BACK ON THESE TWO WEEKS, MY HIGHEST HIGH WAS:

....

MY LOWEST LOW THESE PAST WEEKS WAS:

....

ONE WAY GOD ANSWERED MY PRAYERS WAS:

....

ONE WAY GOD MIGHT USE ME AS A SACRED AGENT TO ANSWER THESE PRAYERS:

....

....

FAMILY COVENANT

We have shared *Highs & Lows* this week, read and highlighted the verses assigned in our Bibles, talked about our lives, prayed for one another's highs and lows, and blessed one another.

....
Parent's Signature   Teen's Signature   Date

THE FINKMANIA QUIZBOWL

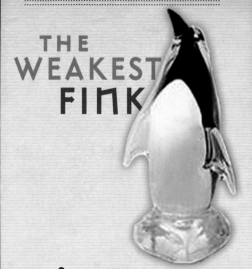

Question 1:

The Third Commandment is:

(A) "Remember the Sabbath day, and keep it holy,"

(B) "Remember the Sabbath day, and keep it occasionally,"

(C) "Honor your parents,"

(D) A or C, depending on whether you order them like a Catholic and Lutheran or like most other Protestants"

Question 2:

The word "Sabbath" in Hebrew means:

(A) Rest,

(B) Recreation,

(C) Wreck Creation,

(D) Sleep in

Question 3:

God commanded that the seventh day be holy because:

(A) Seven is God's lucky number,

(B) Seven rhymes with heaven,

(C) God created the world in seven days,

(D) God rested from creation on the seventh day

Question 4:

The word "holy" means:

(A) Divine,

(B) Sacred, High and Exalted,

(C) Supremely good,

(D) All of the above

Question 5:

Jesus used the Sabbath day to:

(A) Heal the sick,

(B) Go to synagogue, preach and teach,

(C) Read the paper, work on his deck and rest after a tough week,

(D) Both A & B

Question 6:

A person can get to church and still neglect God's Word by:

(A) Being there in body but not hearing the word,

(B) Being there in body but not engaged in prayer, praise and thanksgiving,

(C) Sitting at the coffee table and eating cookies during worship,

(D) All of the above

Question 7:

You can live longer without food than without sleep:

(A) True,

(B) False,

(C) Both A & B,

(D) It depends on what your definition of food is

Question 8:

God commanded people honor Sabbath because:

(A) In the ancient world, people literally worked their animals and slaves to death and God knew we needed rest to survive,

(B) God wanted to go on vacation,

(C) God didn't want union trouble,

(D) God didn't want us cranky every Monday morning

Question 9:

If the word of God is not included in our holy day activities:

(A) We'll just need to do better next time,

(B) We aren't keeping the holy day holy,

(C) Football is a good substitute,

(D) God probably doesn't mind

FINKmania Final Question:

Exodus 20:8 tells us Sabbath is for:

(A) Shopping,

(B) Shopping and football,

(C) Worshipping God, spending time with family, and re-creating in a way that prepares us to be rested for the week ahead,

(D) Packing as much into the weekend as we possibly can

Play this online game using **FINKlink**
LF03 | @ www.faithink.com

THE WEAKEST FINK

SURE, YOU CAN WORSHIP GOD IN THE WOODS. BUT WHEN WAS THE LAST TIME A TREE OFFERED YOU THE FULL AND COMPLETE FORGIVENESS OF ALL YOUR SINS?

ANONYMOUS

TERMS

WRITE A DEFINITION BELOW.

HOLY

RECREATION

REMEMBER

SABBATH

WORSHIP

FAITH
INKUBATORS

"Ruth and Naomi" Dr. He Qi. Order prints at www.heqiarts.com

"HONOR YOUR FATHER AND YOUR MOTHER, SO THAT

YOUR DAYS MAY BE LONG IN THE LAND THAT THE LORD

YOUR GOD IS GIVING YOU."

— EXODUS 20:12

Listen to this song using FINKlink

LF04 | @ www.faithink.com

*I*magine yourself ten or fifteen years from today.
You are older but, in a sense, quite the same.

You are sitting in a hospital room with the person you love more than anyone else in the world, holding your first baby.

You gaze together at the tiny mystery in your arms. This miracle from God—this little bundle of love and hope and possibility—is the best gift you've ever been given. You wipe a tear from your eye and whisper a prayer of thanks. Can you hear it? The whispered prayer? What is this prayer of hope for your baby? What are you asking God for in this moment as a brand new parent?

Fast-forward five years. You stand in a doorway watching your child walk down the street to a waiting bus. It is the first day of school. Your child has lived under your care all her life. Now she is launching into an uncertain world. You can no longer protect her every step. There will be other voices and influences to shape her. There will be dangers and strangers and obstacles. You watch and wait, hoping for the little one to turn, smile and wave before getting on the bus. She takes a step and pauses. Then a beaming broad smile is aimed in your direction. A small hand waves. You wipe a tear from your eye and whisper a prayer. Can you hear it? The whispered prayer? What do you ask of God? What are your dreams for this little one stepping out into the world?

Fast forward ten years ahead. Your baby is now a teenager. You wait in a darkened hallway. You have seen the years pass. A touch of gray graces your temples. You are worried. Car lights momentarily hit the window and your heart races. You rush to the curtain and pull it back. The car passes on. You glance at your watch. This precious gift, this precious child who will always be your baby, is late. Two hours late. You try not to worry, but you love her so much and the night is dark and dangerous. The clock chimes twice. You glance at your watch, waiting and hoping. A car door slams. You whisper a prayer and wipe a tear from your eye. Can you hear it? This whispered prayer? What do you ask of God?

PRAYERS AND CARES AND PARENTS

Parents are crazy. Most parents would do almost anything for their children's safety. They would jump in front of a bus or take a bullet to save their kids. Even on a day when the child yells at them and storms out of the house, they would still die for that child. That's love.

M. Scott Peck in his book *The Road Less Traveled* says love isn't love until it does the work of love—which is to love when you don't feel like it. Parents do that every day. Every day.

MY PARENTS HAVE BEEN VISITING ME FOR A FEW DAYS. I JUST DROPPED THEM OFF AT THE AIRPORT. THEY LEAVE TOMORROW.

MARGARET SMITH

Order this art print using FINKlink
LF04 @ www.faithink.com

IMAGES IN ART

- What do you see in today's painting by Dr. He Qi?

- Where are you in this work of art?

- How do the image and the verse apply to your life today?

So What Does This Mean?

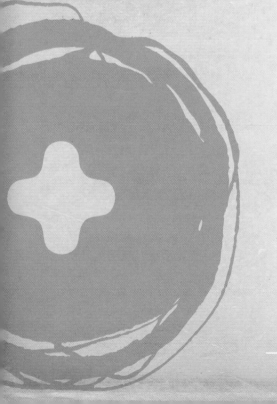

MYSTICAL CONNECTIONS

There is something strange, mystical and wonderful about having a baby. A part of you and the one you love comes alive and walks the face of the earth. A part of your heart will live on even after they have placed your body in the grave. It is a mystery, but if you ever become a parent, your understanding of love will deepen. You may for the first time come to know what real love is all about. Loving someone so much that you would do anything to keep them safe—that is love. Real love. That is how your own parents, even with all their faults, love you. You are a child of a parent's hope. The promise of a parent's tomorrow. The dream of a parent's unspoken tears.

God invites you to honor that kind of love. Will you do it?

BIBLE TIME

Only one of the Ten Commandments was given with a specific promise attached. Read and highlight Exodus 20:12b. What is the promise and what do you think this promise means?

Read Ephesians 6:1-4. What more do you learn about this commandment?

ROLE PLAY

1. You are two hours past curfew and return home, meeting your parents at the door.
2. You believe your parents are abusing alcohol. What do you say? How do you honor them?
3. Jump ahead 50 years. Your mother is going in for a dangerous surgery and may not live. She asks not to be put on a respirator if the surgery fails, but you don't want to lose her. What do you say?

QUESTIONS TO PONDER

1. List five common ways people dishonor their parents. Imagine yourself as a parent of a teenager. Which of these "dis-honoring" ways would bother you most? Why?

2. List five common ways people honor their parents. Imagine yourself as a parent of a teenager. Which of these honoring ways would mean the most to you? Why?

3. Does God expect you to honor a parent who is involved in something illegal, immoral or abusive? How can you?

SMALL GROUP
SHARE, READ, TALK, PRAY, BLESS

1. **SHARE** your highs and lows of the week one-on-one with another person. Listen carefully and record your friend's thoughts in the space below. Then return to small group and share your friend's highs and lows.

MY HIGHS + LOWS THIS WEEK WERE:

....

MY FRIEND'S HIGHS + LOWS THIS WEEK WERE:

....

2. **READ** and highlight the theme verse in your Bibles. Circle key words and learn the verse in song if time permits.

3. **TALK** about how today's verse relates to your highs and lows. Review the art for today, the Quiz Bowl questions, the terms, and the cartoons. Then write a sentence on each of the following:

ONE NEW THING I LEARNED TODAY:

....

ONE THING I ALREADY KNEW THAT IS WORTH REPEATING:

....

ONE THING I WOULD LIKE TO KNOW MORE ABOUT:

....

4. **PRAY** for one another, praising and thanking God for your highs, and asking God to be with you in your lows. Include your friend's highs and lows in your prayers.

A PRAISING PRAYER: ....

A THANKING PRAYER: ....

AN ASKING PRAYER: ....

5. **BLESS** one another using the blessing of the week. (right) Mark each person with the sign of the cross as you bless them.

THE FINK FIVE

THIS WEEK'S BLESSING

(NAME), MAY YOU BE A BLESSING TO YOUR PARENTS, AND MAY ALL THE CHILDREN WHO KNOW YOU RISE UP AND CALL YOU BLESSED. IN JESUS' NAME. AMEN.

THE HOME HUDDLE JOURNAL

SHARE, READ, TALK, PRAY, BLESS

WEEK 1

Read the full devotions using FINKlink

LF04 | @ www.faithink.com

DAY #1

TODAY'S BIBLE VERSE:

EXODUS 20:12

Honor your father and your mother so that your days may be long in the land that the Lord your God is giving you.

MY **HIGH** TODAY WAS:

MY **LOW** TODAY WAS:

MY **PRAYER** TODAY IS:

DAY #2

TODAY'S BIBLE VERSE:

MATTHEW 20:26B

Whoever wishes to be great among you must be your servant.

MY **HIGH** TODAY WAS:

MY **LOW** TODAY WAS:

MY **PRAYER** TODAY IS:

DAY #3

TODAY'S BIBLE VERSE:

LEVITICUS 26:12

And I will walk among you, and will be your God, and you shall be my people.

MY **HIGH** TODAY WAS:

MY **LOW** TODAY WAS:

MY **PRAYER** TODAY IS:

MY **HIGH** TODAY WAS:

MY **LOW** TODAY WAS:

MY **PRAYER** TODAY IS:

DAY #4

TODAY'S BIBLE VERSE:

PSALM 127:3A

Behold, children are a gift of the Lord.

MY **HIGH** TODAY WAS:

MY **LOW** TODAY WAS:

MY **PRAYER** TODAY IS:

DAY #5

TODAY'S BIBLE VERSE:

EPHESIANS 4:26B

Do not let the sun go down on your anger.

MY **HIGH** TODAY WAS:

MY **LOW** TODAY WAS:

MY **PRAYER** TODAY IS:

DAY #6

TODAY'S BIBLE VERSE:

JOHN 15:13

No one has greater love than this, to lay down one's life for one's friends.

MY **HIGHEST HIGH** THIS WEEK WAS:

MY **LOWEST LOW** THIS WEEK WAS:

MY **PRAYER** FOR NEXT WEEK IS:

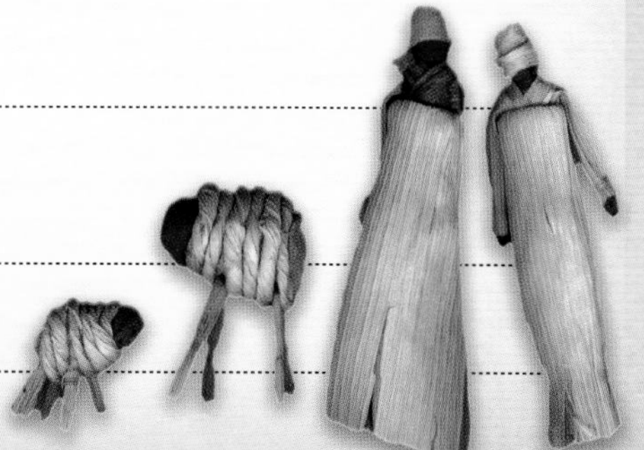

DAY #7

THIS WEEK'S BLESSING

(NAME), MAY YOU BE A BLESSING TO YOUR PARENTS, AND MAY ALL THE CHILDREN WHO KNOW YOU RISE UP AND CALL YOU BLESSED. IN JESUS' NAME. AMEN.

THE HOME HUDDLE jOURNAL
SHARE, READ, tALK, PRAY, BLESS

DAY #1

TODAY'S BIBLE VERSE:

EPHESIANS 6:1

Children, obey your parents in the Lord, for this is right.

MY HIGH TODAY WAS:

MY LOW TODAY WAS:

MY PRAYER TODAY IS:

DAY #2

TODAY'S BIBLE VERSE:

EPHESIANS 6:2-3

"Honor your father and mother"—this is the first commandment with a promise: "so that it may be well with you and you may live long on the earth."

MY HIGH TODAY WAS:

MY LOW TODAY WAS:

MY PRAYER TODAY IS:

DAY #3

TODAY'S BIBLE VERSE:

EPHESIANS 6:4

And, fathers, do not provoke your children to anger, but bring them up in the discipline and instruction of the Lord.

MY HIGH TODAY WAS:

MY LOW TODAY WAS:

MY PRAYER TODAY IS:

1. SHARE HIGHS & LOWS OF THE DAY.

2. READ AND HIGHLIGHT THE VERSE OF THE DAY IN YOUR BIBLES.

3. TALK ABOUT HOW TODAY'S VERSE RELATES TO YOUR HIGHS & LOWS.

4. PRAY FOR YOUR HIGHS & LOWS, FOR YOUR FAMILY AND FOR THE WORLD.

5. BLESS ONE ANOTHER USING THIS WEEK'S BLESSING (ON THE PREVIOUS PAGE).

MY HIGH TODAY WAS:

MY LOW TODAY WAS:

MY PRAYER TODAY IS:

DAY #4

TODAY'S BIBLE VERSE:

HEBREWS 13:17A

Obey your leaders and submit to them, for they are keeping watch over your souls and will give an account.

MY HIGH TODAY WAS:

MY LOW TODAY WAS:

MY PRAYER TODAY IS:

DAY #5

TODAY'S BIBLE VERSE:

PROVERBS 6:20

My child, keep your father's commandment, and do not forsake your mother's teaching.

MY HIGH TODAY WAS:

MY LOW TODAY WAS:

MY PRAYER TODAY IS:

DAY #6

TODAY'S BIBLE VERSE:

PROVERBS 1:8-9

Hear, my child, your fathers instruction and do not reject your mother's teaching ; for they are a fair garland for your head, and pendants for your neck.

THEME IN REVIEW

TEACH YOUR
PARENTS WELL.

GRAHAM NASH

DAY #7

MY FAVORITE VERSE
FROM THE THEME WAS:

....
....
....
....
....

LOOKING BACK ON THESE TWO WEEKS, MY HIGHEST HIGH WAS:

....

MY LOWEST LOW THESE PAST WEEKS WAS:

....

ONE WAY GOD ANSWERED MY PRAYERS WAS:

....

ONE WAY GOD MIGHT USE ME AS A SACRED AGENT
TO ANSWER THESE PRAYERS:

....

....

FAMILY COVENANT

We have shared *Highs & Lows* this week, read and highlighted the verses assigned in our Bibles, talked about our lives, prayed for one another's highs and lows, and blessed one another.

--------------------------------   --------------------------------

Parent's Signature   Teen's Signature   Date

THE FINKMANIA QUIZ BOWL

Question 1:

The commandment that follows "remember the sabbath day" is:

(A) "Honor your father and your mother, so that your days may be long in the land that the Lord your God is giving you,"

(B) "You shall not murder,"

(C) "You shall not steal,"

(D) "Honor your father and your mother, so that you may live at home until you are 38"

Question 2:

Honoring our parents and others in authority truly means:

(A) Irritating them every chance you get,

(B) Treating them with love and respect,

(C) Treating them with love, respect, obedience and service,

(D) Taking them out for a fish taco now and then

Question 3:

Most children on television treat their parents:

(A) With supreme respect and honor,

(B) As dorks who don't know anything,

(C) As wise and loving guides valued for their care and consistent providence,

(D) As superiors in intelligence, wisdom, and experience

Question 4:

When children break the "honor" commandment:

(A) Family life is filled with peace and harmony,

(B) Children and parents are generally happier,

(C) Relationships break apart, families experience more pain, and society suffers,

(D) There is no effect

Question 5:

Common ways teens dishonor their parents today include:

(A) Lying to them,

(B) Ignoring their advice,

(C) Treating them rudely in front of others,

(D) All of the above, and it's not a good way to treat someone who gave you life and would take a bullet for you without thinking twice

Question 6:

The "honor your parents" commandment ends with:

(A) "...or else"

(B) "...that the days may be tolerable in the land that the Lord your God gives you,"

(C) "...that the days may be long in the land the Lord your God gives you,"

(D) "...that you inherit a pile of cash some day"

Question 7:

If a parent breaks the law, one way to still honor them is to:

(A) Ignore their problem and hope it will go away,

(B) Try to help them see God's way,

(C) Criticize them in front of other adults and hope they see the light,

(D) Hire a good lawyer

Question 8:

In the broadest sense of the word, the "honor" commandment tells us we are to respect and obey:

(A) Parents,

(B) Parents and others in authority,

(C) Parents, others in authority, and abusive dictatorial governments,

(D) None of the above

Question 9:

We are to honor our parents because:

(A) God gave them to us as a gift,

(B) God gave them to us as a gift and God commands us to honor them,

(C) God gave them to us as a gift, commands us to honor them, and promises a longer, better life if we do,

(D) All of the above

FINKMANIA Final Question:

Exodus 20:12 tells us:

(A) To respect, obey, love and serve our parents and others in authority,

(B) To respect our parents if they are acting in a respectable manner,

(C) Our parents should respect, obey, love, and serve us,

(D) God doesn't know my parents

 Play this online game using FINKlink

THE WEAKEST FINK

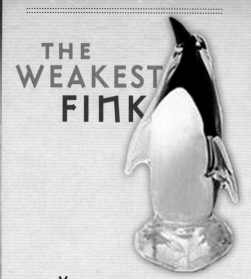

YOUR PARENTS GAVE YOU LIFE. THAT OUGHT TO BE WORTH AT LEAST A SMILE, A "THANKS" AND A COUPLE LOADS OF LAUNDRY EVERY NOW AND THEN.

RICH MELHEIM

TERMS
WRITE A DEFINITION BELOW.

AUTHORITY

CHILDREN

HONOR

PARENTS

RESPECT

"Sacrifice of Abraham" Dr. He Qi: Order prints at www.heqiarts.com

"YOU SHALL NOT MURDER."

— EXODUS 20:13

Listen to this song using FINKlink

LF05 @ www.faithink.com

**A** *Christian farmer witnessed his Moslem enemies enter his village and brutalize his people.*

As a warning to the villagers, the terrorists cut a little girl in half and left her body in the street. That night the farmer vowed revenge. He would find a Moslem child, strangle her, cut her in half, and leave her on her own parents' doorsteps. The angry man plotted and planned his vengeance. When he finally had an opportunity to carry the murder out, however, he found he was unable to harm the child. Revenge would not solve anything. It would make him no different from the butchers he hated.

He looked into the little girls eyes and wept. Then he blessed her, turned and walked away.

Tough Decisions, Tougher People

Every generation has its own set of violent images etched into childhood memories. Every generation has seen insult turn into hatred and watched calls for revenge turn into acts of war and death. Your grandparents may remember the assassination of President Kennedy or the Vietnam war as if it were yesterday. Ask them where they were that morning. They can probably tell you. Your parents may remember Oklahoma City bombing, Tiananmen Square, or the mass murders in Rwanda. Maybe you are old enough to remember the school shooting at Columbine High, the 9/11 attack or the genocide in Darfour.

People do it. Nations do it. Ethnic groups do it. They all strike back. You are tempted to do it, too. When someone hurts you, it is only natural to want to hurt them back. When someone attacks you verbally or physically, it seems perfectly right to want to launch a swift and angry offensive. If you don't fight back, they will only continue to abuse you, right? They'll think you are weak and continue to hurt you if you don't return fire with fire, right?

Revenge is natural, but the Bible tells us that it belongs to God. God will judge the nations and the peoples. We are to love, forgive and heal. We are to leave the judging, revenge, and punishing in God's hands. We are to follow Jesus' example. Easier said than done?

The Killing Commandment

Who is tougher: the person who strikes back when wronged, or the person who has the power to hold back? What does Jesus teach about peace, justice and revenge? What was his reaction to personal violence? How do Christ's words and actions compare with the messages we hear around us?

A follower of Jesus must wrestle with these questions.

> ## Anyone who angers you conquers you.
>
> – Sister Elizabeth

images in Art

- What do you see in today's painting by Dr. He Qi?
- Where are you in this work of art?
- How do the image and the verse apply to your life today?

So What Does This Mean?

THIS IS A DECENT, GODFEARING COUNTRY. WE DON'T ALLOW ANY MURDERS HERE. AND IF YOU BREAK THIS LITTLE RULE WE KILL YOU!

SHERIFF 457

PRAYER

DEAR GOD, WITH MY WORDS, MY ANGER, AND MY PUT-DOWNS, I HAVE KILLED. BY THE THINGS I HAVE DONE AND THE THINGS I HAVE LEFT UNDONE, I HAVE KILLED. WITH MY WORDS AND MY LOOKS, I HAVE KILLED. FORGIVE ME. HEAL ME. CHANGE ME. RESTORE ME. TEACH ME THE POWER THAT HOLDS BACK RATHER THAN THE WEAKNESS THAT STRIKES BACK. I PRAY IN JESUS' NAME.

AMEN.

SO WHAT DOES THIS MEAN?

It may not seem normal, safe or smart, but Jesus didn't lift a finger to defend himself against those who beat him. He didn't lash back against those who mocked him, whipped him, and drove the nails into his hands. He didn't curse, condemn, or even complain. He could have called down armies of angels to punish them on the spot. Instead, our Lord cried out, "Father, forgive them. They know not what they do."

Dignity is, indeed, a crown of thorns. Power, indeed, is in the hand of the one who can hold back rather than strike back. That's what Jesus showed us. That's what he asks his followers to do.

BIBLE TIME

Read and highlight Exodus 20:13. How does this verse connect with each of the following?

Genesis 4:9

Hebrews 10:30

Matthew 5: 21-22a

Matthew 5: 38, 44

Matthew 26:52

Ephesians 4:26

ROLE PLAY

1. A new kid in school is being pushed around by the school bully. What do you say and do?

2. Your best friend comes to you in tears. She is afraid of her father's angry outbursts. She confides in you that he has just bought a gun and is threatening her mother. What do you do? What do you say?

QUESTIONS TO PONDER

1. What would it take for you to have the power to hold back rather than strike back next time someone wrongs you?

2. Justice and mercy are two sides to the same coin. Which is more important to you? Why? Think about this in relationship to capital punishment, mercy killing, and the war against terrorism.

3. How can words, looks, and inaction kill?

Small Group
SHARE, READ, TALK, PRAY, BLESS

1. **SHARE** your highs and lows of the week one-on-one with another person. Listen carefully and record your friend's thoughts in the space below. Then return to small group and share your friend's highs and lows.

   MY HIGHS + LOWS THIS WEEK WERE:

   ....

   MY FRIEND'S HIGHS + LOWS THIS WEEK WERE:

   ....

2. **READ** and highlight the theme verse in your Bibles. Circle key words and learn the verse in song if time permits.

3. **TALK** about how today's verse relates to your highs and lows. Review the art for today, the Quiz Bowl questions, the terms, and the cartoons. Then write a sentence on each of the following:

   ONE NEW THING I LEARNED TODAY:

   ....

   ONE THING I ALREADY KNEW THAT IS WORTH REPEATING:

   ....

   ONE THING I WOULD LIKE TO KNOW MORE ABOUT:

   ....

4. **PRAY** for one another, praising and thanking God for your highs, and asking God to be with you in your lows. Include your friend's highs and lows in your prayers.

   A PRAISING PRAYER: ....

   A THANKING PRAYER: ....

   AN ASKING PRAYER: ....

5. **BLESS** one another using the blessing of the week. (right) Mark each person with the sign of the cross as you bless them.

THE FINK FIVE

THIS WEEK'S BLESSING
(NAME), CHILD OF GOD, MAY YOU BE AN AGENT OF GOD'S HEALING THIS DAY. IN JESUS' NAME. AMEN.

THE HOME HUDDLE JOURNAL
SHARE, READ, TALK, PRAY, BLESS

Read the full devotions using FINKlink
LF 05 | @ www.faithink.com

DAY #1

TODAY'S BIBLE VERSE:

EXODUS 20:13

You shall not murder.

MY **HIGH** TODAY WAS:

MY **LOW** TODAY WAS:

MY **PRAYER** TODAY IS:

DAY #2

TODAY'S BIBLE VERSE:

MATTHEW 5:38-39

You have heard that it was said, "An eye for an eye and a tooth for a tooth." But I say to you, Do not resist an evildoer. But if anyone strikes you on the right cheek, turn the other also.

MY **HIGH** TODAY WAS:

MY **LOW** TODAY WAS:

MY **PRAYER** TODAY IS:

DAY #3

TODAY'S BIBLE VERSE:

MATTHEW 5:43-44

You have heard that it was said, "You shall love your neighbor and hate your enemy." But I say to you, love your enemies and pray for those who persecute you.

MY **HIGH** TODAY WAS:

MY **LOW** TODAY WAS:

MY **PRAYER** TODAY IS:

MY HIGH TODAY WAS:

MY LOW TODAY WAS:

MY PRAYER TODAY IS:

TODAY'S BIBLE VERSE:

HEBREWS 10:30B

Vengeance is mine, I will repay.

MY HIGH TODAY WAS:

MY LOW TODAY WAS:

MY PRAYER TODAY IS:

DAY #5

TODAY'S BIBLE VERSE:

LEVITICUS 19:18

You shall not take vengeance or bear a grudge against any of your people, but you shall love your neighbor as yourself: I am the Lord.

MY HIGH TODAY WAS:

MY LOW TODAY WAS:

MY PRAYER TODAY IS:

DAY #6

TODAY'S BIBLE VERSE:

JAMES 4:2A

You want something and do not have it; so you commit murder. And you covet something and cannot obtain it; so you engage in disputes and conflicts.

MY HIGHEST HIGH THIS WEEK WAS:

MY LOWEST LOW THIS WEEK WAS:

MY PRAYER FOR NEXT WEEK IS:

DAY #7

THIS WEEK'S BLESSING

(NAME), CHILD OF GOD, MAY YOU BE AN AGENT OF GOD'S HEALING THIS DAY. IN JESUS' NAME, AMEN.

THE HOME HUDDLE JOURNAL
SHARE, READ, TALK, PRAY, BLESS

Read the full devotions using FINKlink
LF05 | @ www.faithink.com

DAY #1

TODAY'S BIBLE VERSE:

LUKE 10:29B

Who is my neighbor?

MY **HIGH** TODAY WAS:

MY **LOW** TODAY WAS:

MY **PRAYER** TODAY IS:

DAY #2

TODAY'S BIBLE VERSE:

ROMANS 12:21

Do not be overcome by evil, but overcome evil with good.

MY **HIGH** TODAY WAS:

MY **LOW** TODAY WAS:

MY **PRAYER** TODAY IS:

DAY #3

TODAY'S BIBLE VERSE:

GENESIS 4:9B

Am I my brother's keeper?

MY **HIGH** TODAY WAS:

MY **LOW** TODAY WAS:

MY **PRAYER** TODAY IS:

1. **SHARE** HIGHS & LOWS OF THE DAY.

2. **READ** AND HIGHLIGHT THE VERSE OF THE DAY IN YOUR BIBLES.

3. **TALK** ABOUT HOW TODAY'S VERSE RELATES TO YOUR HIGHS & LOWS.

4. **PRAY** FOR YOUR HIGHS & LOWS, FOR YOUR FAMILY AND FOR THE WORLD.

5. **BLESS** ONE ANOTHER USING THIS WEEK'S BLESSING (ON THE PREVIOUS PAGE).

MY HIGH TODAY WAS:

MY LOW TODAY WAS:

MY PRAYER TODAY IS:

DAY #4

TODAY'S BIBLE VERSE:

PSALM 111:2

Great are the works of the Lord, studied by all who delight in them.

MY HIGH TODAY WAS:

MY LOW TODAY WAS:

MY PRAYER TODAY IS:

DAY #5

TODAY'S BIBLE VERSE:

MATTHEW 26:52B

Put your sword back into its place. For all who take the sword will perish by the sword.

MY HIGH TODAY WAS:

MY LOW TODAY WAS:

MY PRAYER TODAY IS:

DAY #6

TODAY'S BIBLE VERSE:

MATTHEW 25:40

And the king will answer them, "Truly I tell you, just as you did it to one of the least of these who are members of my family, you did it to me."

THEME iN REVIEW

THE LESSON IS:
OUR GOD IS VENGEFUL!
O SPITEFUL ONE, SHOW
ME WHO TO SMITE AND
THEY SHALL BE SMOTEN!

HOMER SIMPSON

DAY #7

MY FAVORITE **VERSE**
FROM THE THEME WAS:

....
....
....
....
....
....
....
....
....

LOOKING BACK ON THESE TWO WEEKS, MY HIGHEST **HIGH** WAS:
....

MY LOWEST **LOW** THESE PAST WEEKS WAS:
....

ONE WAY GOD ANSWERED MY **PRAYERS** WAS:
....

ONE WAY GOD MIGHT USE ME AS A **SACRED AGENT**
TO ANSWER THESE PRAYERS:
....
....

FAMILY COVENANT

We have shared *Highs & Lows* this week, read and highlighted the verses assigned in our Bibles, talked about our lives, prayed for one another's highs and lows, and blessed one another.

....
Parent's Signature   Teen's Signature   Date

THE FINKMANIA QUIZ BOWL

QUESTION 1:

The "killing" commandment states:

(A) "You shall not murder,"

(B) "You shall not kill animals for food,"

(C) "You shall not kill brain cells with hours upon hours of mindless video games,"

(D) "You shall not kill, unless you can kill a lot of people all at once and call it a 'just war'"

QUESTION 2:

Which of the following is a type of murder?

(A) Physically harming someone,

(B) Emotionally harming someone,

(C) Spiritually harming someone,

(D) All of the above

QUESTION 3:

How might someone be "murdered" emotionally?

(A) By being neglected, criticized and ignored

(B) By being gossiped about,

(C) By being dipped in honey and tied to a stake outside a colony of Fire Ants while being forced to listen to 37 of our pastor's old sermons

(D) A and B and maybe C

QUESTION 4:

How might someone be "murdered" spiritually?

(A) By neglecting prayer,

(B) By ignoring God's word,

(C) By staying away from worship and fellowship with the Body of Christ,

(D) All of the above and then some

QUESTION 5:

According to Jesus, who is our neighbor?

(A) Anyone who lives next door,

(B) Anyone who lives in your town,

(C) Anyone in trouble, even a feared or hated foreigner,

(D) Only people with your skin color

QUESTION 6:

How does gossip break the murder commandment?

(A) It kills a person's reputation,

(B) It kills someone's spirit,

(C) Both A & B,

(D) None of the above

QUESTION 7:

How does yelling at parents or siblings break the killing commandment?

(A) It doesn't - yell away!

(B) It might cause them to pop a few blood vessels, killing cells in their brain,

(C) It hurts them and one definition of killing includes hurting people in any way,

(D) I haven't the foggiest

QUESTION 8:

What are we supposed to do for our neighbors to truly keep the intent of this commandment?

(A) Leave them alone,

(B) Ignore their problems,

(C) Help them in all their physical needs,

(D) Buy them tickets to a "Barney on Ice" concert

QUESTION 9:

According to the intent of this commandment, killing is only ending a life:

(A) True,

(B) False,

(C) Both A & B,

(D) It depends on what your definition of "is" is

FINKMANIA FINAL QUESTION:

Exodus 20:13 tells us:

(A) We are not to harm our neighbors in any way,

(B) We are to help our neighbors in all of their physical needs,

(C) Both A & B,

(D) We are to only harm our neighbors when we feel threatened by them

Play this online game using FINKlink
LF05 | @ www.faithink.com

THE WEAKEST FINK

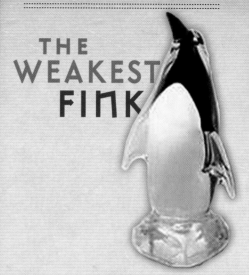

WHY DOES MAN KILL? HE KILLS FOR FOOD. BUT, OFTEN TIMES THERE MUST ALSO BE A BEVERAGE INVOLVED.

WOODY ALLEN

TERMS

WRITE A DEFINITION BELOW.

CAPITAL PUNISHMENT

KILL

MURDER

NEIGHBOR

WAR

FAITH INKUBATORS

ADULTERY

"Samaritan Woman at the Well" Dr. He Qi. Order prints at www.heqiarts.com

"YOU SHALL NOT COMMIT ADULTERY."

—EXODUS 20:14

Listen to this song using FINKlink

LF06 | @ www.faithink.com

Late one afternoon, King David rose from a nap and stepped out onto his palace rooftop.

From his high vantage point, he spotted a woman bathing. Bathsheba was stunningly beautiful. He was intoxicated by her and, although she was married to one of his loyal generals, David wanted her for himself. With her husband off fighting a war, David sent for her. She could not refuse the king. He slept with her, then sent her home. The secret affair wouldn't stay secret for long. Within a short time, she realized she was pregnant.

David devised a plan to cover up his sin. He sent for her husband, Uriah, and ordered him to return home to report on the war. David was sure the general would spend some time with his beautiful wife, but the soldier stayed near the palace the whole time and refused to go home. David's plan failed. Caught in his sin and lie, he made a deadly decision. David sent Uriah to the front lines and set him up to be ambushed and killed. When Uriah's wife heard that her husband was dead, she grieved deeply. Then King David sent for her again. She became his wife and bore him a son.

Wait a minute! David was God's chosen ruler. God raised him up from a shepherd boy to become king over all of Israel. God had blessed David and given him success over all of his enemies. Yet, even with all of these gifts and blessings, David still wanted more. His lust led to adultery. Adultery led to lies. Lies led to treachery. Treachery led to murder. Something that should have been so beautiful—love—turned to lust and destroyed a marriage, ended a life, and almost derailed God's plans for that nation.

So What?

When a Christian man and woman fall in love and choose to marry, they stand before God and their families to make a sacred promise. They vow that the special gifts of their hearts, their minds, and their bodies will only be shared in the most intimate ways with each other. A ring is given as a sign of this love and faithfulness as God places a divine blessing upon their promises.

In a world where sex fills magazines and flashes across movie screens, why would a young person consider staying sexually pure? Why would anyone even think of getting married and limiting their options like this?

The answer?

It is God's will. The God who created you loves you and knows what is best for your life. You can settle for less than God's best, but why would you?

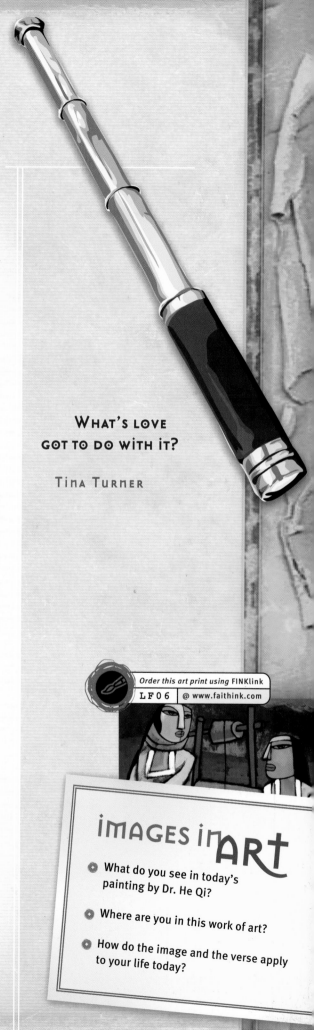

WHAT'S LOVE GOT TO DO WITH IT?

Tina Turner

Order this art print using FINKlink
LF06 @ www.faithink.com

IMAGES in ART

- What do you see in today's painting by Dr. He Qi?

- Where are you in this work of art?

- How do the image and the verse apply to your life today?

SO WHAT DOES THIS MEAN?

CREATIVE GOD,
THANK YOU FOR THE POWER
OF PHYSICAL LOVE AND HUMAN
PASSION. I KNOW YOU CREATED
IT AS A GIFT, AND ALL OF YOUR
GIFTS ARE GOOD. TEACH ME
TO TREAT SEX AND MY SEXUAL-
ITY AS THE SACRED EXPERIENCE
YOU INTEND IT TO BE. GIVE ME
THE STRENGTH TO ALWAYS TREAT
THE GIFT WITH CARE, RESPECT,
THANKSGIVING AND HONOR.

AMEN.

THE PROMISE

The sacred promise of marriage binds man and wife together into the beautiful and fulfilling plan and purpose God has for them. Jesus made it clear: God's will is that "the two shall be one" and "what God has joined together, let no one tear apart." Adultery tears apart the bind and cheats the cheater as much as it cheats the person who is cheated.

When we break the adultery commandment, we break more than one of God's laws. Betraying the oneness you have promised to your spouse is also break-ing the stealing commandment. It is stealing something precious that doesn't belong to you. It also breaks the false witness commandment. It is murder on families. Adultery in also idolatry—putting something else above God. Break-ing this commandment also breaks hearts, homes, and futures. It pollutes the purity, tears apart the oneness, and destroys the joys God intends in marriage.

BIBLE TIME

Read and highlight Exodus 20:15. Write "Sexual Purity" in the margin. Now read the following verses. What are five goals God has in mind for marriage?

Genesis 1:27-28

Genesis 2:24

Matthew 19:4-6

I Corinthians 6:19-20

Hebrews 13:4

ROLE PLAY

1. A friend says: "OK, I believe adultery is wrong, but I'm not married. This commandment doesn't say anything about sex outside of marriage with another unmarried person." What do you say?

2. You suspect a friend is being sexually abused. What do you say?

3. A friend spends a lot of time on pornographic web sites: "There's nothing wrong with that!" they say. "Didn't God make bodies?" What do you say?

QUESTIONS TO PONDER

1. What does this ancient commandment on adultery have to do with teenagers living today?

2. If someone is guilty of a sexual sin, what should he or she do according to I John 1:9?

3. What are some ways to keep temptation from getting control of your life?

Small Gr⊕up
SHARE, READ, TALK, PRAY, BLESS

1. **SHARE** your highs and lows of the week one-on-one with another person. Listen carefully and record your friend's thoughts in the space below. Then return to small group and share your friend's highs and lows.

   MY HIGHS + LOWS THIS WEEK WERE:

   ....

   MY FRIEND'S HIGHS + LOWS THIS WEEK WERE:

   ....

2. **READ** and highlight the theme verse in your Bibles. Circle key words and learn the verse in song if time permits.

3. **TALK** about how today's verse relates to your highs and lows. Review the art for today, the Quiz Bowl questions, the terms, and the cartoons. Then write a sentence on each of the following:

   ONE NEW THING I LEARNED TODAY:

   ....

   ONE THING I ALREADY KNEW THAT IS WORTH REPEATING:

   ....

   ONE THING I WOULD LIKE TO KNOW MORE ABOUT:

   ....

4. **PRAY** for one another, praising and thanking God for your highs, and asking God to be with you in your lows. Include your friend's highs and lows in your prayers.

   A PRAISING PRAYER: ....

   A THANKING PRAYER: ....

   AN ASKING PRAYER: ....

5. **BLESS** one another using the blessing of the week. (right) Mark each person with the sign of the cross as you bless them.

THIS WEEK'S BLESSING

(NAME), CHILD OF GOD, IN ALL MATTERS OF SEX MAY YOUR WORDS AND CONDUCT BE PURE AND HONORABLE. MAY YOU KEEP YOUR PROMISES IN LOVE AND RESPECT TO ALL. IN CHRIST. AMEN.

THE HOME HUDDLE JOURNAL
SHARE, READ, TALK, PRAY, BLESS

Read the full devotions using FINKlink
LF06 @ www.faithink.com

DAY #1

TODAY'S BIBLE VERSE:

EXODUS 20:14

You shall not commit adultery.

MY **HIGH** TODAY WAS:

MY **LOW** TODAY WAS:

MY **PRAYER** TODAY IS:

DAY #2

TODAY'S BIBLE VERSE:

GENESIS 1:31A

God saw everything that he had made, and indeed, it was very good.

MY **HIGH** TODAY WAS:

MY **LOW** TODAY WAS:

MY **PRAYER** TODAY IS:

DAY #3

TODAY'S BIBLE VERSE:

MATTHEW 19:5B

For this reason a man shall leave his father and mother and be joined to his wife, and the two shall become one flesh.

MY **HIGH** TODAY WAS:

MY **LOW** TODAY WAS:

MY **PRAYER** TODAY IS:

my **HIGH** today was: _____

my **LOW** today was: _____

my **PRAYER** today is: _____

_____

DAY #4

TODAY'S BIBLE VERSE:
Matthew 19:6
So they are no longer two, but one flesh. Therefore what God has joined together, let no one separate.

---

my **HIGH** today was: _____

my **LOW** today was: _____

my **PRAYER** today is: _____

_____

DAY #5

TODAY'S BIBLE VERSE:
2 Corinthians 6:19
Or do you not know that your body is a temple of the Holy Spirit within you, which you have from God?

---

my **HIGH** today was: _____

my **LOW** today was: _____

my **PRAYER** today is: _____

_____

DAY #6

TODAY'S BIBLE VERSE:
2 Corinthians 6:20
And that you are not your own? For you were bought with a price; therefore glorify God in your body.

---

my **HIGHEST HIGH** this week was: _____

my **LOWEST LOW** this week was: _____

my **PRAYER** for next week is: _____

DAY #7

THIS WEEK'S BLESSING
(NAME), CHILD OF GOD, IN ALL MATTERS OF SEX MAY YOUR WORDS AND CONDUCT BE PURE AND HONORABLE. MAY YOU KEEP YOUR PROMISES IN LOVE AND RESPECT TO ALL. IN CHRIST. AMEN.

THE HOME HUDDLE jOURNAL

SHARE, READ, TALK, PRAY, BLESS

Read the full devotions using FINKlink
LF06 | @ www.faithink.com

DAY #1

TODAY'S BIBLE VERSE:

GENESIS 1:27

So God created humankind in his image, in the image of God he created them; male and female he created them.

MY HIGH TODAY WAS:

MY LOW TODAY WAS:

MY PRAYER TODAY IS:

DAY #2

TODAY'S BIBLE VERSE:

GENESIS 1:28a

God blessed them, and God said to them, "Be fruitful and multiply..."

MY HIGH TODAY WAS:

MY LOW TODAY WAS:

MY PRAYER TODAY IS:

DAY #3

TODAY'S BIBLE VERSE:

HEBREWS 13:4

Let marriage be held in honor by all, and let the marriage bed be kept undefiled; for God will judge fornicators and adulterers.

MY HIGH TODAY WAS:

MY LOW TODAY WAS:

MY PRAYER TODAY IS:

1. **SHARE** HIGHS & LOWS OF THE DAY.

2. **READ** AND HIGHLIGHT THE VERSE OF THE DAY IN YOUR BIBLES.

3. **TALK** ABOUT HOW TODAY'S VERSE RELATES TO YOUR HIGHS & LOWS.

4. **PRAY** FOR YOUR HIGHS & LOWS, FOR YOUR FAMILY AND FOR THE WORLD.

5. **BLESS** ONE ANOTHER USING THIS WEEK'S BLESSING (ON THE PREVIOUS PAGE).

MY HIGH TODAY WAS:

MY LOW TODAY WAS:

MY PRAYER TODAY IS:

DAY #4

TODAY'S BIBLE VERSE:

PHILIPPIANS 4:8B

Whatever is true, whatever is honorable, whatever is just, whatever is pure, whatever is pleasing, whatever is commendable, if there is anything worthy of praise, think about these things.

MY HIGH TODAY WAS:

MY LOW TODAY WAS:

MY PRAYER TODAY IS:

DAY #5

TODAY'S BIBLE VERSE:

2 SAMUEL 12:13B

I have sinned against the Lord.

MY HIGH TODAY WAS:

MY LOW TODAY WAS:

MY PRAYER TODAY IS:

DAY #6

TODAY'S BIBLE VERSE:

1 CORINTHIANS 14:1A

Pursue love...

S | M | T | W | TH | F | S

THEME IN REVIEW

> THERE IS NOTHING
> TO KEEP US HERE. NOTHING.
> NOTHING EXCEPT HONOR.
>
> ASHLEY WILKES TO
> SCARLETT O'HARA
> (EXPLAINING WHY HE WON'T
> RUN AWAY WITH HER IN
> "GONE WITH THE WIND")

DAY #7

MY FAVORITE VERSE
FROM THE THEME WAS:

....

....

....

....

....

....

....

LOOKING BACK ON THESE TWO WEEKS, MY HIGHEST HIGH WAS:

....

MY LOWEST LOW THESE PAST WEEKS WAS:

....

ONE WAY GOD ANSWERED MY PRAYERS WAS:

....

ONE WAY GOD MIGHT USE ME AS A SACRED AGENT
TO ANSWER THESE PRAYERS:

....

....

FAMILY COVENANT

We have shared *Highs & Lows* this week, read and highlighted the verses assigned in our Bibles, talked about our lives, prayed for one another's highs and lows, and blessed one another.

_____   _____   _____

Parent's Signature   Teen's Signature   Date

THE FINKMANIA QUIZBOWL

QUESTION 1:

The commandment that speaks of sex is:

(A) "You shall not admit adultery,"

(B) "You shall not omit adultery,"

(C) "You shall not commit adultery,"

(D) "You shall not get caught"

QUESTION 2:

The dictionary defines adultery as:

(A) Sex,

(B) Sex with someone who is not your spouse,

(C) Sex between adults,

(D) Sex between non-consenting adults

QUESTION 3:

According to a recent study, sexual content appears in what percentage of television programs?:

(A) 64%,

(B) 70%,

(C) 50%,

(D) 13%

QUESTION 4:

Adultery and betrayal are related because:

(A) Both break a bond, trust or agreement,

(B) Both deal with marriage exclusively,

(C) Both are mild offenses,

(D) Both are never done by Christians

QUESTION 5:

God's design and plan for sex includes:

(A) Pleasure,

(B) Procreation (making babies),

(C) Bonding two people for life (according to Jesus),

(D) All of the above and then some

QUESTION 6:

God's plan for sex does not include:

(A) Pleasure,

(B) Procreation (making babies),

(C) Bonding two people for life,

(D) Coupling and uncoupling like so many boxcars

QUESTION 7:

The "sex" commandment has to do with:

(A) Sexual language being pure and honorable,

(B) Sexual conduct being pure and honorable,

(C) Husbands and wives loving and respecting each other,

(D) All of the above

QUESTION 8:

If someone is guilty of sexual sin, according to I John 1:9, they should:

(A) Be stoned,

(B) Go to jail, go directly to jail,

(C) Confess and sin no more,

(D) Appear on Oprah

QUESTION 9:

Which of the following did Jesus not say about sex?:

(A) "A man shall leave his father and mother and be joined to his wife,"

(B) "The two shall become one flesh. They are no longer two, but one,"

(C) "What God has joined together let no one separate,"

(D) "If you can't be with the one you love, love the one you're with"

FINKMANIA FINAL QUESTION:

Exodus 20:14 is really about:

(A) Respect and honesty,

(B) Love and commitment,

(C) Treating sex as a wonderful gift within the bonds of marriage,

(D) All of the above and then some

 Play this online game using FINKlink
LF06 @ www.faithink.com

THE WEAKEST FINK

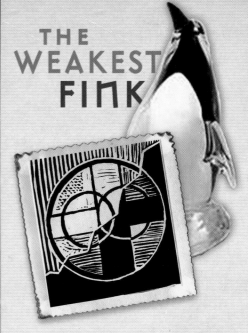

DO NOT DO WHAT YOU WOULD UNDO IF CAUGHT.

LEAH ARENDT

TERMS
WRITE A DEFINITION BELOW.

ADULTERY

HONORABLE

MARRIAGE

PURE

SEX

 FAITH INKUBATORS

STEALING

"David and Jonathan" Dr. He Qi. Order prints at www.heqiarts.com

"YOU SHALL NOT STEAL."

— EXODUS 20:15

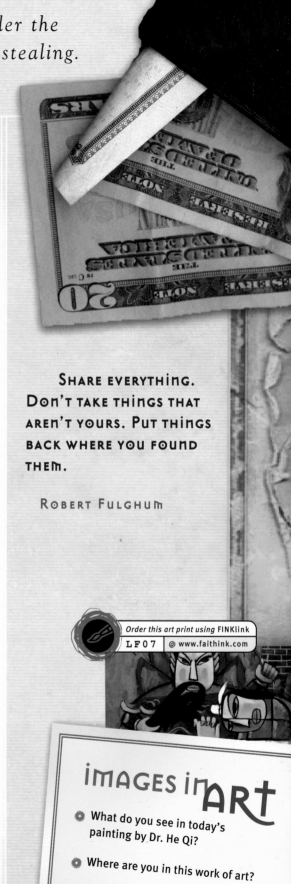

God must have heard every excuse under the sun a billion times when it comes to stealing.

Finder's keepers... Every day people find and keep things that do not belong to them. Is it really stealing, or just good luck?

It's only fair considering... Every day people believe that an error in their favor is designed to even out all the other times unfair things have happened to them. Is it really stealing, or just evening the score?

It's not hurting anyone... Every day people steal from large corporations or stores because of the company's multimillion-dollar profits. Is it really stealing if a company is too big to notice?

I was only borrowing it... Every day people believe they can designate something as a long-term loan. Is it really stealing if you were going to eventually, possibly, maybe return it? (If you remembered?)

They deserved it... Every day people steal from others as an act of revenge. Is it really stealing if they had it coming?

I haven't really taken anything... Every day people steal when they lie about their age or age of children, download copyrighted material, or bootleg services. Is it really stealing if you didn't actually lift something from a store shelf?

Everyone else does it... Every day people steal with this thought in mind. Is it really stealing if everyone is doing it?

I work here—I earn it... Every day employees take advantage of their companies with this thought and this is stealing through embezzlement. Is it really stealing if you are taking it from your place of work?

It's not stealing—I would have known the answer if I had time to study... Is taking an answer you didn't get on your own really stealing, or just good time management?

Integrity

Think about these two words: integrity and integrate. What is an "integrated" person? What is a person of integrity? Go to your favorite dictionary and define both words. God desires our words and actions to fit together. That is what it means to integrate. You do what you say and say what you do. It's another word for honesty. Look into someone's eyes and say:

"I will be a person of integrity. My actions and my words will fit together."

Share everything. Don't take things that aren't yours. Put things back where you found them.

Robert Fulghum

Order this art print using FINKlink
LF07 @ www.faithink.com

Images in Art

- What do you see in today's painting by Dr. He Qi?
- Where are you in this work of art?
- How do the image and the verse apply to your life today?

So What Does This Mean?

MRS. FENSTER, WOULD YOU KINDLY MAKE ME THIRTY COPIES OF THIS SONG ON THE 7th COMMANDMENT?

YOU SHALL NOT STEAL

COPIES #.08

PRAYER

DEAR GOD, MAKE ME THINK TWICE BEFORE I EVER TAKE SOMETHING THAT ISN'T MINE. HELP ME TO BE FAITHFUL EVEN IN LITTLE THINGS THAT DON'T SEEM TO MATTER—ANSWERS ON TESTS, POCKET CHANGE ON THE TABLE, AND SMALL WORDS OF GOSSIP. TEACH ME TO LIVE IN INTEGRITY AND DO WHAT IS RIGHT WHETHER ANYONE IS LOOKING OR NOT. I PRAY IN JESUS' NAME.

AMEN.

SO WHAT?

What's the big deal about stealing? It's not like murder or adultery. No one gets hurt, right?

Wrong.

Someone always gets hurt, and that someone is often you! Stealing was important enough for God to include in the Big Ten. And remember Christ's "Golden Rule?" We are to treat others in the same way we would want them to treat us. We are to love our neighbors as ourselves. You don't like to be ripped off.

So don't do it to others.

BIBLE TIME

In this commandment, God not only seeks to protect our valuables, but also to protect our lives from being robbed. Read and highlight each of the following verses, writing "Stealing" in the margin. What does each say about stealing?

Exodus 20:15

Leviticus 19:11

Malachi 3:8

Romans 2:21

Luke 19:8

I John 3:18

ROLE PLAY

1. You are working at the local burger joint. Your friends come in and expect you to slip them some free food. What do you say? What do you do?

2. You meet friends at the mall for lunch. One friend brags how easy it is to walk out of a store with T-shirts. Everyone dares you to do it. What do you say?

QUESTIONS TO PONDER

1. Describe a time in your life when something you valued was stolen from you. How did you feel? What did you do about it?

2. How do people justify each of the following?

Shoplifting

Cheating on income tax

Cheating on a term paper

Underpaying a worker

Copying a DVD or CD

Loafing on the job

Cheating a poor gambler

Spending all their money selfishly

SMALL GROUP
SHARE, READ, TALK, PRAY, BLESS

1. **SHARE** your highs and lows of the week one-on-one with another person. Listen carefully and record your friend's thoughts in the space below. Then return to small group and share your friend's highs and lows.

    MY HIGHS + LOWS THIS WEEK WERE:

    ....

    MY FRIEND'S HIGHS + LOWS THIS WEEK WERE:

    ....

2. **READ** and highlight the theme verse in your Bibles. Circle key words and learn the verse in song if time permits.

3. **TALK** about how today's verse relates to your highs and lows. Review the art for today, the Quiz Bowl questions, the terms, and the cartoons. Then write a sentence on each of the following:

    ONE NEW THING I LEARNED TODAY:

    ....

    ONE THING I ALREADY KNEW THAT IS WORTH REPEATING:

    ....

    ONE THING I WOULD LIKE TO KNOW MORE ABOUT:

    ....

4. **PRAY** for one another, praising and thanking God for your highs, and asking God to be with you in your lows. Include your friend's highs and lows in your prayers.

    A PRAISING PRAYER: ....

    A THANKING PRAYER: ....

    AN ASKING PRAYER: ....

5. **BLESS** one another using the blessing of the week. (right) Mark each person with the sign of the cross as you bless them.

THE FINK 5

THIS WEEK'S BLESSING

(NAME), CHILD OF GOD, MAY GOD BE GENEROUS TO YOU AND YOU DO LIKEWISE. IN CHRIST'S NAME, AMEN.

Lot No. AA3157

014

PIECE NO.

THE HOME HUDDLE jOURNAL

SHARE, READ, tALK, PRAY, BLESS

WEEK I

Read the full devotions using FINKlink

LF07 | @ www.faithink.com

DAY #1

tODAY'S BIBLE VERSE:

EXODUS 20:15

You shall not steal.

MY HIGH tODAY WAS:

_____

MY LOW tODAY WAS:

_____

MY PRAYER tODAY IS:

_____

_____

DAY #2

tODAY'S BIBLE VERSE:

LUKE 19:8B

If I have defrauded anyone of anything, I will pay back four times as much.

MY HIGH tODAY WAS:

_____

MY LOW tODAY WAS:

_____

MY PRAYER tODAY IS:

_____

_____

DAY #3

tODAY'S BIBLE VERSE:

ACTS 20:35B

It is more blessed to give than to receive.

MY HIGH tODAY WAS:

_____

MY LOW tODAY WAS:

_____

MY PRAYER tODAY IS:

_____

_____

my HIGH today was:

my LOW today was:

my PRAYER today is:

DAY #4

today's Bible verse:

Matthew 25:35

For I was hungry and you gave me food, I was thirsty and you gave me something to drink, I was a stranger and you welcomed me.

---

my HIGH today was:

my LOW today was:

my PRAYER today is:

DAY #5

today's Bible verse:

Matthew 25:36

I was naked and you gave me clothing, I was sick and you took care of me, I was in prison and you visited me.

---

my HIGH today was:

my LOW today was:

my PRAYER today is:

DAY #6

today's Bible verse:

Ephesians 4:28

Thieves must give up stealing; rather let them labor and work honestly with their own hands, so as to have something to share with the needy.

---

my HIGHEST HIGH this week was:

my LOWEST LOW this week was:

my PRAYER for next week is:

DAY #7

this week's blessing

(NAME), child of God, may God be generous to you and you do likewise. In Christ's name. Amen.

THE HOME HUDDLE JOURNAL
SHARE, READ, TALK, PRAY, BLESS

WEEK 2

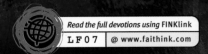

Read the full devotions using FINKlink
LF07 @ www.faithink.com

DAY #1

TODAY'S BIBLE VERSE:

1 JOHN 3:18

Little children, let us love, not in word or speech, but in truth and action.

MY HIGH TODAY WAS:

MY LOW TODAY WAS:

MY PRAYER TODAY IS:

DAY #2

TODAY'S BIBLE VERSE:

MARK 8:36

What will it profit them to gain the whole world and forfeit their life?

MY HIGH TODAY WAS:

MY LOW TODAY WAS:

MY PRAYER TODAY IS:

DAY #3

TODAY'S BIBLE VERSE:

JUDGES 17:2

He said to his mother, "The eleven hundred pieces of silver that were taken from you, about which you uttered a curse, and even spoke it in my hearing,—that silver is in my possession; I took it; but now I will return it to you." And his mother said, "May my son be blessed by the Lord!"

MY HIGH TODAY WAS:

MY LOW TODAY WAS:

MY PRAYER TODAY IS:

1. SHARE HIGHS & LOWS OF THE DAY.

2. READ AND HIGHLIGHT THE VERSE OF THE DAY IN YOUR BIBLES.

3. TALK ABOUT HOW TODAY'S VERSE RELATES TO YOUR HIGHS & LOWS.

4. PRAY FOR YOUR HIGHS & LOWS, FOR YOUR FAMILY AND FOR THE WORLD.

5. BLESS ONE ANOTHER USING THIS WEEK'S BLESSING (ON THE PREVIOUS PAGE).

MY HIGH TODAY WAS:

MY LOW TODAY WAS:

MY PRAYER TODAY IS:

DAY #4

TODAY'S BIBLE VERSE:

Leviticus 19:11

You shall not steal; you shall not deal falsely; you shall not lie to one another.

MY HIGH TODAY WAS:

MY LOW TODAY WAS:

MY PRAYER TODAY IS:

DAY #5

TODAY'S BIBLE VERSE:

Matthew 20:26b

Whoever wishes to be great among you must be your servant.

MY HIGH TODAY WAS:

MY LOW TODAY WAS:

MY PRAYER TODAY IS:

DAY #6

TODAY'S BIBLE VERSE:

John 10:10

The thief comes only to steal and kill and destroy. I came that they may have life, and have it abundantly.

THEME IN REVIEW

THE LOUDER HE
TALKED OF HIS HONOUR,
THE FASTER WE COUNTED
OUR SPOONS.

RALPH WALDO EMERSON

DAY #7

MY FAVORITE **VERSE**
FROM THE THEME WAS:

LOOKING BACK ON THESE TWO WEEKS, MY HIGHEST **HIGH** WAS:

MY LOWEST **LOW** THESE PAST WEEKS WAS:

ONE WAY **GOD** ANSWERED MY **PRAYERS** WAS:

ONE WAY **GOD** MIGHT USE ME AS A **SACRED AGENT**
TO ANSWER THESE PRAYERS:

FAMILY COVENANT

We have shared *Highs & Lows* this week, read and highlighted the verses assigned in our Bibles, talked about our lives, prayed for one another's highs and lows, and blessed one another.

Parent's Signature   Teen's Signature   Date

THE FINKMANIA QUIZBOWL

Question 1:

The commandment that follows "you shall not kill" is:

(A) "You shall not commit adultery,"

(B) "You shall not steal,"

(C) "You shall not bear false witness against your neighbor"

(D) A or B, depending on if you are Catholic and Lutheran or another Protestant denomination

Question 2:

To steal means:

(A) To take something without permission,

(B) To use something without permission, then put it back before anyone notices,

(C) To borrow something for an extended duration and forget to return it,

(D) A, B and sometimes C

Question 3:

Which of the following is not stealing?:

(A) Loafing on the job,

(B) Shoplifting,

(C) Copying MP3s, DVDs, and software,

(D) None of the above

Question 4:

If you steal something and no one sees you:

(A) Good for you,

(B) You got away with it so it's okay,

(C) You didn't really get away with it because God sees everything

(D) God sees you but it really doesn't matter because God's not going to turn you in

Question 5:

Integrity means:

(A) Your words and conduct—what you say and what you do—match (integrate) with each other,

(B) You are a person of honor, honesty, morality and ethics,

(C) Both A & B,

(D) Neither A nor B

Question 6:

"Do unto others as you would have them do unto you" is sometimes called:

(A) The Golden Rule,

(B) The Bill of Rights,

(C) The Great Commission,

(D) The Great Omission

Question 7:

Most wars are caused by:

(A) Oil,

(B) Religion,

(C) Greed, followed by someone breaking the Seventh Commandment,

(D) Greed, followed by someone breaking the First, Second, Third, Fourth, Fifth, Sixth, Seventh, Eighth, Ninth and Tenth Commandments

Question 8:

Breaking the "stealing" commandment includes:

(A) Taking our neighbor's money,

(B) Taking our neighbor's property,

(C) Getting things in dishonest ways,

(D) All of the above

Question 9:

Keeping the "stealing" commandment involves:

(A) Helping our neighbors improve and protect their property,

(B) Helping our neighbors improve and protect their means of making a living,

(C) Both A & B,

(D) Buying Lotto tickets whenever it reaches one hundred million or more and donating to charity

FINKMANIA Final Question:

Exodus 20:15 tells us:

(A) We should only steal from the rich and give to the poor,

(B) We should only steal when we're sure we won't get caught,

(C) We should never steal—never, never, never,

(D) Gambling isn't stealing

Play this online game using FINKlink

LF07 @ www.faithink.com

THE WEAKEST FINK

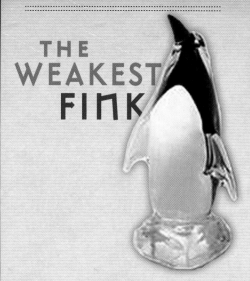

DAD, IS IT ALL RIGHT TO TAKE THINGS FROM PEOPLE YOU DON'T LIKE?

LISA SIMPSON

TERMS
WRITE A DEFINITION BELOW.

DISHONESTY

HONESTY

INTEGRITY

PRESERVE

STEAL

FAITH INKUBATORS

False Witness

"Judgment of Solomon" Dr. He Qi. Order prints at www.heqiarts.com

"YOU SHALL NOT BEAR FALSE WITNESS

AGAINST YOUR NEIGHBOR."

— EXODUS 20:16

Listen to this song using FINKlink
LF08 @ www.faithink.com

**N**icole lay awake in too much pain to sleep, but it wasn't the hairline fracture in her arm or the thigh-to-ankle plaster casts on her legs that hurt the most.

It was the pain from a lie her "so-called best friend" had spread about her that was keeping her up. She could not remember much about the night before or the accident. Oncoming headlights, the loud crash, and spinning across the wet pavement were all a blur. She wished she could say the same about the argument which preceded her frenzied drive. That memory was crystal clear.

Someone had been spreading a terrible rumor about her in school. That night she drove to her best friend's house, hoping to find some comfort. Much to her despair, Nicole discovered it was her friend who had started the rumors. With tears clouding her eyes, she ran from the house, jumped into her car, and sped off down the street.

Eight weeks later Nicole was sitting in school, marveling at the wonder of touching skin instead of plaster on her legs. She had not heard from her friend in all that time. Not a card. Not a visit. Nothing. The bell rang as she grabbed her crutches. Looking up, she was startled to meet her former friend's eyes. The girl looked as though she had something to say. Nicole was not ready to deal with her. She brushed by, then turned quickly back. "Sticks and stones."

"What?" asked the friend.

"The old saying isn't true." She smiled a half-smile. "Sticks and stones are nothing. Words can really hurt you."

Why Lie?

Is lying ever right? Are some lies worse than others? According to a *New York Times* survey, ninety-one percent of people confess they regularly don't tell the truth. Twenty percent admit they can't get through a day without conscious, premeditated lies. The article suggests the moral landscape of people today has changed as it relates to bearing false witness. Lying is now openly accepted.

Some people lie to make themselves look good. Some people lie to hurt others. Some lie to cover up mistakes. Some find themselves lying in order to cover up their other lies. Once a lie starts, it is often impossible to stop. Once the toothpaste is out of the tube, it is almost impossible to put it back in.

Lies come in many shapes, forms and sizes. Some destroy relationships. Some destroy reputations. Some destroy countries.

All destroy trust.

CHARLIE BROWN:
WE'RE SUPPOSED TO WRITE HOME TO OUR PARENTS AND TELL THEM WHAT A GREAT TIME WE'RE HAVING HERE AT CAMP.

Linus:
EVEN IF WE'RE NOT? ISN'T THAT A LIE?

CHARLIE BROWN:
WELL... IT'S SORT OF A WHITE LIE.

Linus:
LIES COME IN COLORS?

IMAGES in ART

- What do you see in today's painting by Dr. He Qi?

- Where are you in this work of art?

- How do the image and the verse apply to your life today?

SO WHAT DOES THIS MEAN?

I MAKE iT A POINT **NEVER** TO TELL A LiE ABOUT ANY ONE UNLESS iT'S A REAL **GOOD** ONE!

YOU SHALL NOT BEAR FALSE WITNESS AGAINST YOUR NEIGHBOR

SO WHAT?

The Bible says God considers lying a sin. Period. It is a major wrong – the breaking of a commandment – to tell a falsehood. "There are six things that the Lord hates… a lying tongue…" Proverbs 6:16-17. One of the main attributes of God is justice. Truth is a precondition of justice. Lying is more than just not telling the truth. A liar creates injustice, distrust, and misery. God commands us to be people of truth. What are you going to do about it?

BIBLE TIME

Read and highlight Exodus 20:16 in your Bible, writing "Truth!" in the margin. Now look at these other commandments. How might breaking the "false witness" commandment be related to:

Worshiping Other Gods   Honoring Parents

Killing   Adultery

Stealing   Coveting

ROLE PLAY

1. You notice your teacher gave you a higher grade than you deserved on a test. You approach her desk and...

2. One of your roommates smokes marijuana on the church youth trip. A chaperone walks into your room, smells smoke and asks about it. How do you respond?

3. A friend is spreading rumors about a new kid in school. Whether they are true or not, they are costing this new kid friends. What do you do and say?

QUESTIONS TO PONDER

1. Where do you draw the line between talking about other people, gossip and bearing false witness?

2. What could you do to make things right if you have said something that harmed another person's reputation?

3. Think about a time when someone told a lie about you. What did that individual take from you by doing that? What did they gain? What did they lose? Why did they do it? How did you respond? What would you do differently if that situation had been reversed?

PRAYER

OH GOD, iT HURTS TO BE LiED TO AND LiED ABOUT. PLEASE MAKE ME THINK TWICE NEXT TIME I START TO SAY ANYTHING UNTRUE, HURTFUL OR CRUEL ABOUT ANYONE. HELP ME TO LIVE WITH SUCH INTEGRITY THAT I SPEAK THE SAME TO PEOPLES' FACES AS I SPEAK WHEN THEY ARE NOT AROUND. IN JESUS' NAME.

AMEN.

SMALL GR✛UP
SHARE, READ, TALK, PRAY, BLESS

1. **S H A R E** your highs and lows of the week one-on-one with another person. Listen carefully and record your friend's thoughts in the space below. Then return to small group and share your friend's highs and lows.

MY HIGHS + LOWS THIS WEEK WERE:

....

MY FRIEND'S HIGHS + LOWS THIS WEEK WERE:

....

2. **R E A D** and highlight the theme verse in your Bibles. Circle key words and learn the verse in song if time permits.

3. **T A L K** about how today's verse relates to your highs and lows. Review the art for today, the Quiz Bowl questions, the terms, and the cartoons. Then write a sentence on each of the following:

ONE NEW THING I LEARNED TODAY:

....

ONE THING I ALREADY KNEW THAT IS WORTH REPEATING:

....

ONE THING I WOULD LIKE TO KNOW MORE ABOUT:

....

4. **P R A Y** for one another, praising and thanking God for your highs, and asking God to be with you in your lows. Include your friend's highs and lows in your prayers.

A PRAISING PRAYER: ....

A THANKING PRAYER: ....

AN ASKING PRAYER: ....

5. **B L E S S** one another using the blessing of the week. (right) Mark each person with the sign of the cross as you bless them.

THIS WEEK'S BLESSING
(NAME), CHILD OF
GOD, MAY YOU BE A
PERSON OF TRUTH THIS
DAY. AMEN.

THE HOME HUDDLE jOURNAL
SHARE, READ, tALK, PRAY, BLESS

Read the full devotions using FINKlink
LF08 | @ www.faithink.com

DAY #1

tODAY'S BiBLE VERSE:

EXODUS 20:16

You shall not bear false witness against your neighbor.

MY HiGH tODAY WAS:

MY LOW tODAY WAS:

MY PRAYER tODAY iS:

DAY #2

tODAY'S BiBLE VERSE:

LUKE 22:48B

Jesus said to him, "Judas, is it with a kiss that you are betraying the son of man?

MY HiGH tODAY WAS:

MY LOW tODAY WAS:

MY PRAYER tODAY iS:

DAY #3

tODAY'S BiBLE VERSE:

PROVERBS 22:1

A good name is to be chosen rather than great riches; and favor is better than silver or gold.

MY HiGH tODAY WAS:

MY LOW tODAY WAS:

MY PRAYER tODAY iS:

my HIGH today was:

my LOW today was:

my PRAYER today is:

TODAY'S BIBLE VERSE:
PROVERBS 11:13
A gossip goes around telling secrets, but one who is trustworthy in spirit keeps a confidence.

---

my HIGH today was:

my LOW today was:

my PRAYER today is:

DAY #5

TODAY'S BIBLE VERSE:
EXODUS 23:1
You shall not spread a false report. You shall not join hands with the wicked to act as a malicious witness.

---

my HIGH today was:

my LOW today was:

my PRAYER today is:

DAY #6

TODAY'S BIBLE VERSE:
PROVERBS 25:18
Like a war club, a sword, or a sharp arrow is one who bears false witness against a neighbor.

---

my HIGHEST HIGH this week was:

my LOWEST LOW this week was:

my PRAYER for next week is:

DAY #7

THIS WEEK'S BLESSING
(NAME), CHILD OF GOD, MAY YOU BE A PERSON OF TRUTH THIS DAY. AMEN.

THE HOME HUDDLE JOURNAL

SHARE, READ, TALK, PRAY, BLESS

WEEK 2

Read the full devotions using FINKlink

LF08 @ www.faithink.com

DAY #1

TODAY'S BIBLE VERSE:

PROVERBS 11:9

With their mouths the god-less would destroy their neighbors, but by knowledge the righteous are delivered.

MY HIGH TODAY WAS:

MY LOW TODAY WAS:

MY PRAYER TODAY IS:

DAY #2

TODAY'S BIBLE VERSE:

EPHESIANS 4:29

Let no evil talk come out of your mouths, but only what is useful for building up, as there is need, so that your words may give grace to those who hear.

MY HIGH TODAY WAS:

MY LOW TODAY WAS:

MY PRAYER TODAY IS:

DAY #3

TODAY'S BIBLE VERSE:

PROVERBS 15:1

A soft answer turns away wrath, but a harsh word stirs up anger.

MY HIGH TODAY WAS:

MY LOW TODAY WAS:

MY PRAYER TODAY IS:

1. **SHARE** HIGHS & LOWS OF THE DAY.

2. **READ** AND HIGHLIGHT THE VERSE OF THE DAY IN YOUR BIBLES.

3. **TALK** ABOUT HOW TODAY'S VERSE RELATES TO YOUR HIGHS & LOWS.

4. **PRAY** FOR YOUR HIGHS & LOWS, FOR YOUR FAMILY AND FOR THE WORLD.

5. **BLESS** ONE ANOTHER USING THIS WEEK'S BLESSING (ON THE PREVIOUS PAGE).

MY HIGH TODAY WAS:

MY LOW TODAY WAS:

MY PRAYER TODAY IS:

DAY #4

TODAY'S BIBLE VERSE:

PROVERBS 6:16-19A

There are six things the Lord hates... haughty eyes, a lying tongue, hands that shed innocent blood, a heart that devises wicked plans, feet that hurry to run to evil, a lying witness who testifies falsely...

MY HIGH TODAY WAS:

MY LOW TODAY WAS:

MY PRAYER TODAY IS:

DAY #5

TODAY'S BIBLE VERSE:

EPHESIANS 4:11-12

The gifts he gave were that some would be apostles, some prophets, some evangelists, some pastors and teachers, to equip the saints for the work of ministry, for building up the body of Christ.

MY HIGH TODAY WAS:

MY LOW TODAY WAS:

MY PRAYER TODAY IS:

DAY #6

TODAY'S BIBLE VERSE:

PSALM 82:3-4

Give justice to the weak and the orphan; maintain the right of the lowly and the destitute. Rescue the weak and the needy; deliver them from the hand of the wicked.

THEME IN REVIEW

S|M|T|W|TH|F|S

THERE IS A DEMON WHO PUTS WINGS ON CERTAIN STORIES AND WHO LAUNCHES THEM LIKE EAGLES INTO THE AIR.

ALEXANDER DUMAS

DAY #7

MY FAVORITE VERSE FROM THE THEME WAS:

....

....

....

....

....

....

LOOKING BACK ON THESE TWO WEEKS, MY HIGHEST HIGH WAS:

....

MY LOWEST LOW THESE PAST WEEKS WAS:

....

ONE WAY GOD ANSWERED MY PRAYERS WAS:

....

ONE WAY GOD MIGHT USE ME AS A SACRED AGENT TO ANSWER THESE PRAYERS:

....

....

FAMILY COVENANT

We have shared *Highs & Lows* this week, read and highlighted the verses assigned in our Bibles, talked about our lives, prayed for one another's highs and lows, and blessed one another.

....
Parent's Signature   Teen's Signature   Date

THE FINKMANIA QUIZBOWL

QUESTION 1:

The commandment that follows "you shall not steal" is:

(A) "You shall not kill,"

(B) "You shall not commit adultery,"

(C) "You shall not steal,"

(D) "You shall not bear false witness against your neighbor"

QUESTION 2:

False witness includes:

(A) Lies,

(B) Gossip,

(C) Rumors,

(D) All of the above and then some

QUESTION 3:

A good reputation:

(A) Takes a long time to earn but an even longer time to lose,

(B) Takes a long time to earn but a short time to lose to a gossip,

(C) Is quite expensive to buy,

(D) Really isn't all that important

QUESTION 4:

A lie told intentionally is called:

(A) Slander,

(B) Payback,

(C) Misnomer,

(D) Politics as usual

QUESTION 5:

What did Jesus say about people who are hurt by lies?:

(A) They should get even,

(B) They should get a lawyer,

(C) They should rejoice, feel blessed, and return good for the evil done to them,

(D) They should rejoice, feel blessed, then get a lawyer and cheerfully sue the socks off the offender

QUESTION 6:

How can you make things right if you have told a lie about someone?

(A) Confess and offer to make things up,

(B) Confess and offer to lie about someone else from now on,

(C) Forget the whole thing happened,

(D) Pay them in cash from your dad's sock drawer before they sue you

QUESTION 7:

Breaking the "false witness" commandment involves:

(A) Betrayal, slander and lies,

(B) Betrayal, slander and lies,

(C) Betrayal, slander and lies,

(D) All of the above, plus betrayal, slander and lies

QUESTION 8:

To truly keep the intent of the "false witness" commandment, we are to:

(A) Defend our neighbors,

(B) Speak well of our neighbors,

(C) Both A & B, and explain their actions in the kindest ways,

(D) Both A & B, but not try to explain their actions

QUESTION 9:

Breaking the "false witness" commandment also breaks the:

(A) Killing and stealing commandments because we are killing and stealing someone's reputation,

(B) Golden Rule,

(C) First Amendment to the US Constitution,

(D) Both A and B

FINKMANIA FINAL QUESTION:

Exodus 20:16 tells us:

(A) We are not to bear false witness against our neighbor,

(B) We are not to betray, slander, or lie about our neighbor,

(C) We are to defend, speak well of, and explain our neighbor's actions in the kindest ways,

(D) All of the above and then some

 Play this online game using FINKlink | LF08 | @ www.faithink.com

---

THE WEAKEST FINK

PEOPLE DO NOT LIVE BY WORDS ALONE, ALTHOUGH THEY SOMETIMES MUST EAT THEM.

ADLAI STEVENSON

TERMS
WRITE A DEFINITION BELOW.

BETRAY

FALSE WITNESS

GOSSIP

LIE

SLANDER

◆ FAITH INKUBATORS

Coveting

"Joseph's Coat" Dr. He Qi. Order prints at www.heqiarts.com

"YOU SHALL NOT COVET YOUR NEIGHBOR'S HOUSE; YOU

SHALL NOT COVET YOUR NEIGHBOR'S WIFE, OR MALE OR

FEMALE SLAVE, OR OX, OR DONKEY, OR ANYTHING THAT

BELONGS TO YOUR NEIGHBOR."

— EXODUS 20:17

Listen to this song using FINKlink
LF09 | @ www.faithink.com

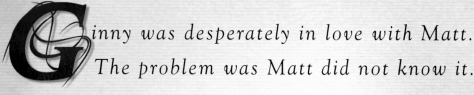

Ginny was desperately in love with Matt. The problem was Matt did not know it.

She was too frightened to tell him. What if he didn't feel the same way? Matt had been like a brother to her since he moved into the neighborhood in grade school. They hung out together and talked about everything from feelings to fads to their futures. Then, during junior high, Matt started paying attention to some of Ginny's friends. All of a sudden, Ginny became sarcastic and critical. Whenever Matt would ask her about a certain girl, Ginny would put the friend down and tell Matt all the dirt she knew. Matt did not understand everything that was going on. He was seeing an ugly side of her and he didn't like it. The more she "dissed" the girls Matt liked, the less he wanted to be around her. Ginny was jealous, and it wasn't pretty.

When Matt told her he was asking one of her friends to Homecoming, Ginny began to scheme up ways to make Matt think less of the girl. She told some lies, but Matt didn't believe her. Finally she stormed over to the girl's house and ordered her to leave Matt alone. "If you are any friend of mine, you will stay away from him!" she screamed.

WANTING AND COVETING

What is the difference between wanting something and coveting it? What's the difference between a healthy desire for something or someone and an unhealthy greed that leads you to scheme? At the tail end of the Ten Commandments, we find two clear orders from God. We are not to covet our neighbor's house or their spouse! We are not to covet their things or their relationships. That goes for tempting and coaxing loyalty away from relationships, as well as for plotting and scheming to get possessions that don't belong to us.

Like most sin, coveting usually begins in the mind. It starts with jealous thoughts, desires, and feelings. It gets amplified through self-talk—conversations that go on in our heads. Some psychologists suggest that most people are holding an unending dialogue with themselves every waking and sleeping minute of the day. That dialogue colors their every experience and shapes how they view themselves and the world. A person can speak out loud at a rate of 150-200 words a minute. Our private conversation, however, speeds on at the rate of approximately 1300 words a minute! It is a challenge to learn to control thoughts and feelings at that speed! Thoughts can take on a life of their own. Wants can turn into desires, desires into jealousy, jealousy into schemes, and schemes into coveting actions before we know what hit us.

That's when you get in trouble.

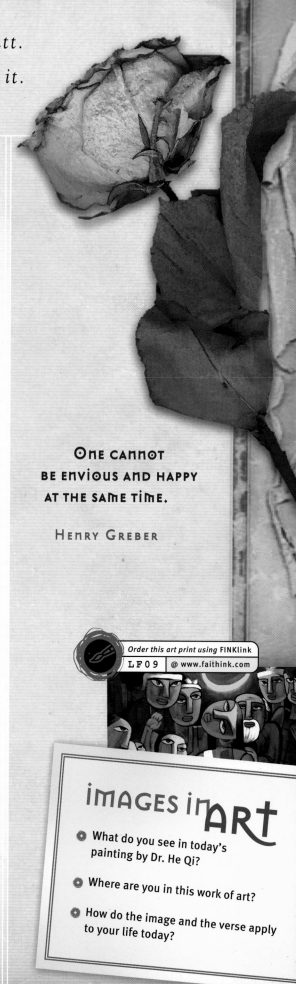

ONE CANNOT BE ENVIOUS AND HAPPY AT THE SAME TIME.

HENRY GREBER

Order this art print using FINKlink
LF09 @ www.faithink.com

IMAGES in ART

○ What do you see in today's painting by Dr. He Qi?

○ Where are you in this work of art?

○ How do the image and the verse apply to your life today?

SO WHAT DOES THIS MEAN?

JUST REMEMBER TONIGHT WHEN I TAKE YOUR MONEY, IT'S NOT GAMBLING. IT'S **GAMING**

IF YOU REALLY WANT SOMETHING IN THIS LIFE, YOU HAVE TO WORK FOR IT— NOW QUIET, THEY'RE ABOUT TO ANNOUNCE THE LOTTERY NUMBERS!

HOMER SIMPSON

SO WHAT?

There is nothing wrong with wanting something. Wants can lead us to creativity, teamwork, and the motivation to get off our rear ends, work hard, and earn it. When wants become obsessions with things we can't have, those obsessions can lead to plots and scheming. That's when the danger flags raise. Envy, jealousy, and greed result. Those things destroy. There is enough destruction in the world. Children of God are called to be people who build up in a world that tears down. Will you give up the coveting when it rears its ugly head and be a person who builds for God?

BIBLE TIME

God wants to help shape your self talk and desires. How do the following verses suggest that could happen?

Psalm 27:4	I Samuel 16:7b
Exodus 20:17	Proverbs 16:28-9
Philippians 4:8	Mark 8:36

ROLE PLAY

1. A friend says: "If I'm not number one in my sport I feel miserable and I'm out to get whoever is ahead of me. Is there anything wrong with that?"

2. Your friend appears to have everything: looks, good grades, money, a great family. You start to become aware that you are jealous. What do you do?

QUESTIONS TO PONDER

1. What was the last thing you really wanted but couldn't possess?

2. When might wanting something badly be good?

3. How might coveting and cheating someone be related? How might coveting and gambling be connected?

PRAYER

DEAR GOD, IT'S LIKE I HAVE THIS EMPTY HOLE I KEEP TRYING TO FILL. I WANT MORE, AND MORE, AND MORE. BUT THE MORE I GET THE EMPTIER I FEEL. I KNOW YOU ALONE CAN FILL THAT EMPTY SPACE. WILL YOU COME INTO ALL THE EMPTY SPACES IN MY HEART? FILL ME UP WITH YOUR THOUGHTS AND DESIRES. I WANT TO FOLLOW YOU. AMEN.

SMALL GROUP
SHARE, READ, TALK, PRAY, BLESS

1. **SHARE** your highs and lows of the week one-on-one with another person. Listen carefully and record your friend's thoughts in the space below. Then return to small group and share your friend's highs and lows.

   MY HIGHS + LOWS THIS WEEK WERE:

   ....

   MY FRIEND'S HIGHS + LOWS THIS WEEK WERE:

   ....

2. **READ** and highlight the theme verse in your Bibles. Circle key words and learn the verse in song if time permits.

3. **TALK** about how today's verse relates to your highs and lows. Review the art for today, the Quiz Bowl questions, the terms, and the cartoons. Then write a sentence on each of the following:

   ONE NEW THING I LEARNED TODAY:

   ....

   ONE THING I ALREADY KNEW THAT IS WORTH REPEATING:

   ....

   ONE THING I WOULD LIKE TO KNOW MORE ABOUT:

   ....

4. **PRAY** for one another, praising and thanking God for your highs, and asking God to be with you in your lows. Include your friend's highs and lows in your prayers.

   A PRAISING PRAYER: ....

   A THANKING PRAYER: ....

   AN ASKING PRAYER: ....

5. **BLESS** one another using the blessing of the week. (right) Mark each person with the sign of the cross as you bless them.

Hey! You're all going the wrong way!

THIS WEEK'S BLESSING
MAY THE SPIRIT OF THE LIVING GOD BE ALL THAT YOU NEED THIS DAY. IN CHRIST'S NAME, AMEN.

THE HOME HUDDLE JOURNAL
SHARE, READ, TALK, PRAY, BLESS

WEEK 1

Read the full devotions using FINKlink
LF09 @ www.faithink.com

DAY #1

TODAY'S BIBLE VERSE:

EXODUS 20:17

You shall not covet your neighbor's house.

my HIGH today was:

my LOW today was:

my PRAYER today is:

DAY #2

TODAY'S BIBLE VERSE:

PROVERBS 16:28-29

A perverse person spreads strife, and a whisperer separates close friends. The violent entice their neighbors, and lead them in a way that is not good.

my HIGH today was:

my LOW today was:

my PRAYER today is:

DAY #3

TODAY'S BIBLE VERSE:

PHILIPPIANS 4:11-12A

Not that I am referring to being in need; for I have learned to be content with whatever I have. I know what it is to have little, and I know what it is to have plenty.

my HIGH today was:

my LOW today was:

my PRAYER today is:

my HIGH today was:

my LOW today was:

my PRAYER today is:

TODAY'S BIBLE VERSE:
HEBREWS 13:5
Keep your lives free from the love of money, and be content with what you have; for he has said, "I will never leave you or forsake you."

---

my HIGH today was:

my LOW today was:

my PRAYER today is:

DAY #5

TODAY'S BIBLE VERSE:
1 TIMOTHY 6:10
For the love of money is a root of all kinds of evil, and in their eagerness to be rich some have wandered away from the faith and pierced themselves with many pains.

---

my HIGH today was:

my LOW today was:

my PRAYER today is:

DAY #6

TODAY'S BIBLE VERSE:
GALATIANS 5:22B-23A
The fruit of the Spirit is love, joy, peace, patience, kindness, generosity, faithfulness, gentleness, and self-control.

---

my HIGHEST HIGH this week was:

my LOWEST LOW this week was:

my PRAYER for next week is:

DAY #7

THIS WEEK'S BLESSING
MAY THE SPIRIT OF THE LIVING GOD BE ALL THAT YOU NEED THIS DAY. IN CHRIST'S NAME. AMEN.

THE HOME HUDDLE JOURNAL

SHARE, READ, TALK, PRAY, BLESS

WEEK 2

Read the full devotions using FINKlink

LF09 @ www.faithink.com

DAY #1

TODAY'S BIBLE VERSE:

Matthew 5:27-28

"You have heard that it was said, 'You shall not commit adultery.' But I say to you that everyone who looks at a woman with lust has already committed adultery with her in his heart.

MY **HIGH** TODAY WAS:

MY **LOW** TODAY WAS:

MY **PRAYER** TODAY IS:

DAY #2

TODAY'S BIBLE VERSE:

Amos 8:4, 7

Hear this, you that trample on the needy, and bring to ruin the poor of the land... The Lord has sworn by the pride of Jacob: "Surely I will never forget any of their deeds."

MY **HIGH** TODAY WAS:

MY **LOW** TODAY WAS:

MY **PRAYER** TODAY IS:

DAY #3

TODAY'S BIBLE VERSE:

Job 5:13

He takes the wise in their own craftiness; and the schemes of the wily are brought to a quick end.

MY **HIGH** TODAY WAS:

MY **LOW** TODAY WAS:

MY **PRAYER** TODAY IS:

1. **SHARE** HIGHS & LOWS OF THE DAY.

2. **READ** AND HIGHLIGHT THE VERSE OF THE DAY IN YOUR BIBLES.

3. **TALK** ABOUT HOW TODAY'S VERSE RELATES TO YOUR HIGHS & LOWS.

4. **PRAY** FOR YOUR HIGHS & LOWS, FOR YOUR FAMILY AND FOR THE WORLD.

5. **BLESS** ONE ANOTHER USING THIS WEEK'S BLESSING (ON THE PREVIOUS PAGE).

MY HIGH TODAY WAS:

MY LOW TODAY WAS:

MY PRAYER TODAY IS:

DAY #4

TODAY'S BIBLE VERSE:

EXODUS 23:4

When you come upon your enemy's ox or donkey going astray, you shall bring it back.

MY HIGH TODAY WAS:

MY LOW TODAY WAS:

MY PRAYER TODAY IS:

DAY #5

TODAY'S BIBLE VERSE:

LUKE 9:25

What does it profit them if they gain the whole world, but lose or forfeit themselves.?

MY HIGH TODAY WAS:

MY LOW TODAY WAS:

MY PRAYER TODAY IS:

DAY #6

TODAY'S BIBLE VERSE:

EXODUS 20:17B

You shall not covet your neighbor's wife, or male or female slave, or ox, or donkey, or anything that belongs to your neighbor.

THEME IN REVIEW

THE ONLY THING HE DIDN'T HAVE WAS MORE.

RICH MELHEIM

DAY #7

MY FAVORITE **VERSE** FROM THE THEME WAS:

LOOKING BACK ON THESE TWO WEEKS, MY HIGHEST **HIGH** WAS:

MY LOWEST **LOW** THESE PAST WEEKS WAS:

ONE WAY GOD ANSWERED MY **PRAYERS** WAS:

ONE WAY GOD MIGHT USE ME AS A **SACRED AGENT** TO ANSWER THESE PRAYERS:

FAMILY COVENANT

We have shared *Highs & Lows* this week, read and highlighted the verses assigned in our Bibles, talked about our lives, prayed for one another's highs and lows, and blessed one another.

Parent's Signature   Teen's Signature   Date

THE FINKMANIA QUIZ BOWL

QUESTION 1:

The final commandments relate to:

(A) Coveting property,
(B) Coveting relationships,
(C) Neither A nor B,
(D) Both A and B

QUESTION 2:

The word "covet" means:

(A) To want,
(B) To steal,
(C) To want something so much that you scheme to get it,
(D) To want something so much that you work for it

QUESTION 3:

Most of the wars in the history of the world can be linked to:

(A) Oil,
(B) Gold,
(C) Coveting,
(D) Bad breath

QUESTION 4:

The first murder in the Bible was a result of:

(A) Miscommunication between Cain and Abel,
(B) Coveting and jealousy between Cain and Abel,
(C) Girl problems between Cain and Abel,
(D) Bad breath

QUESTION 5:

Another murder in the Old Testament involved:

(A) King David coveting another man's house,
(B) King David coveting another man's spouse,
(C) King David coveting another man's mouse,
(D) King David coveting tickets to the first Olympics

QUESTION 6:

To covet someone's house means:

(A) To want it so much that you scheme to get it from them,
(B) To want it so much that you make an offer on it through a realtor,
(C) To want it so much that you paint your name on the garage door,
(D) None of the above

QUESTION 7:

The "house" commandment is really about:

(A) All possessions of any kind,
(B) Scheming to get things that don't belong to you,
(C) Pretending to a have a right to something that isn't yours,
(D) All of the above

QUESTION 8:

The "spouse" commandment is really about:

(A) All of a person's relationships,
(B) All of a person's loyalties,
(C) All of a person's friends and workers,
(D) All of the above

QUESTION 9:

To truly keep these commandments we are to:

(A) Give up all earthly desires and become Buddhists,
(B) Help our neighbors keep their possessions,
(C) Encourage all to remain loyal to their spouses, bosses and commitments,
(D) B & C

FINKMANIA FINAL QUESTION:

Exodus 20:17 tells us:

(A) "You shall not covet your neighbor's possessions,"
(B) "You shall not covet your neighbor's relationships,"
(C) Both A & B
(D) A & B, but not C

Play this online game using FINKlink
LF09 @ www.faithink.com

THE WEAKEST FINK

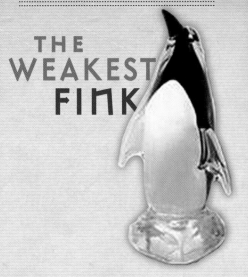

IN THIS WORLD THERE ARE ONLY TWO TRAGEDIES. ONE IS NOT GETTING WHAT ONE WANTS, AND THE OTHER IS GETTING IT.

OSCAR WILDE

TERMS
WRITE A DEFINITION BELOW.

COVET

_____

ENVY

_____

JEALOUSY

_____

SCHEMING

_____

TEMPT

_____

FAITH INKUBATORS

"Red Sea Crossing" Dr. He Qi. Order prints at www.heqiarts.com

"ALL THE ENDS OF THE EARTH SHALL REMEMBER AND TURN TO THE LORD; AND ALL THE FAMILIES OF THE NATIONS SHALL WORSHIP BEFORE HIM. TO HIM, INDEED, SHALL ALL WHO SLEEP IN THE EARTH BOW DOWN; BEFORE HIM SHALL BOW ALL WHO GO DOWN TO THE DUST, AND I SHALL LIVE FOR HIM. POSTERITY WILL SERVE HIM; FUTURE GENERATIONS WILL BE TOLD ABOUT THE LORD, AND PROCLAIM HIS DELIVERANCE TO A PEOPLE YET UNBORN, SAYING THAT HE HAS DONE IT."

— PSALM 22:27, 29-31

Listen to this song using FINKlink
LF10 @ www.faithink.com

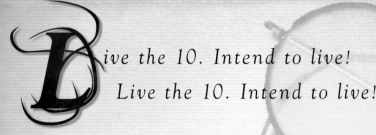

Live the 10. Intend to live!

Bryan Sirchio wrote a fun song about the Ten Commandments called "Live the Ten!" Give yourself a beat or go online to FINKlink LF10 and try it out:

LIVE THE 10   BY BRYAN SIRCHIO

Now I know you've all heard of the
    10 commandments,
But have you taken time to
    understand them?
They're more than a list of rules
    to memorize,
They're the Holy Torah—a way of life.
Now I've laid down a rhythm
    and it's bumpin' burnin'
Move your body while you
    do some learnin,
I'm gonna give 'em to you
    right out straight and then
    I'm gonna take time to elaborate.

Now check this out…
    now remember right off
There's only 1 Lord
    and I didn't say 2 and I didn't say 4
and whatever you do
    you don't bow down before
    anything you make with your hands.
And when you smack your thumb hard
    with a hammer some day
don't get all mad and
    shout out God's name,
'cause God's not to blame
    for your lousy aim
    and that's right—that's right!

And remember the Sabbath
    or whatever you call it
that means pray and rest
    don't be a playaholic
and you love mom and dad
    even when they're not wise,
and don't ever kill—
    does that go for flies?
(Hey that's a good question man)
And when you marry someday
    don't you be a cheat,
and don't you ever steal,
    and don't lie through your teeth,
and don't want the things
    that your friends' got so bad
    you'd take it if you could.

And there you have it my friend
    if you count 'em there's 10
and might I suggest that
    you rap it again,
but if you have a little trouble
    getting all 10 down,
Jesus took 10 and made 'em
    2 somehow,
He said, "Love God the most
    and your neighbor as yourself.
That's right, love God the most
    and your neighbor as yourself."

RULES, RULES, RULES!

It's easy to see laws and rules as negative and restrictive, but think for a moment. If there were no speed limit, you could have a lot of fun driving, but you'd be in much more danger on the road. If there were no laws against stealing, people could walk right into your house and take your stuff. If there were no law of gravity, you'd float off the planet. (Okay, that's a stretch.)

The point is, we need laws and rules to have a safe, fair, and decent society. Without laws, life would be difficult and dangerous. In Jesus' day, the religious leaders had laws about everything. They told you what you could eat and when. They told you when you could work and when you had to rest. They told you under what circumstances you could get a divorce, and what you had to do if your brother died. (Marry his wife and raise sons for him!) They even told you what direction to turn if you had to relieve yourself. (A bit much?)

IMAGES in ART

- What do you see in today's painting by Dr. He Qi?

- Where are you in this work of art?

- How do the image and the verse apply to your life today?

SO WHAT DOES THIS MEAN?

I AM NOT POSITIVE, FENSTER, BUT I MAY NOT HAVE BEEN CLEAR ENOUGH ABOUT THE ROLE OF THE TEN COMMANDMENTS IN THE CHRISTIAN LIFE.

PRAYER

DEAR GOD, HELP ME TO BE THE KIND OF PERSON YOU WANT ME TO BE AND TO LOVE YOU WITH MY WHOLE HEART, MIND, SOUL, AND STRENGTH. IN JESUS' NAME.

AMEN.

SO WHAT?

Every day you make small decisions that don't appear all that earth-shattering. So what if you cheated on that test? No one gets hurt, right? So what if you break a promise? So what if you yell at your parents? So what if you sleep in on Sunday? So what? So what! When you add up all of these small "so-what's" you end up with a life lacking goodness, meaning, and direction. And we end up with a heartless, God-less society. Without God's guidance, our lives lack the purpose, value, integrity and the joy God intends. When it comes right down to it, God isn't about rules. God is about life. Joy. Fullness. Love.

When Jesus was asked what the greatest commandment was, he made it clear there were two: Love God above all else and love your neighbor as yourself. Everything else falls into these two categories. The only law a Christian needs to worry about is love.

BIBLE TIME

Read and highlight the theme verse, Psalm 22:27, 19-31, in your Bible, writing "Remember!" in the margin. Then do the same with the following verses. What connection is there with the Ten Commandments?

Psalm 119:11   Deuteronomy 5:32-33

Matthew 22:34-40   John 10:10

ROLE PLAY

1. You chair the city council of your town. Mrs. Glemp is offended by the "Ten Commandments" replica stone in the front entrance of the city library and wants it removed. What is your opinion? On what do you base it?

2. You chair the same city council. The owner of a private building has hung a giant painting of the Nativity as a Christmas decoration for the city. Mrs. Glemp wants it removed. What is your opinion? On what do you base it?

QUESTIONS TO PONDER

1. What are the Top Ten highlights of your past year? What are the great moments you remember? Write them out in the back of this book.

2. What are the Top Ten highlights of your Christian life? Start with your baptism? Write them out in the back of this book as well.

3. Summarize the Ten Commandments in one sentence.

Small Group
SHARE, READ, TALK, PRAY, BLESS

1. **SHARE** your highs and lows of the week one-on-one with another person. Listen carefully and record your friend's thoughts in the space below. Then return to small group and share your friend's highs and lows.

   MY HIGHS + LOWS THIS WEEK WERE:

   ....

   MY FRIEND'S HIGHS + LOWS THIS WEEK WERE:

   ....

2. **READ** and highlight the theme verse in your Bibles. Circle key words and learn the verse in song if time permits.

3. **TALK** about how today's verse relates to your highs and lows. Review the art for today, the Quiz Bowl questions, the terms, and the cartoons. Then write a sentence on each of the following:

   ONE NEW THING I LEARNED TODAY:

   ....

   ONE THING I ALREADY KNEW THAT IS WORTH REPEATING:

   ....

   ONE THING I WOULD LIKE TO KNOW MORE ABOUT:

   ....

4. **PRAY** for one another, praising and thanking God for your highs, and asking God to be with you in your lows. Include your friend's highs and lows in your prayers.

   A PRAISING PRAYER: ....

   A THANKING PRAYER: ....

   AN ASKING PRAYER: ....

5. **BLESS** one another using the blessing of the week. (right) Mark each person with the sign of the cross as you bless them.

THIS WEEK'S BLESSING

(NAME), CHILD OF GOD, MAY YOU LIVE A LIFE THAT IS PURE AND MAY THE SPIRIT OF LOVE CAPTURE YOUR HEART THIS DAY. AMEN.

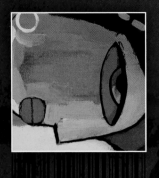

THE HOME HUDDLE JOURNAL

SHARE, READ, TALK, PRAY, BLESS

Read the full devotions using FINKlink
LF10 @ www.faithink.com

DAY #1

TODAY'S BIBLE VERSE:

PSALM 22:27

All the ends of the earth shall remember and turn to the LORD; and all the families of the nations shall worship before him.

MY **HIGH** TODAY WAS:

MY **LOW** TODAY WAS:

MY **PRAYER** TODAY IS:

DAY #2

TODAY'S BIBLE VERSE:

EXODUS 20:2-3

I am the Lord your God, who brought you out of the land of Egypt, out of the house of slavery; you shall have no other gods before me.

MY **HIGH** TODAY WAS:

MY **LOW** TODAY WAS:

MY **PRAYER** TODAY IS:

DAY #3

TODAY'S BIBLE VERSE:

EXODUS 20:4

You shall not make for yourself an idol, whether in the form of anything that is in heaven above, or that is on the earth beneath, or that is in the water under the earth.

MY **HIGH** TODAY WAS:

MY **LOW** TODAY WAS:

MY **PRAYER** TODAY IS:

DAY #4

MY HIGH today was:

MY LOW today was:

MY PRAYER today is:

EXODUS 20:7

You shall not make wrongful use of the name of the Lord your God, for the Lord will not acquit anyone who misuses his name.

DAY #5

MY HIGH today was:

MY LOW today was:

MY PRAYER today is:

today's bible verse:

EXODUS 20:8

Remember the sabbath day, and keep it holy.

DAY #6

MY HIGH today was:

MY LOW today was:

MY PRAYER today is:

today's bible verse:

EXODUS 20:12

Honor your father and your mother, so that your days may be long in the land that the Lord your God is giving you.

DAY #7

MY HIGHEST HIGH this week was:

MY LOWEST LOW this week was:

MY PRAYER for next week is:

THIS WEEK'S BLESSING

(NAME), CHILD OF GOD, MAY YOU LIVE A LIFE THAT IS PURE AND MAY THE SPIRIT OF LOVE CAPTURE YOUR HEART THIS DAY.

THE HOME HUDDLE JOURNAL

SHARE, READ, TALK, PRAY, BLESS

WEEK 2

Read the full devotions using FINKlink
LF10 @ www.faithink.com

DAY #1

TODAY'S BIBLE VERSE:

EXODUS 20:13

You shall not murder.

MY HIGH TODAY WAS:

MY LOW TODAY WAS:

MY PRAYER TODAY IS:

DAY #2

TODAY'S BIBLE VERSE:

EXODUS 20:14

You shall not commit adultery.

MY HIGH TODAY WAS:

MY LOW TODAY WAS:

MY PRAYER TODAY IS:

DAY #3

TODAY'S BIBLE VERSE:

EXODUS 20:15

You shall not steal.

MY HIGH TODAY WAS:

MY LOW TODAY WAS:

MY PRAYER TODAY IS:

1. SHARE HIGHS & LOWS OF THE DAY.

2. READ AND HIGHLIGHT THE VERSE OF THE DAY IN YOUR BIBLES.

3. TALK ABOUT HOW TODAY'S VERSE RELATES TO YOUR HIGHS & LOWS.

4. PRAY FOR YOUR HIGHS & LOWS, FOR YOUR FAMILY AND FOR THE WORLD.

5. BLESS ONE ANOTHER USING THIS WEEK'S BLESSING (ON THE PREVIOUS PAGE).

MY HIGH TODAY WAS:

MY LOW TODAY WAS:

MY PRAYER TODAY IS:

DAY #4

TODAY'S BIBLE VERSE:

EXODUS 20:16

You shall not bear false witness against your neighbor.

MY HIGH TODAY WAS:

MY LOW TODAY WAS:

MY PRAYER TODAY IS:

DAY #5

TODAY'S BIBLE VERSE:

EXODUS 20:17A

You shall not covet your neighbor's house.

MY HIGH TODAY WAS:

MY LOW TODAY WAS:

MY PRAYER TODAY IS:

DAY #6

TODAY'S BIBLE VERSE:

EXODUS 20:17B

You shall not covet your neighbor's wife, or male or female slave, or ox, or donkey, or anything that belongs to your neighbor.

THEME IN REVIEW

WE MIGHT THINK GOD SIMPLY WANTS OBE-DIENCE TO A SET OF RULES; WHEREAS GOD REALLY WANTS PEOPLE OF A PARTICULAR SORT.

C.S. LEWIS

DAY #7

MY FAVORITE VERSE FROM THE THEME WAS:

....

....

....

....

....

....

....

SO IF MOSES BROKE ALL OF THE TEN COMMANDMENTS AT ONCE, WHAT'S THE BIG PROBLEM WITH ME BREAKING ONE OR TWO?

LOOKING BACK ON THESE TWO WEEKS, MY HIGHEST HIGH WAS:

....

MY LOWEST LOW THESE PAST WEEKS WAS:

....

ONE WAY GOD ANSWERED MY PRAYERS WAS:

....

ONE WAY GOD MIGHT USE ME AS A SACRED AGENT TO ANSWER THESE PRAYERS:

....

....

FAMILY COVENANT

We have shared *Highs & Lows* this week, read and highlighted the verses assigned in our Bibles, talked about our lives, prayed for one another's highs and lows, and blessed one another.

_____   _____   _____

Parent's Signature   *Teen's Signature*   *Date*

THE FINKMANIA QUIZBOWL

QUESTION 1:

The First Commandment is:

(A) "Don't get caught,"

(B) "Do unto others as you would have them do unto you,"

(C) "I am the Lord your God, you shall have no other gods before me,"

(D) "You shall not take the name of the Lord your God in vain"

QUESTION 2:

The Second Commandment is:

(A) "You shall not take the name of the Lord your God in vain,"

(B) "You shall not make for yourself an idol,"

(C) "You shall not steal,"

(D) A or B, depending on if you order them the way the Faiths and Catholics do, or the way most other Protestants do

QUESTION 3:

The commandment that follows "name in vain" is:

(A) "Remember the Sabbath day,"

(B) "Remember the Sabbath day, and keep it holy,"

(C) "Remember the Sabbath day, and keep it frequently,"

(D) "Remember the Sabbath day, and keep it occasionally,"

QUESTION 4:

The commandment that follows "Sabbath" is:

(A) The only Commandment that comes with a promise attached,

(B) "Honor your father and mother when they aren't embarrassing you,"

(C) "Honor your father and mother that the days may be long in the land the Lord your God gives you,"

(D) A & C

QUESTION 5:

The commandment that follows "parents" is:

(A) "You shall not kill,"

(B) "You shall not steal,"

(C) "You shall not kill on the fifth,"

(D) "You shall not steal on the fifth,"

QUESTION 6:

The commandment that follows "killing" is:

(A) About honoring marriage,

(B) About keeping sex pure,

(C) Directly related to all of the rest because breaking it causes you to place something before God, kill a trust, steal a relationship, lie and covet all at the same time,

(D) All of the above and then some

QUESTION 7:

The commandment that follows "adultery" is:

(A) "You shall not steal,"

(B) "You shall not steal,"

(C) "You shall not steal,"

(D) All of the above

QUESTION 8:

The commandment that follows "stealing" is:

(A) We aren't to betray, gossip, lie about, or slander our neighbor,

(B) We are to defend, speak well of, and explain our neighbor's actions in the kindest ways,

(C) "You shall not bear false witness against your neighbor,"

(D) All of the above

QUESTION 9:

The final commandments are about:

(A) Coveting and scheming to get things and relationships that don't belong to you,

(B) Working to get things you want through honest means,

(C) A & B,

(D) Proper dental hygiene

FINKMANIA Final Question:

Rabbi Jesus said all the commandments can be summed up by one four letter word:

(A) Love,

(B) Obey,

(C) Work,

(D) Food

 Play this online game using FINKlink
LF10 @ www.faithink.com

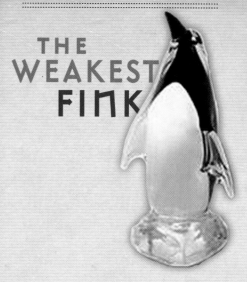

THE WEAKEST FINK

DO THE RIGHT THING.

SPIKE LEE

TERMS
WRITE A DEFINITION BELOW.

CONSEQUENCES

LAW

OBEDIENCE

RULES

TORAH

THE LORD'S PRAYER

1. OUR FATHER
2. HALLOWED
3. KINGDOM COME
4. WILL BE DONE
5. DAILY BREAD
6. FORGIVE
7. SAVE US FROM TRIAL
8. DELIVER US FROM EVIL
9. THE DOXOLOGY
10. LORD'S PRAYER REVIEW

OUR FATHER

"Escape to Egypt" Dr. He Qi. Order prints at www.heqiarts.com

"OUR FATHER IN HEAVEN..."

—MATTHEW 6:9A

*I*magine floating back in time one thousand, two thousand years to a dusty hillside in Palestine.

The sun hangs hot in the afternoon sky and a dry, blistering wind bites you with sand. You are a little child, walking hand in hand with Jesus. You are thirsty, so thirsty. You look up at the Master and ask for a drink, but there is no water in sight. What does Jesus say? You are hungry, so hungry, but there is no food. You ask Jesus for something to eat. What does Jesus do?

You tell Jesus what you need in your own words. He looks directly into your soul. His eyes are deep, like a well of clear water. They are filled with compassion. You have never seen eyes quite like his before. It is hard to look away. "I tell you the truth," he says, "ask and it will be given you; seek, and you will find; knock, and it will be opened." Everything within you desires to connect with this Jesus. His invitation draws you closer. Closer.

You continue walking. A stone hut comes in sight. Without a word, Jesus smiles and motions you in. You recline on beautiful red satin pillows by a low table set with cool water and fresh, steaming bread. You eat and drink. There are others in the room—your friends—and he speaks to you all: "What father among you, if his child asks for a fish, will instead of a fish give him a snake; or if he asks for an egg, will give him a scorpion? If you then, who are evil, know how to give good gifts to your children, how much more will the heavenly Father give the Holy Spirit to those who ask him?"

The Holy Spirit? All I asked for was food and water. You want to give me more? Jesus smiles again, as if reading your thoughts. He steps up, places his hand on your shoulder, and says: "This is my child! I would do anything for this one. I would even die for this one I love. And I will never leave you alone. Never."

You are God's child. Jesus claims you. You belong.

TEACH US TO PRAY

While he was on earth, Jesus spent a lot of time alone in prayer. One day his disciples asked him, "Lord, teach us to pray, just like John (the Baptist) also taught his disciples." (Luke 11:1) They had seen their Lord do so much – from walking on water to healing people. Maybe his power had something to do with prayer? They wanted to have that same kind of connection with God. They wanted to know how to pray like their friend and teacher. So they asked for a lesson on prayer, and the Son of God taught them what we now call the Lord's Prayer. It is a prayer known and recited by two billion people today across the globe. It starts like this:

"Our Father in heaven..."

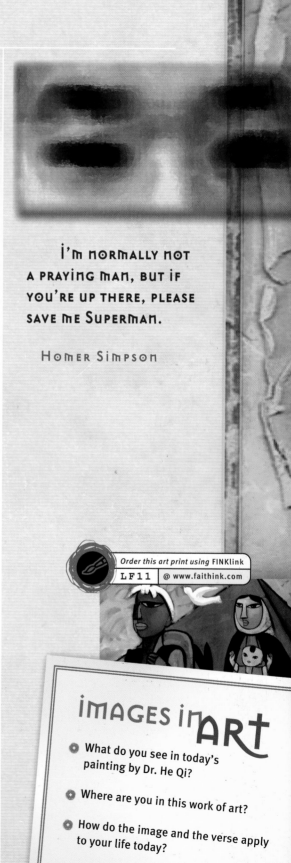

I'M NORMALLY NOT A PRAYING MAN, BUT IF YOU'RE UP THERE, PLEASE SAVE ME SUPERMAN.

HOMER SIMPSON

Order this art print using FINKlink
LF11 | @ www.faithink.com

IMAGES IN ART

- What do you see in today's painting by Dr. He Qi?

- Where are you in this work of art?

- How do the image and the verse apply to your life today?

SO WHAT DOES THIS MEAN?

I CAN ALWAYS TELL THE UNSPIRITUAL PEOPLE IN THIS HERE CHURCH 'CAUSE THEY'RE THE ONES WHO KEEP THEIR EYES OPEN WHEN WE PRAY!

PRAYER

DEAR GOD,

DO YOU REALLY LOVE ME LIKE A PARENT? DO YOU STILL LOVE ME EVEN WHEN I IGNORE YOU, TREAT YOU POORLY, AND FORGET TO SAY THANKS?

IT'S HARD FOR ME TO IMAGINE YOU LOVE ME THAT MUCH.

HELP ME TO LOVE YOU, TRUST YOU, AND COME TO YOU AS MY LOVING HEAVENLY FATHER. IN JESUS' NAME.

AMEN.

SO WHAT?

Our Father? How could anyone in Jesus' day dare to address God as Father? People didn't even risk saying the word for God (*Yahweh*) out loud for fear of taking God's name in vain. Instead, they called God words like "Lord" (*Adonai*) and other terms of reverence, but never Father! Another time, Jesus even used the word *Abba* (daddy) in addressing God in prayer.

Jesus was saying a lot by beginning his prayer this way. To Christ, God wasn't a distant god at all. Nor was God simply a generic Mother Nature. To him, God was a loving parent who loved him, knew his needs, and wanted to give good gifts to all the children of the world. Prayer was connecting with this loving parent, not pleading with some distant force or begging trinkets off of some uncaring stone statue. This *Abba* God was different from all the other gods of the day, and different from all other fathers. This God was bigger than time and space. Bigger than bullies and governments. Bigger than a person's biggest problems. And this God loved, cared, and provided like the best of parents. When you pray, fix your mind upon God as a loving parent, waiting to give you the very best gifts—gifts of the Holy Spirit!

BIBLE TIME

Read and highlight both places where the Lord's Prayer is found in your Bible. Write "Lord's Prayer" in the margins:

Matthew 6:9-13   Luke 11:1-4

ROLE PLAY

1. You invite a friend to a meal at your home. Before eating, you pause and say a prayer. Your friend asks: "What's that prayer all about?" How do you respond?

2. A friend says: "I don't believe in prayer or in God. I prayed when my grandma was sick and she died anyway. Prayer doesn't work." How do you respond?

QUESTIONS TO PONDER

1. What makes a good parent? How is God like this and more?

2. Do you think you can or should pray to God saying "Our Mother"? Why or why not?

3. What does the introduction to the Lord's Prayer have to say about the confidence we can have in coming to God with our needs?

SMALL GROUP
SHARE, READ, TALK, PRAY, BLESS

1. **SHARE** your highs and lows of the week one-on-one with another person. Listen carefully and record your friend's thoughts in the space below. Then return to small group and share your friend's highs and lows.

   MY HIGHS + LOWS THIS WEEK WERE:

   ....

   MY FRIEND'S HIGHS + LOWS THIS WEEK WERE:

   ....

2. **READ** and highlight the theme verse in your Bibles. Circle key words, and learn the verse in song if time permits.

3. **TALK** about how today's verse relates to your highs and lows. Review the art for today, the Quiz Bowl questions, the terms, and the cartoons. Then write a sentence on each of the following:

   ONE NEW THING I LEARNED TODAY:

   ....

   ONE THING I ALREADY KNEW THAT IS WORTH REPEATING:

   ....

   ONE THING I WOULD LIKE TO KNOW MORE ABOUT:

   ....

4. **PRAY** for one another, praising and thanking God for your highs, and asking God to be with you in your lows. Include your friend's highs and lows in your prayers.

   A PRAISING PRAYER: ....

   A THANKING PRAYER: ....

   AN ASKING PRAYER: ....

5. **BLESS** one another using the blessing of the week. (right) Mark each person with the sign of the cross as you bless them.

THIS WEEK'S BLESSING

(NAME), CHILD OF GOD, MAY YOUR DAYS BE LIVED WITH COURAGE AND YOUR NIGHTS BE BLESSED WITH PEACE IN THE ARMS OF THE GOD WHO LOVES YOU.

THE HOME HUDDLE JOURNAL
SHARE, READ, TALK, PRAY, BLESS

Read the full devotions using FINKlink
LL06 @ www.faithink.com

DAY #1

TODAY'S BIBLE VERSE:
Matthew 6:9a

Pray then in this way: "Our Father in heaven..."

MY **HIGH** TODAY WAS:

MY **LOW** TODAY WAS:

MY **PRAYER** TODAY IS:

DAY #2

TODAY'S BIBLE VERSE:
Malachi 2:10

Have we not all one father? Has not one God created us? Why then are we faithless to one another, profaning the covenant of our ancestors?

MY **HIGH** TODAY WAS:

MY **LOW** TODAY WAS:

MY **PRAYER** TODAY IS:

DAY #3

TODAY'S BIBLE VERSE:
Psalm 103:13

As a father has compassion for his children, so the Lord has compassion for those who fear him.

MY **HIGH** TODAY WAS:

MY **LOW** TODAY WAS:

MY **PRAYER** TODAY IS:

MY HIGH TODAY WAS:

....

MY LOW TODAY WAS:

....

MY PRAYER TODAY IS:

....

....

TODAY'S BIBLE VERSE:

JOHN 14:9B

Whoever has seen me has seen the Father. How can you say, "Show us the Father?"

MY HIGH TODAY WAS:

....

MY LOW TODAY WAS:

....

MY PRAYER TODAY IS:

....

....

DAY #5

TODAY'S BIBLE VERSE:

1 Corinthians 8:6

Yet for us there is one God, the Father, from whom are all things and for whom we exist, and one Lord, Jesus Christ, through whom are all things and through whom we exist.

MY HIGH TODAY WAS:

....

MY LOW TODAY WAS:

....

MY PRAYER TODAY IS:

....

....

DAY #6

TODAY'S BIBLE VERSE:

Galatians 4:6

And because you are children, God has sent the Spirit of his Son into our hearts, crying, "Abba! Father!"

MY HIGHEST HIGH THIS WEEK WAS:

....

MY LOWEST LOW THIS WEEK WAS:

....

MY PRAYER FOR NEXT WEEK IS:

....

....

DAY #7

THIS WEEK'S BLESSING

(NAME), CHILD OF GOD, MAY YOUR DAYS BE LIVED WITH COURAGE AND YOUR NIGHTS BE BLESSED WITH PEACE IN THE ARMS OF THE GOD WHO LOVES YOU.

THE HOME HUDDLE JOURNAL
SHARE, READ, TALK, PRAY, BLESS

Read the full devotions using FINKlink
LF11 @ www.faithink.com

DAY #1

TODAY'S BIBLE VERSE:

ROMANS 8:15B-16

When we cry, "Abba! Father!' it is that very Spirit bearing witness with our spirit that we are children of God.

MY **HIGH** TODAY WAS:

MY **LOW** TODAY WAS:

MY **PRAYER** TODAY IS:

DAY #2

TODAY'S BIBLE VERSE:

ROMANS 5:1-2A

Therefore, since we are justified by faith, we have peace with God through our Lord Jesus Christ, through whom we have obtained access to this grace in which we stand...

MY **HIGH** TODAY WAS:

MY **LOW** TODAY WAS:

MY **PRAYER** TODAY IS:

DAY #3

TODAY'S BIBLE VERSE:

JOHN 14:6

I am the way, and the truth, and the life. No one comes to the Father except through me.

MY **HIGH** TODAY WAS:

MY **LOW** TODAY WAS:

MY **PRAYER** TODAY IS:

1. SHARE HIGHS & LOWS OF THE DAY.

2. READ AND HIGHLIGHT THE VERSE OF THE DAY IN YOUR BIBLES.

3. TALK ABOUT HOW TODAY'S VERSE RELATES TO YOUR HIGHS & LOWS.

4. PRAY FOR YOUR HIGHS & LOWS, FOR YOUR FAMILY AND FOR THE WORLD.

5. BLESS ONE ANOTHER USING THIS WEEK'S BLESSING (ON THE PREVIOUS PAGE).

MY HIGH TODAY WAS:

MY LOW TODAY WAS:

MY PRAYER TODAY IS:

DAY #4

TODAY'S BIBLE VERSE:

1 John 3:1a

See what love the Father has given us, that we should be called children of God; and that is what we are.

MY HIGH TODAY WAS:

MY LOW TODAY WAS:

MY PRAYER TODAY IS:

DAY #5

TODAY'S BIBLE VERSE:

1 Thessalonians 5:17

...pray without ceasing...

MY HIGH TODAY WAS:

MY LOW TODAY WAS:

MY PRAYER TODAY IS:

DAY #6

TODAY'S BIBLE VERSE:

Hebrews 4:16

Let us therefore approach the throne of grace with boldness, so that we may receive mercy and find grace to help in time of need.

THEME IN REVIEW

LEARNING WHO GOD IS BY NAME IS THE ANSWER TO EVERY SITUATION IN LIFE.

KAY AUTHOR

DAY #7

MY FAVORITE **VERSE** FROM THE THEME WAS:

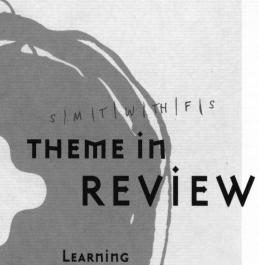

BY SAYING "OUR FATHER" JESUS IS TELLING US THAT GOD IS MORE THAN SOME VAGUE DISINTERESTED FORCE WHO DOESN'T KNOW WHAT'S GOING ON IN YOUR LIFE FLOATING AROUND IN SPACE.

BUT WHAT IF I WANT A VAGUE DISINTERESTED FORCE WHO DOESN'T KNOW WHAT'S GOING ON IN MY LIFE?

I GUESS YOU'LL JUST HAVE TO FIND YOURSELF ANOTHER GOD THEN...

GUESS SO...

LOOKING BACK ON THESE TWO WEEKS, MY HIGHEST **HIGH** WAS:

MY LOWEST **LOW** THESE PAST WEEKS WAS:

ONE WAY GOD ANSWERED MY **PRAYERS** WAS:

ONE WAY GOD MIGHT USE ME AS A **SACRED AGENT** TO ANSWER THESE PRAYERS:

FAMILY COVENANT

We have shared *Highs & Lows* this week, read and highlighted the verses assigned in our Bibles, talked about our lives, prayed for one another's highs and lows, and blessed one another.

_____   _____   _____
Parent's Signature   Teen's Signature   Date

Phone Home

THE FINKMANIA QUIZBOWL

QUESTION 1:

Jesus began the Lord's Prayer with the words:

(A) Our Father,

(B) Our Father in heaven, hollowed be your name,

(C) Our Father in heaven, Harold be your name,

(D) Immortal, Eternal, Omnipotent and Most Mystical Ground of All Ontological Being,

QUESTION 2:

What does "Our Father" mean?:

(A) God is an Episcopalian,

(B) God is like an ancient watch maker who built the world, wound it up and walked away forever,

(C) We can pray to God with complete confidence just as children speak to a loving father,

(D) God is too busy for our measly problems

QUESTION 3:

Where does God live?

(A) In the sky,

(B) In the church steeple with the bats,

(C) In, with, and under everything, but not held by space, time or any other dimensions of the physical universe,

(D) Just north of Toledo

QUESTION 4:

Another name Jesus used for God in prayer was:

(A) Abba (daddy),

(B) Abu (uncle),

(C) Addis Ababa (city),

(D) A boo boo (ouch)

QUESTION 5:

Calling God "Father" or "Abba" was shocking to most people in Jesus' day because:

(A) God was seen as mysterious and unapproachable,

(B) God was known mostly as a God of war, death and destruction,

(C) God was always referred to in the feminine,

(D) Most people didn't like their fathers back then

QUESTION 6:

The most common names for God in the Hebrew Bible were:

(A) Yahweh (I Am) and Adonai (Lord),

(B) Yassir and a donut,

(C) Rabbi (Teacher) and Shalom (Peace),

(D) Kobe and Shaq

QUESTION 7:

A good earthly parent:

(A) Always lets us off the hook when we mess up,

(B) Always gives us everything we want when we want it and demand it without asking any questions,

(C) Always loves and forgives us if we are good enough and deserve it,

(D) Loves and forgives, even when we don't deserve it

QUESTION 8:

What did Jesus tell his disciples about prayer?:

(A) Only use written prayers from witty blue handbooks,

(B) Always pray out loud at church and make a big deal of it in public,

(C) Cover your heads when you pray, especially if they are female,

(D) Pray in secret and God will reward you in secret

QUESTION 9:

God cares for us:

(A) When we are obedient,

(B) When we give lots of money to charity,

(C) When it is in God's best interest to do so,

(D) All the time—like a loving parent cares for a child

FINKMANIA FINAL QUESTION:

The Lord's Prayer is found in:

(A) Matthew 6:9a,

(B) Luke 11:2,

(C) Ringo 22:6

(D) A & B

 Play this online game using FINKlink

THE WEAKEST FINK

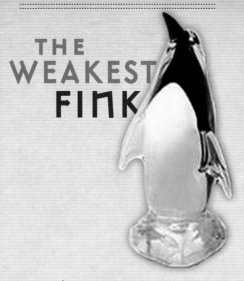

IF ONLY GOD WOULD GIVE ME SOME CLEAR SIGN! LIKE MAKING A LARGE DEPOSIT IN MY NAME AT A SWISS BANK.

WOODY ALLEN

TERMS
WRITE A DEFINITION BELOW.

ABBA

FATHER

HEAVEN

THE LORD'S PRAYER

YAHWEH

HALLOWED

"The Magi" Dr. He Qi. Order prints at www.heqiarts.com

"HALLOWED BE YOUR NAME."

— MATTHEW 6:9B

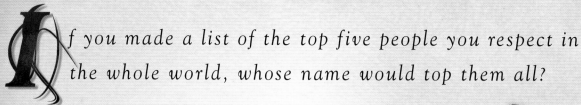

If you made a list of the top five people you respect in the whole world, whose name would top them all?

A movie star? A sports star? The captain of your high school football team? A soldier back from Iraq? A former president? The person who runs your local food shelf? Your mom or dad? The creator of *American Idol*?

What would you call this person if you saw them? Are you close enough to call them by their first name? Do you only know them well enough to call them Mr. or Mrs. or Miss So-and-So?

A great person's name deserves respect. If they have done something wonderful, astounding, or unusually sacrificial, they deserve to have their name treated with the highest esteem. Honor, even.

There is one name that calls for more respect and reverence than any other name in the universe. It has been spoken throughout history in every language on every continent, though sometimes the name takes on different forms. That name is God's name. God's name by its very nature is great. It speaks of hope, love, power, creativity, majesty and forgiveness. It sometime begs, sometimes demands, but always needs to be treated with respect. In the First Petition (requesting statement) of the Lord's Prayer, Jesus taught his disciples to pray: "Hallowed be your name!" He wanted all people to know they were praying to the greatest being in the universe, and that being deserved respect.

Hallowed be God's name!

THE FIRST PETITION

Have you ever wondered why people stand whenever the music for the *Hallelujah Chorus* plays? The composer, George Frederick Handel, wrote this marvelous piece of music to honor and hallow God's name. As he put the finishing strokes on *The Messiah* he felt inspired! The notes, the feeling, the music had come together in such a powerful way. Legend has it, the first time it was played, the Queen agreed. She was so moved by the chorus that she rose to honor the Great Composer who had given the gift of music. In those days, when a Queen stood, everybody stood. From that day on, people still rise to hallow—to honor—the God who reigns above all.

Are you standing for God?

Order this art print using FINKlink
LF12 @ www.faithink.com

iMAGES iN ART

- What do you see in today's painting by Dr. He Qi?

- Where are you in this work of art?

- How do the image and the verse apply to your life today?

So What Does This Mean?

I GOT EVERYTHING YOU SAID ABOUT THAT "HALLOWED BE THY NAME" STUFF EXCEPT THE PART YOU SAID AFTER "YOU MAY NOW BE SEATED."

PRAYER

HOLY, HOLY, HOLY ARE YOU GOD! THE WHOLE EARTH IS FULL OF YOUR GLORY. YOU ARE THE CENTER OF EVERYTHING. YOU WERE, YOU ARE, AND YOU ARE TO COME. I WANT TO KNOW YOU AND YOUR WISDOM. I WANT TO HONOR AND PRAISE YOU WITH MY LIFE, MY ACTIONS, MY WORDS, AND MY RELATIONSHIPS. HOLY, HOLY, HOLY ARE YOU GOD. LET ME HALLOW YOU IN EVERY WAY, IN ALL I DO AND ALL I SAY TODAY!

AMEN.

BIBLE TIME

Acknowledging God's name as holy is a way of honoring God. Read and highlight Matthew 6:9b, writing "Hallowed!" in the margin. Then highlight the following verses. What does each say about God? Does God have feelings?

Genesis 1:27

Exodus 20:5

Jeremiah 31:32

Romans 8:26

John 3:16

ROLE PLAY

1. You just discovered your mom took an extra job so you could play a club sport that you otherwise couldn't afford. What do you say? How do you show thanks?

2. Your coaches swear a lot at your team mates, the referees and at you. They misuse and abuse God's name in practically every other sentence. What do you say?

QUESTIONS TO PONDER

1. What was the last thing someone did that honored you? How did you feel?

2. Do you think God has the same feelings as people when honored or dishonored? Why or why not?

3. What does swearing have to do with the First Petition of the Lord's Prayer? Does the way we use God's name matter? What does it say about us? About our opinion of God?

Small Group
SHARE, READ, TALK, PRAY, BLESS

1. **SHARE** your highs and lows of the week one-on-one with another person. Listen carefully and record your friend's thoughts in the space below. Then return to small group and share your friend's highs and lows.

   MY HIGHS + LOWS THIS WEEK WERE:

   ....

   MY FRIEND'S HIGHS + LOWS THIS WEEK WERE:

   ....

2. **READ** and highlight the theme verse in your Bibles. Circle key words, and learn the verse in song if time permits.

3. **TALK** about how today's verse relates to your highs and lows. Review the art for today, the Quiz Bowl questions, the terms, and the cartoons. Then write a sentence on each of the following:

   ONE NEW THING I LEARNED TODAY:

   ....

   ONE THING I ALREADY KNEW THAT IS WORTH REPEATING:

   ....

   ONE THING I WOULD LIKE TO KNOW MORE ABOUT:

   ....

4. **PRAY** for one another, praising and thanking God for your highs, and asking God to be with you in your lows. Include your friend's highs and lows in your prayers.

   A PRAISING PRAYER: ....

   A THANKING PRAYER: ....

   AN ASKING PRAYER: ....

5. **BLESS** one another using the blessing of the week. (right) Mark each person with the sign of the cross as you bless them.

THE FINE 5

THIS WEEK'S BLESSING

(NAME), CHILD OF GOD, MAY YOUR WORDS, THOUGHTS, AND ACTIONS THIS DAY BRING HONOR AND PRAISE TO THE NAME OF OUR HOLY GOD. AMEN.

THE HOME HUDDLE JOURNAL
SHARE, READ, TALK, PRAY, BLESS

Read the full devotions using FINKlink
LF12 @ www.faithink.com

DAY #1

TODAY'S BIBLE VERSE:

MATTHEW 6:9B
Hallowed be your name.

MY HIGH TODAY WAS:

MY LOW TODAY WAS:

MY PRAYER TODAY IS:

DAY #2

TODAY'S BIBLE VERSE:

ISAIAH 6:3B

Holy, holy, holy is the Lord of hosts; the whole earth is full of his glory.

MY HIGH TODAY WAS:

MY LOW TODAY WAS:

MY PRAYER TODAY IS:

DAY #3

TODAY'S BIBLE VERSE:

PSALM 99:1-3

The Lord is king; let the peoples tremble! He sits enthroned upon the cherubim; let the earth quake! The Lord is great in Zion; he is exalted over all the peoples. Let them praise your great and awesome name. Holy is he!

MY HIGH TODAY WAS:

MY LOW TODAY WAS:

MY PRAYER TODAY IS:

my HIGH today was: _____

my LOW today was: _____

my PRAYER today is: _____

_____

_____

TODAY'S BIBLE VERSE:

REVELATION 4:8B

Holy, holy, holy, the Lord God the Almighty, who was and is and is to come.

---

my HIGH today was: _____

my LOW today was: _____

my PRAYER today is: _____

_____

_____

DAY #5

TODAY'S BIBLE VERSE:

1 SAMUEL 2:2

There is no Holy One like the Lord, no one besides you; there is no Rock like our God.

---

my HIGH today was: _____

my LOW today was: _____

my PRAYER today is: _____

_____

_____

DAY #6

TODAY'S BIBLE VERSE:

JOHN 17:17

Sanctify them in the truth; your word is truth.

---

my HIGHEST HIGH this week was: _____

my LOWEST LOW this week was: _____

my PRAYER for next week is: _____

_____

DAY #7

THIS WEEK'S BLESSING

(NAME), CHILD OF GOD, MAY YOUR WORDS, THOUGHTS, AND ACTIONS THIS DAY BRING HONOR AND PRAISE TO THE NAME OF OUR HOLY GOD. AMEN.

DAY #1

tODAY'S BiBLE VERSE:

CoLossians 3:16

Let the word of Christ dwell in you richly; teach and admonish one another in all wisdom; and with gratitude in your hearts sing psalms, hymns, and spiritual songs to God.

MY HiGH tODAY WAS:

MY LOW tODAY WAS:

MY PRAYER tODAY is:

DAY #2

tODAY'S BiBLE VERSE:

Leviticus 21:6a

They shall be holy to their God, and not profane the name of their God!

MY HiGH tODAY WAS:

MY LOW tODAY WAS:

MY PRAYER tODAY is:

DAY #3

tODAY'S BiBLE VERSE:

james 1:22

But be doers of the word, and not merely hearers who deceive themselves.

MY HiGH tODAY WAS:

MY LOW tODAY WAS:

MY PRAYER tODAY is:

1. SHARE HIGHS & LOWS OF THE DAY.

2. READ AND HIGHLIGHT THE VERSE OF THE DAY IN YOUR BIBLES.

3. TALK ABOUT HOW TODAY'S VERSE RELATES TO YOUR HIGHS & LOWS.

4. PRAY FOR YOUR HIGHS & LOWS, FOR YOUR FAMILY AND FOR THE WORLD.

5. BLESS ONE ANOTHER USING THIS WEEK'S BLESSING (ON THE PREVIOUS PAGE).

MY HIGH TODAY WAS:

MY LOW TODAY WAS:

MY PRAYER TODAY IS:

DAY #4

TODAY'S BIBLE VERSE:

PSALM 30:4

Sing praises to the Lord, O you his faithful ones, and give thanks to his holy name.

MY HIGH TODAY WAS:

MY LOW TODAY WAS:

MY PRAYER TODAY IS:

DAY #5

TODAY'S BIBLE VERSE:

PROVERBS 30:8B-9

Give me neither poverty nor riches; feed me with the food that I need, or I shall be full and deny you, and say, "Who is the Lord?" or I shall be poor, and steal, and profane the name of my God.

MY HIGH TODAY WAS:

MY LOW TODAY WAS:

MY PRAYER TODAY IS:

DAY #6

TODAY'S BIBLE VERSE:

2 TIMOTHY 1:3

I am grateful to God—whom I worship with a clear conscience, as my ancestors did—when I remember you constantly in my prayers night and day.

THEME IN REVIEW

Silent gratitude isn't much use to anyone.

GLADYS BROWN STERN

DAY #7

MY FAVORITE VERSE FROM THE THEME WAS:

....
....
....
....
....
....
....

WHAT'S HALLOWED?

HALLOWED MEANS HOLY. SPECIAL. SACRED.

WELL THEN, WHAT'S HOLLOWED?

EMPTY.

OH.

DO YOU 'SPOSE GOD FEELS HOLLOWED WHEN HIS NAME ISN'T HALLOWED?

LOOKING BACK ON THESE TWO WEEKS, MY HIGHEST HIGH WAS:

....

MY LOWEST LOW THESE PAST WEEKS WAS:

....

ONE WAY GOD ANSWERED MY PRAYERS WAS:

....

ONE WAY GOD MIGHT USE ME AS A SACRED AGENT TO ANSWER THESE PRAYERS:

....
....

FAMILY COVENANT

We have shared *Highs & Lows* this week, read and highlighted the verses assigned in our Bibles, talked about our lives, prayed for one another's highs and lows, and blessed one another.

....
Parent's Signature   *Teen's Signature*   *Date*

THE FINKMANIA QUIZBOWL

Question 1:

The First Petition of the Lord's Prayer is:

(A) "Our Father in heaven,"

(B) "Hollowed be your name,"

(C) "Hollywood be your name,"

(D) None of the above

Question 2:

"Holy, special, sacred, worthy of honor and praise" is a good way to define the word:

(A) Happy,

(B) Hokey,

(C) Hollowed,

(D) Hallowed

Question 3:

The word "respect" literally means:

(A) To get your vision checked,

(B) Aretha Franklin,

(C) To see the stars,

(D) To "look again" or take a second look

Question 4:

How do people "dis" (disrespect) God?:

(A) By harming and polluting creation,

(B) By ignoring God's holy Word,

(C) By using God's name to curse, yelling at their parents and others in authority, and refusing to take out the garbage when asked,

(D) All of the above and then some

Question 5:

God's name is certainly holy in and of itself, but we ask in this prayer:

(A) That we may keep it holy in the language we choose to use,

(B) That we may keep it holy in the way we live our lives,

(C) Both A & B,

(D) That God doesn't mind if we curse and swear like a drunken sailor

Question 6:

When is God's name hallowed?:

(A) When God's Word is taught in its truth and purity,

(B) When God's children live in harmony with God's Word,

(C) When people use God's name to justify wars, bigotry or racism,

(D) A & B, but never C

Question 7:

Why should we show honor to God's name?:

(A) God is worth it,

(B) God commands it,

(C) Both A & B,

(D) Because if we don't, God will probably place a zit on our nose during class picture day

Question 8:

How is taking care of our bodies a way of showing respect to God?:

(A) Our bodies are a temple of the Holy Spirit and taking care of the temple honors God's creation,

(B) God wants Christians buff so they can impress others into the kingdom,

(C) God loves washboard abs,

(D) None of the above

Question 9:

How does regular worship honor and hallow God's holy name?:

(A) It shows God that we aren't ungrateful brats,

(B) It shows the world what God means to us,

(C) It shows God how thankful we are for all God's gifts and how aware we are of God's greatness,

(D) All of the above and then some

FINKmania Final Question:

The First Petition of the Lord's Prayer, Matthew 6:9b, tells us:

(A) "Hallowed be your name,"

(B) We are to give God respect and reverence in our words, thoughts, worship and actions,

(C) A & B,

(D) Not much, it's too short

Play this online game using FINKlink

LF12 @ www.faithink.com

THE WEAKEST FINK

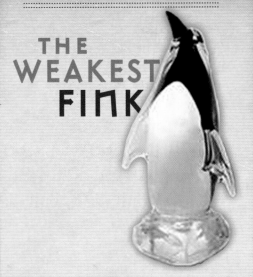

I'M NO THEOLOGIAN. I DON'T KNOW WHO OR WHAT GOD IS. ALL I KNOW IS HE'S MORE POWERFUL THAN MOM AND DAD PUT TOGETHER.

LISA SIMPSON

TERMS

WRITE A DEFINITION BELOW.

HALLOWED

HOLY

HONOR

PETITION

RESPECT

◆ FAITH INKUBATORS

KINGDOM COME

"The Visitation" Dr. He Qi. Order prints at www.heqiarts.com

"YOUR KINGDOM COME..."

— MATTHEW 6:10A

Listen to this song using FINKlink
LF13 @ www.faithink.com

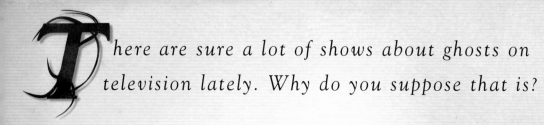

There are sure a lot of shows about ghosts on television lately. Why do you suppose that is?

Maybe people are bored with the world they see and hungry for something more. Maybe we are not satisfied with our material lives. Maybe we are longing for something eternal—hoping and groping to find something that lasts beyond this world.

Some people hold séances to get in touch with the spirits. Some play with *Ouiji* boards. Some practice witchcraft. But followers of Jesus don't seek the eternal in the presence of the dead. We don't need answers from the grave. We are seeking the presence of the living God. Some people empty themselves in meditation and chant so they can be void of all feeling and emotion. Followers of Jesus empty themselves in order to be filled with the presence of the living God. Some look for the kingdom of God in synods and ceremonies, political systems, or bank accounts. Followers of Jesus look for the kingdom of God in their hearts. "You will seek me and find me when you seek me with your whole heart," says God. "Seek the Lord while he may be found…" The kingdom—God's true reign—starts with Jesus coming into our hearts and the power of the Holy Spirit calling, gathering, enlightening and making us clean.

God Knocking

Picture yourself in a dark and dirty room. The shades are drawn. There are things you don't want exposed in this room, a room of your deepest thoughts. What are the sins that must be washed away? What are the thoughts that need to be thrown out before Christ can enter? Think for a moment of a sin that haunts you. As you slowly exhale, whisper: "Spirit cleanse me. Spirit cleanse me." The room is emptying. The ugly, the hidden, and the dark sins of a guilty soul are clearing away. The Spirit whispers in your ear: "If you confess your sins, God will forgive and cleanse you." You fling the windows open. Fresh air bursts through with the Spirit's whisper: "As far as the east is from the west, so have I removed your sins." You are now clean in God's sight. You inhale slowly, whispering the words: "Spirit fill me. Spirit fill me." Then, from the other side of the door, you hear the voice of Jesus: "Behold, I stand at the door and knock. If anyone hears my voice and opens the door I will come in…" There is a knocking at the door. You step toward the sound and pause. You grip the knob, then turn it slowly. Jesus is standing with joy-filled eyes and a broad smile. He is so proud, so happy you have opened the door. Do you invite him in? Ask him to enter now using your own words. The Spirit has helped prepare the room of your heart. And now you pray:

"Your kingdom come. Your kingdom come. Your kingdom come to me."

THERE IS NO TELLING WHAT TO EXPECT WHEN CHRIST WALKS IN THE DOOR.

THE TABLE SET FOR FOUR MUST OFTEN BE ENLARGED, AND DECORUM THROWN TO THE WINDS.

IT'S HIS VOICE THAT CALLS THEM, AND IT'S NO USE TO BOLT AND BAR THE DOOR.

GOD'S KINGDOM KNOWS NO BOUNDS OF ROOF, OF WALL OR FLOOR.

MARCELLA HOLLOWAY

Order this art print using FINKlink
LF13 @ www.faithink.com

IMAGES in ART

- What do you see in today's painting by Dr. He Qi?
- Where are you in this work of art?
- How do the image and the verse apply to your life today?

So What Does This Mean?

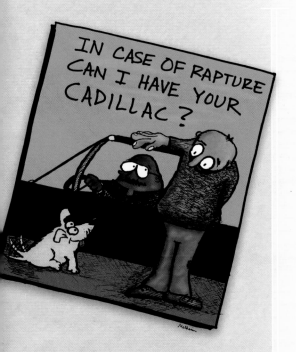

PRAYER

BREAKING GOD, BREAK IN ON ME! YOUR KINGDOM COME TO ME, THROUGH ME. I AM OPEN.

I PRAY FOR THAT PEACE AND POWER AND PRESENCE WITH ALL MY HEART. IN THE NAME OF JESUS.

AMEN.

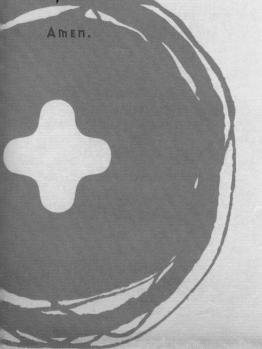

THE SECOND PETITION

Have you ever felt especially close to God? Have you ever experienced a time when God's Spirit seemed to be breaking in on you? Maybe it was on the mountainside or a beach watching a beautiful sunset. Maybe it was at a campfire at Bible camp or on a retreat. Maybe it in was a hospital when you watched a life enter or exit the world. Maybe it happened in worship or at a concert and you prayed for help from God. How did you feel? How was this a "kingdom" moment?

The kingdom of God is not some "pie in the sky in the sweet bye and bye" that you only reach when you die. The kingdom of God has to do with the here and now. God is present with us every moment. God's kingdom is not a theory, a proposition, or theological doctrine or teaching. The kingdom comes whenever God gives the Holy Spirit and, in faith, we live as God's people and bring Christ's presence, love, forgiveness, hope, and joy to others.

The kingdom is coming. Pray that it also comes to you and through you!

BIBLE TIME

What exactly are you praying for when you pray the Second Petition? Read and highlight Matthew 6:10a, writing "Kingdom come!" in the margin. Next, read the following verses. What do these say about kingdom life here and now?

Mark 10:14   Matthew 6:33

Mark 1:15   Mark 12: 28-34

ROLE PLAY

1. A classmate is making racist remarks. What do you say and do?

2. You are in charge of creating a rap or dance that expresses God's Kingdom breaking into the world. Don't just sit there—do it now!

QUESTIONS TO PONDER

1. Do you think people will ever build a perfect society on earth? Why or why not?

2. List five elements that would have to be in place in order to have a perfect society according to God's standards.

3. What is one thing you can do today to bring a little bit of God's kingdom to someone who is hurting?

Small Group
SHARE, READ, TALK, PRAY, BLESS

1. **SHARE** your highs and lows of the week one-on-one with another person. Listen carefully and record your friend's thoughts in the space below. Then return to small group and share your friend's highs and lows.

   MY HIGHS + LOWS THIS WEEK WERE:

   ....

   MY FRIEND'S HIGHS + LOWS THIS WEEK WERE:

   ....

2. **READ** and highlight the theme verse in your Bibles. Circle key words, and learn the verse in song if time permits.

3. **TALK** about how today's verse relates to your highs and lows. Review the art for today, the Quiz Bowl questions, the terms, and the cartoons. Then write a sentence on each of the following:

   ONE NEW THING I LEARNED TODAY:

   ....

   ONE THING I ALREADY KNEW THAT IS WORTH REPEATING:

   ....

   ONE THING I WOULD LIKE TO KNOW MORE ABOUT:

   ....

4. **PRAY** for one another, praising and thanking God for your highs, and asking God to be with you in your lows. Include your friend's highs and lows in your prayers.

   A PRAISING PRAYER: ....

   A THANKING PRAYER: ....

   AN ASKING PRAYER: ....

5. **BLESS** one another using the blessing of the week. (right) Mark each person with the sign of the cross as you bless them.

THIS WEEK'S BLESSING

(NAME), CHILD OF GOD, MAY GOD'S KINGDOM COME TO YOU AND THROUGH YOU THIS DAY. IN JESUS' PRECIOUS NAME. AMEN.

THE HOME HUDDLE jOURNAL

SHARE, READ, tALK, PRAY, BLESS

Read the full devotions using FINKlink
LF13 | @ www.faithink.com

DAY #1

tODAY'S BiBLE VERSE:

Matthew 6:10a

Your kingdom come.

my HiGH tODAY WAS:

my LOW tODAY WAS:

my PRAYER tODAY iS:

DAY #2

tODAY'S BiBLE VERSE:

Matthew 3:2

Repent, for the kingdom of heaven has come near.

my HiGH tODAY WAS:

my LOW tODAY WAS:

my PRAYER tODAY iS:

DAY #3

tODAY'S BiBLE VERSE:

Luke 12:32

Do not be afraid, little flock, for it is your Father's good pleasure to give you the kingdom.

my HiGH tODAY WAS:

my LOW tODAY WAS:

my PRAYER tODAY iS:

MY HIGH TODAY WAS:

MY LOW TODAY WAS:

MY PRAYER TODAY IS:

DAY #4

TODAY'S BIBLE VERSE:

Matthew 5:3

Blessed are the poor in spirit, for theirs is the kingdom of heaven.

MY HIGH TODAY WAS:

MY LOW TODAY WAS:

MY PRAYER TODAY IS:

DAY #5

TODAY'S BIBLE VERSE:

Psalm 145:10-11

All your works shall give thanks to you, O Lord, and all your faithful shall bless you. They shall speak of the glory of your kingdom, and tell of your power...

MY HIGH TODAY WAS:

MY LOW TODAY WAS:

MY PRAYER TODAY IS:

DAY #6

TODAY'S BIBLE VERSE:

Psalm 145:12-13a

...to make known to all people your mighty deeds, and the glorious splendor of your kingdom. Your kingdom is an everlasting kingdom, and your dominion endures throughout all generations.

MY HIGHEST HIGH THIS WEEK WAS:

MY LOWEST LOW THIS WEEK WAS:

MY PRAYER FOR NEXT WEEK IS:

DAY #7

THIS WEEK'S BLESSING

(NAME), CHILD OF GOD, MAY GOD'S KINGDOM COME TO YOU AND THROUGH YOU THIS DAY. IN JESUS' NAME.

THE HOME HUDDLE JOURNAL
SHARE, READ, TALK, PRAY, BLESS

Read the full devotions using FINKlink
LF13 | @ www.faithink.com

DAY #1

TODAY'S BIBLE VERSE:

PSALM 25:5

Lead me in your truth, and teach me, for you are the God of my salvation; for you I wait all day long.

MY **HIGH** TODAY WAS:

MY **LOW** TODAY WAS:

MY **PRAYER** TODAY IS:

DAY #2

TODAY'S BIBLE VERSE:

JOHN 14:1-2

Do not let your hearts be troubled. Believe in God, believe also in me. In my Father's house there are many dwelling places. If it were not so, would I have told you that I go to prepare a place for you?

MY **HIGH** TODAY WAS:

MY **LOW** TODAY WAS:

MY **PRAYER** TODAY IS:

DAY #3

TODAY'S BIBLE VERSE:

MATTHEW 6:33

But strive first for the kingdom of God and his righteousness, and all these things will be given to you as well.

MY **HIGH** TODAY WAS:

MY **LOW** TODAY WAS:

MY **PRAYER** TODAY IS:

1. **SHARE** HIGHS & LOWS OF THE DAY.

2. **READ** AND HIGHLIGHT THE VERSE OF THE DAY IN YOUR BIBLES.

3. **TALK** ABOUT HOW TODAY'S VERSE RELATES TO YOUR HIGHS & LOWS.

4. **PRAY** FOR YOUR HIGHS & LOWS, FOR YOUR FAMILY AND FOR THE WORLD.

5. **BLESS** ONE ANOTHER USING THIS WEEK'S BLESSING (ON THE PREVIOUS PAGE).

MY HIGH TODAY WAS:

MY LOW TODAY WAS:

MY PRAYER TODAY IS:

DAY #4

TODAY'S BIBLE VERSE:

MATTHEW 5:10

Blessed are those who are persecuted for righteousness' sake, for theirs is the kingdom of heaven.

MY HIGH TODAY WAS:

MY LOW TODAY WAS:

MY PRAYER TODAY IS:

DAY #5

TODAY'S BIBLE VERSE:

REVELATION 11:15b

The kingdom of the world has become the kingdom of our Lord and of his Messiah, and he will reign forever and ever.

MY HIGH TODAY WAS:

MY LOW TODAY WAS:

MY PRAYER TODAY IS:

DAY #6

TODAY'S BIBLE VERSE:

2 TIMOTHY 2:1-2

You then, my child, be strong in the grace that is in Christ Jesus; and what you have heard from me through many witnesses entrust to faithful people who will be able to teach others as well.

S | M |T | W | TH | F | S

THEME iN
REViEW

THE FUTURE WiLL BE
BETTER TOMORROW

j. DANFORTH QUAYLE

DAY #7

MY FAVORITE VERSE
FROM THE THEME WAS:

LOOKING BACK ON THESE TWO WEEKS, MY HIGHEST HIGH WAS:

....

MY LOWEST LOW THESE PAST WEEKS WAS:

....

ONE WAY GOD ANSWERED MY PRAYERS WAS:

....

ONE WAY GOD MIGHT USE ME AS A SACRED AGENT
TO ANSWER THESE PRAYERS:

....

....

FAMILY COVENANT

We have shared *Highs & Lows* this week, read and highlighted the verses assigned in our Bibles,
talked about our lives, prayed for one another's highs and lows, and blessed one another.

....

Parent's Signature   Teen's Signature   Date

THE FINKMANIA QUIZ BOWL

QUESTION 1:

The Second Petition to the Lord's Prayer is:

(A) "Our Father in heaven,"

(B) "Hallowed be your name,"

(C) "Your kingdom come,"

(D) "Your will be done"

QUESTION 2:

What does it mean to ask for God's kingdom to come?:

(A) We are asking God to take over the White House,

(B) We are asking Jesus to wipe out all the infidels,

(C) We are asking Jesus to set up a new world order,

(D) We are asking that God's reign of justice, peace and love come directly into our lives and world

QUESTION 3:

What is a "petition" in prayer?

(A) A request signed by at least 10,000 people asking God to listen and pay attention,

(B) A demand made to God,

(C) A request made to God,

(D) A request made by a pet

QUESTION 4:

When does God's kingdom come?:

(A) When God gives us the Holy Spirit,

(B) When, by God's grace, we believe God's word,

(C) When we live a godly life on earth,

(D) All of the above, and one day it will come in a big way in heaven

QUESTION 5:

What would have to change in order for this world to look more like heaven on earth?:

(A) All Democrats would have to turn Republican,

(B) All Republicans would have to turn Democrat,

(C) Sponge Bob SquarePants would have to be elected dictator of the world,

(D) People's hearts

QUESTION 6:

What does the Holy Spirit do to usher God's kingdom to us?:

(A) Calls us through the gospel,

(B) Gathers us together with other Christians

(C) Enlightens our minds, sanctifies us (makes us holy) and keeps us united with Jesus in the one true faith,

(D) All of the above

QUESTION 7:

Jesus said, "Very truly I tell you, no one can see the kingdom...":

(A) "...without earning it,"

(B) "...without going to church, and saying their prayers,"

(C) "...without being born from above,"

(D) "...without burning all their parent's old disco albums"

QUESTION 8:

When will the world end and God's final kingdom come?

(A) Hopefully before my algebra final,

(B) Only our pastor knows,

(C) Only God knows, and Jesus said not even the angels are in on it,

(D) It already happened and you missed it

QUESTION 9:

Why won't we ever have a perfect kingdom of God here on earth?

(A) People don't have very good management skills,

(B) Human nature is flawed by sin,

(C) We do (it's called Disney World),

(D) We do (it's called North Dakota)

FINKMANIA FINAL QUESTION:

The Second Petition to the Lord's Prayer, Matthew 6:10a, tells us:

(A) Not much—it's too short,

(B) God's kingdom won't come unless we pray for it,

(C) God's kingdom will come whether we pray for it or not, but we ask in this prayer that it may come also to us,

(D) Only 144,000 will be saved and you didn't make the cut

Play this online game using FINKlink

THE WEAKEST FINK

I HAVE A DREAM THAT MY FOUR CHILDREN WILL ONE DAY LIVE IN A NATION WHERE THEY WILL NOT BE JUDGED BY THE COLOR OF THEIR SKIN BUT BY THE CONTENT OF THEIR CHARACTER.

MARTIN LUTHER KING, JR.

TERMS
WRITE A DEFINITION BELOW.

BORN ANEW

HEAVEN

HOLY SPIRIT

KINGDOM OF GOD

PETITION

WILL BE DONE

"Women at Tomb" Dr. He Qi. Order prints at www.heqiarts.com

"YOUR WILL BE DONE ON EARTH AS IN HEAVEN."

— MATTHEW 6:10B

You are running through a steaming jungle, holding a baby. Someone is chasing you and shooting. Your heart is beating faster and faster.

You can barely catch your breath, but you know if you stop they will kill you. Shouts are getting close, closer. You come upon a clearing to the place your house once stood. All that is left is a smoldering pile of rubble. The shouts and shots are getting near, nearer. You lay your child down. She is barely breathing. You begin to weep and close your eyes. "God help me," you cry, "God help me." Slowly the scene changes.

You are at a stop light near a group of peaceful protesters. Their skin is a different color than yours, and their signs are printed with the blood-red word "Justice." A smaller group of angry faces heckles the crowd, swearing and calling them names. Suddenly a scuffle breaks out. One of the protesters is wrestled to the ground. He is being kicked again and again and again. The light changes, and you drive on. Looking back, you see the angry mob close in around the man. You whisper a prayer, "God help him. God help him."

Do these two situations seem impossible to you? Improbable? Like something you'll never experience? Is your life so safe and secure—so blessed—that you'll never see such things? Most people pray Christ's words "your kingdom come, your will be done" with eyes closed. Some never open them to see the suffering in the world around them. If you live in a safe town, a safe home, and have food on the table, it's easy to think everyone is in your identical situation. The truth is, the majority of children in the world are not. Clean water, good food, a safe place to stay, a good education, secure streets—these are a luxury afforded only to a minority in the world at any given moment.

Even in a rich industrialized country, children go to bed hungry. Even in lands of the rich and famous, a quiet, grueling war against poverty continues to rage. Even in a land that sings "God Bless America!" the good and gracious will of God is not always done. People still are hungry. What can you do about it?

SEEING AND BEING

It takes very little thought and effort to pray "your will be done on earth as it is in heaven" week after week. It takes much more maturity, thought and effort to pray this prayer and mean it. To be looking for God's will is one thing. To be working for it is something entirely different.

Some pray to *see* the will of God.

Some pray to *be* the will of God.

Which will you pray today?

> **TO LOVE IS TO RECEIVE A GLIMPSE OF HEAVEN.**
>
> KAREN SUNDE

Order this art print using FINKlink
LF14 @ www.faithink.com

IMAGES IN ART

- What do you see in today's painting by Dr. He Qi?
- Where are you in this work of art?
- How do the image and the verse apply to your life today?

So What Does This Mean?

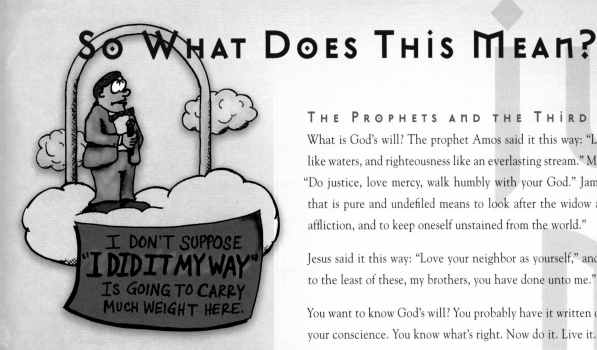

I DON'T SUPPOSE "I DID IT MY WAY" IS GOING TO CARRY MUCH WEIGHT HERE.

PRAYER

DEAR GOD, ARE YOU REALLY IN CHARGE OF THE WORLD? IF SO, WHY IS THERE SUFFERING? I DON'T UNDERSTAND EVERYTHING, BUT I HEAR JESUS CALLING ME TO PRAY FOR YOUR KINGDOM TO COME AND YOUR WILL TO BE DONE.

I KNOW YOU LOVE THE WORLD. IT MUST HURT YOUR HEART TO SEE SO MUCH EVIL AND PAIN. USE ME TODAY, GOD, AS YOUR SACRED AGENT TO BRING YOUR GOOD AND GRACIOUS WILL TO THIS HURTING WORLD. I PRAY IN JESUS' NAME AND FOR HIS POWER.

AMEN.

THE PROPHETS AND THE THIRD PETITION

What is God's will? The prophet Amos said it this way: "Let justice roll down like waters, and righteousness like an everlasting stream." Micah said it this way: "Do justice, love mercy, walk humbly with your God." James wrote: "Religion that is pure and undefiled means to look after the widow and orphan in their affliction, and to keep oneself unstained from the world."

Jesus said it this way: "Love your neighbor as yourself," and "Whatever you do to the least of these, my brothers, you have done unto me."

You want to know God's will? You probably have it written on your heart and in your conscience. You know what's right. Now do it. Live it. Be it.

BIBLE TIME

Read and highlight Matthew 6:10b in your Bible, writing "God's Will" in the margin. Now turn to Genesis chapter three and write "The Fall" in the margin. The Bible teaches that the very first sin of all—original sin—came about when humans wanted to be their own gods. The attitude towards God was "my will be done" and not "thy will be done." Is that what sin is today?

ROLE PLAY

1. A classmate says, "I can't believe in a God who would allow wars, starvation and all this evil in the world. Either God isn't all powerful, or God isn't all loving." How do you respond?

2. There are people alive today who sincerely believe it is the will of God for them to strap explosives on their bodies and blow themselves up in order to kill enemies, soldiers, civilians, and children. How do you respond?

QUESTIONS TO PONDER

1. Why do we need to pray for God's will to be done? If God is God, can't God do it without us?

2. List five things happening in the world today that are definitely not the will of God.

3. List one thing you could do to bring God's will to one of the situations above. Will you do it?

Small Group
SHARE, READ, TALK, PRAY, BLESS

1. **SHARE** your highs and lows of the week one-on-one with another person. Listen carefully and record your friend's thoughts in the space below. Then return to small group and share your friend's highs and lows.

MY HIGHS + LOWS THIS WEEK WERE:

....

MY FRIEND'S HIGHS + LOWS THIS WEEK WERE:

....

2. **READ** and highlight the theme verse in your Bibles. Circle key words, and learn the verse in song if time permits.

3. **TALK** about how today's verse relates to your highs and lows. Review the art for today, the Quiz Bowl questions, the terms, and the cartoons. Then write a sentence on each of the following:

ONE NEW THING I LEARNED TODAY:

....

ONE THING I ALREADY KNEW THAT IS WORTH REPEATING:

....

ONE THING I WOULD LIKE TO KNOW MORE ABOUT:

....

4. **PRAY** for one another, praising and thanking God for your highs, and asking God to be with you in your lows. Include your friend's highs and lows in your prayers.

A PRAISING PRAYER: ....

A THANKING PRAYER: ....

AN ASKING PRAYER: ....

5. **BLESS** one another using the blessing of the week. (right) Mark each person with the sign of the cross as you bless them.

THIS WEEK'S BLESSING
(NAME), CHILD OF GOD,
BE A SACRED AGENT OF
THE GOOD AND GRACIOUS
WILL OF GOD THIS DAY. IN
JESUS' NAME, AMEN.

THE HOME HUDDLE jOURNAL
SHARE, READ, tALK, PRAY, BLESS

Read the full devotions using FINKlink
LL06 | @ www.faithink.com

DAY #1

tODAY'S BiBLE VERSE:

Matthew 6:10b

Your will be done on earth as it is in heaven.

mY HiGH tODAY WAS:

mY LOW tODAY WAS:

mY PRAYER tODAY is:

DAY #2

tODAY'S BiBLE VERSE:

Psalm 25:4

Make me to know your ways, O Lord; teach me your paths...

mY HiGH tODAY WAS:

mY LOW tODAY WAS:

mY PRAYER tODAY is:

DAY #3

tODAY'S BiBLE VERSE:

Psalm 40:8

I delight to do your will, O my God; your law is within my heart.

mY HiGH tODAY WAS:

mY LOW tODAY WAS:

mY PRAYER tODAY is:

MY HIGH TODAY WAS:
....

MY LOW TODAY WAS:
....

MY PRAYER TODAY IS:
....
....
....

MY HIGH TODAY WAS:
....

MY LOW TODAY WAS:
....

MY PRAYER TODAY IS:
....
....
....

MY HIGH TODAY WAS:
....

MY LOW TODAY WAS:
....

MY PRAYER TODAY IS:
....
....
....

MY HIGHEST HIGH THIS WEEK WAS:
....

MY LOWEST LOW THIS WEEK WAS:
....

MY PRAYER FOR NEXT WEEK IS:
....

DAY #4

TODAY'S BIBLE VERSE:

1 TIMOTHY 2:3-4

This is right and is acceptable in the sight of God our Savior, who desires everyone to be saved and to come to the knowledge of the truth.

DAY #5

TODAY'S BIBLE VERSE:

1 THESSALONIANS 4:3-4

For this is the will of God, your sanctification: that you abstain from fornication; that each one of you know how to control your own body in holiness and honor...

DAY #6

TODAY'S BIBLE VERSE:

1 THESSALONIANS 4:6-7

...that no one wrong or exploit a brother or sister in this matter, because the Lord is an avenger in all these things... God did not call us to impurity but in holiness.

DAY #7

THIS WEEK'S BLESSING

(NAME), CHILD OF GOD, BE A SACRED AGENT OF THE GOOD AND GRACIOUS WILL OF GOD THIS DAY. IN JESUS' NAME, AMEN.

THE HOME HUDDLE JOURNAL
SHARE, READ, TALK, PRAY, BLESS

Read the full devotions using FINKlink
LF14 | @ www.faithink.com

DAY #1

TODAY'S BIBLE VERSE:

ROMANS 12:2

Do not be conformed to this world, but be transformed by the renewing of your minds, so that you may discern what is the will of God—what is good and acceptable and perfect.

MY **HIGH** TODAY WAS:

MY **LOW** TODAY WAS:

MY **PRAYER** TODAY IS:

DAY #2

TODAY'S BIBLE VERSE:

GALATIANS 1:3-4

Grace to you and peace from God our Father and the Lord Jesus Christ, who gave himself for our sins to set us free from the present evil age, according to the will of our God and Father, to whom be the glory forever and ever. Amen.

MY **HIGH** TODAY WAS:

MY **LOW** TODAY WAS:

MY **PRAYER** TODAY IS:

DAY #3

TODAY'S BIBLE VERSE:

JOB 42:2

I know that you can do all things, and that no purpose of yours can be thwarted.

MY **HIGH** TODAY WAS:

MY **LOW** TODAY WAS:

MY **PRAYER** TODAY IS:

1. **SHARE** HIGHS & LOWS OF THE DAY.

2. **READ** AND HIGHLIGHT THE VERSE OF THE DAY IN YOUR BIBLES.

3. **TALK** ABOUT HOW TODAY'S VERSE RELATES TO YOUR HIGHS & LOWS.

4. **PRAY** FOR YOUR HIGHS & LOWS, FOR YOUR FAMILY AND FOR THE WORLD.

5. **BLESS** ONE ANOTHER USING THIS WEEK'S BLESSING (ON THE PREVIOUS PAGE).

MY HIGH TODAY WAS:

MY LOW TODAY WAS:

MY PRAYER TODAY IS:

DAY #4

TODAY'S BIBLE VERSE:
MATTHEW 26:42B
My Father, if this cannot pass unless I drink it, your will be done.

MY HIGH TODAY WAS:

MY LOW TODAY WAS:

MY PRAYER TODAY IS:

DAY #5

TODAY'S BIBLE VERSE:
REVELATION 11:15
...there were loud voices in heaven, saying, "The kingdom of the world has become the kingdom of our Lord and of his Messiah, and he will reign forever and ever."

MY HIGH TODAY WAS:

MY LOW TODAY WAS:

MY PRAYER TODAY IS:

DAY #6

TODAY'S BIBLE VERSE:
PSALM 143:10
Teach me to do your will, for you are my God. Let your good spirit lead me on a level path.

THEME iN REViEW

THE THiRD PETiTiON
OF THE LORD'S PRAYER iS
REPEATED DAiLY BY MiLLiONS
WHO HAVE NOT THE SLiGHTEST
iNTENTiON OF LETTiNG ANY-
ONE'S WiLL BE DONE BUT
THEiR OWN.

ALDOUS HUXLEY

DAY #7

MY FAVORiTE VERSE
FROM THE THEME WAS:

....
....
....
....
....
....
....

LOOKiNG BACK ON THESE TWO WEEKS, MY HiGHEST HiGH WAS:

....

MY LOWEST LOW THESE PAST WEEKS WAS:

....

ONE WAY GOD ANSWERED MY PRAYERS WAS:

....

ONE WAY GOD MiGHT USE ME AS A SACRED AGENT
TO ANSWER THESE PRAYERS:

....

....

FAMiLY COVENANT

We have shared *Highs & Lows* this week, read and highlighted the verses assigned in our Bibles, talked about our lives, prayed for one another's highs and lows, and blessed one another.

....
Parent's Signature   Teen's Signature   Date

THE FINKMANIA QUIZBOWL

QUESTION 1:

The Third Petition of the Lord's Prayer is:

(A) My will be done,

(B) Thy will be done,

(C) Thy will be done on earth,

(D) Thy will be done on earth as it is in heaven

QUESTION 2:

What does "Thy will be done on earth as it is in heaven" mean?:

(A) Just what it says,

(B) God desires that the people of the world live in faith, love, harmony and peace,

(C) Both A & B,

(D) It depends on what your definition of "done" is

QUESTION 3:

When is God's will done?

(A) When I pick up the dirty underwear on my floor,

(B) When God defeats every evil that would prevent us from keeping God's name holy and the kingdom from coming,

(C) When God strengthens our faith and keeps us firm in the Word,

(D) All of the above and then some

QUESTION 4:

What's the difference between my will and God's will?:

(A) God's will is always good for me and the world,

(B) My will is often short-sighted and selfish,

(C) God doesn't always have my best interest in mind,

(D) Both A & B

QUESTION 5:

Which of the following classic ad campaigns encourages us to fulfill God's will, not our own?:

(A) "Just do it!"

(B) "Have it your way,"

(C) "Get more,"

(D) None of the above

QUESTION 6:

Why didn't God make us like puppets and control us that way?:

(A) We couldn't truly love God without the ability to reject God,

(B) We wouldn't be human without a free will and the ability to decide between good and evil,

(C) Both A & B,

(D) God didn't have enough string

QUESTION 7:

God's will includes:

(A) Justice for the poor,

(B) Mercy for the hurting,

(C) Both A & B,

(D) Big profits for the oil industry at the expense of the working poor

QUESTION 8:

How can people best bring God's will to earth:

(A) On the space shuttle,

(B) By complaining constantly,

(C) By isolating themselves away with other Christians to keep themselves unstained and untouched by the world,

(D) By doing the work of Christ in the world and sharing God's love every where they go

QUESTION 9:

Why do we have to pray for God's will to be done on earth as in heaven?:

(A) We don't,

(B) Praying for God's will helps us focus on what that will is, and helps us see how we might bring God's will into our world,

(C) If we don't pray, God won't act,

(D) If we don't pray, Jesus won't love us as much

FINKMANIA FINAL QUESTION:

The Third Petition of the Lord's Prayer, Matthew 6:10b, tells us:

(A) Our will is best,

(B) God's will is going to be accomplished whether we're in on it or not, but we ought to get in on it,

(C) God's will won't be accomplished unless we talk God into it,

(D) God will do anything we want

 Play this online game using FINKlink
LF14 @ www.faithink.com

THE WEAKEST FINK

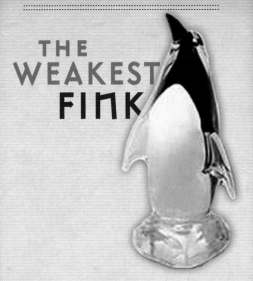

IF YOU WANT TO MAKE GOD LAUGH, TELL HIM ABOUT YOUR PLANS.

WOODY ALLEN

TERMS
WRITE A DEFINITION BELOW.

HEAVEN

THE FALL

ORIGINAL SIN

PETITION

WILL (GOD'S)

 FAITH INKUBATORS

DAILY BREAD

"Elijah and the Ravens" Dr. He Qi. Order prints at www.heqiarts.com

"GIVE US THIS DAY OUR DAILY BREAD."

— MATTHEW 6:11

 Listen to this song using FINKlink
LF15 @ www.faithink.com

The old man walked down the same mountain path in East Germany every day to buy his bread and milk.

He had seen it all in those forty years: war, hunger, change, disappointment, death, despair.

He had lived through the horrors of WWI, the terrible depression that followed, and the rise of Adolph Hitler. After the Nazis and the Second World War, he suffered the occupation of the Russians, years of barely making ends meet, political persecution and finally, the collapse of the Berlin Wall. Through it all, he had managed to walk down from his little chalet to the village every day to purchase his meager supplies.

When Germany finally reunited in 1989, grandchildren he had never known came from the West to pay him a visit. These high tech relatives were appalled that Grandpa had to walk every day. They went out and bought him a new refrigerator so he could shop once a week and not be forced into making the long trip to town every day.

The old man thanked his well-meaning family, waited until they left, then set the fridge outside on the porch and promptly, turned it into a flower planter. The daily walk was no nuisance to him. It was both his prayer time and his therapy. It was his way of remembering who he was and whose he was. To him, "daily bread" was much more than a phrase or expression. The walk, the prayer, and the acknowledgement of God's providence were his way of life. Every day. He wasn't about to change that.

True story.

THE FOURTH PETITION

The Children of Israel were wandering in the wilderness without food. God told Moses not to worry. There would be bread from heaven every morning and quail for meat every night. The next morning, they woke, looked out on the fields and exclaimed, "What is it?" (*Manna* in Hebrew literally means "What is it?") Manna was the daily gift God sent—the first bread from heaven. God gave them just enough for each day. If they collected too much and tried to hoard the manna, it became wormy, rotted and started to smell. The Provider was training them to trust in God one day at a time.

God gives life one day at a time. The joys, pains, challenges and struggles all come in bite-size chunks. Don't spend your time worrying about tomorrow. You will miss out on today. Let tomorrow's worries be tomorrow's worries. Today is all you have. Don't waste it. It is too precious a gift to lose.

> GOD GIVES
> EVERY BIRD ITS FOOD,
> BUT GOD DOES NOT
> THROW IT INTO THE NEST.
>
> JOSIAH HOLLAND

Order this art print using FINKlink
LF15 @ www.faithink.com

IMAGES IN ART

- What do you see in today's painting by Dr. He Qi?

- Where are you in this work of art?

- How do the image and the verse apply to your life today?

So What Does This Mean?

HEY DAD, HOW'S ABOUT A LITTLE DAILY BREAD?

DEAR LORD: THE GODS HAVE BEEN GOOD TO ME. FOR THE FIRST TIME IN MY LIFE, EVERYTHING IS ABSOLUTELY PERFECT JUST THE WAY IT IS. SO HERE'S THE DEAL: YOU FREEZE EVERYTHING THE WAY IT IS, AND I WON'T ASK FOR ANYTHING MORE. IF THAT IS OK, PLEASE GIVE ME ABSOLUTELY NO SIGN. OK, DEAL. IN GRATITUDE, I PRESENT YOU THIS OFFERING OF COOKIES AND MILK. IF YOU WANT ME TO EAT THEM FOR YOU, GIVE ME NO SIGN. THY WILL BE DONE.

HOMER SIMPSON

BIBLE TIME

Read and highlight the theme verse, Matthew 6:11, writing "Daily Bread" in the margin. Connect it to one or more of the following verses:

Isaiah 55: 1-2   Matthew 4:4

Matthew 26:26   John 6: 35

John 6: 48-51

PRAYER

Jesus, sometimes I get my wants and my needs mixed up. Help me to understand what really matters, and to trust in you for my daily bread. Make me a thankful person. Teach me to live one day at a time. Help me to share all I have been given with others so they may have daily bread, too. Amen.

ROLE PLAY

1. A friend has lost a lot of weight. You notice she runs off to the bathroom every day after you eat lunch together at school. You are worried that she may have an eating disorder. What do you say?

2. You have saved up money for months to buy your friend a wonderful birthday present. You can't wait to give it to him. When he opens it, however, he seems less than impressed and hardly acknowledges it. How do you feel? What do you say? How does this relate to God's good gifts?

QUESTIONS TO PONDER

1. How would you explain the difference between a need and a want?

2. What are three things that worry people your age the most? What worried you today?

3. What would it take for you to give this worry totally and completely over to God? Will you dare do it?

Small Group
SHARE, READ, TALK, PRAY, BLESS

1. **S H A R E** your highs and lows of the week one-on-one with another person. Listen carefully and record your friend's thoughts in the space below. Then return to small group and share your friend's highs and lows.

   MY HIGHS + LOWS THIS WEEK WERE:

   ....

   MY FRIEND'S HIGHS + LOWS THIS WEEK WERE:

   ....

2. **R E A D** and highlight the theme verse in your Bibles. Circle key words, and learn the verse in song if time permits.

3. **T A L K** about how today's verse relates to your highs and lows. Review the art for today, the Quiz Bowl questions, the terms, and the cartoons. Then write a sentence on each of the following:

   ONE NEW THING I LEARNED TODAY:

   ....

   ONE THING I ALREADY KNEW THAT IS WORTH REPEATING:

   ....

   ONE THING I WOULD LIKE TO KNOW MORE ABOUT:

   ....

4. **P R A Y** for one another, praising and thanking God for your highs, and asking God to be with you in your lows. Include your friend's highs and lows in your prayers.

   A PRAISING PRAYER: ....

   A THANKING PRAYER: ....

   AN ASKING PRAYER: ....

5. **B L E S S** one another using the blessing of the week. (right) Mark each person with the sign of the cross as you bless them.

THIS WEEK'S BLESSING
(NAME), CHILD OF GOD, MAY THE LORD OF LOVE SUPPLY ALL YOUR NEEDS AND MAKE YOU A BLESSING TO THE WORLD. IN CHRIST'S NAME.

THE HOME HUDDLE jOURNAL

SHARE, READ, TALK, PRAY, BLESS

Read the full devotions using FINKlink
LL06 | @ www.faithink.com

DAY #1

TODAY'S BIBLE VERSE:

Matthew 6:11

Give us this day our daily bread.

my HIGH today was:

my LOW today was:

my PRAYER today is:

DAY #2

TODAY'S BIBLE VERSE:

Psalm 145:15

The eyes of all look to you, and you give them their food in due season.

my HIGH today was:

my LOW today was:

my PRAYER today is:

DAY #3

TODAY'S BIBLE VERSE:

Psalm 78:23-24

(God) ...opened the doors of heaven; he rained down on them manna to eat, and gave them the grain of heaven.

my HIGH today was:

my LOW today was:

my PRAYER today is:

my HIGH today was:

my LOW today was:

my PRAYER today is:

TODAY'S BIBLE VERSE:

PSALM 34:10

The young lions suffer want and hunger, but those who seek the Lord lack no good thing.

my HIGH today was:

my LOW today was:

my PRAYER today is:

DAY #5

TODAY'S BIBLE VERSE:

MARK 4:39-40

He woke up and rebuked the wind, and said to the sea, "Peace! Be still!" Then the wind ceased, and there was a dead calm. He said to them, "Why are you afraid. Have you still no faith?"

my HIGH today was:

my LOW today was:

my PRAYER today is:

DAY #6

TODAY'S BIBLE VERSE:

JOHN 6:35

Jesus said to them, "I am the bread of life. Whoever comes to me will never be hungry, and whoever believes in me will never be thirsty."

my HIGHEST HIGH this week was:

my LOWEST LOW this week was:

my PRAYER for next week is:

DAY #7

THIS WEEK'S BLESSING

(NAME), CHILD OF GOD, MAY THE LORD OF LOVE SUPPLY ALL YOUR NEEDS AND MAKE YOU A BLESSING TO THE WORLD. IN CHRIST'S NAME.

THE HOME HUDDLE jOURNAL

SHARE, READ, tALK, PRAY, BLESS

Read the full devotions using FINKlink
LF15 @ www.faithink.com

DAY #1

todAY'S BiBLE VERSE:

PsALM 90:17A

Let the favor of the Lord our God be upon us, and prosper for us the work of our hands—O prosper the work of our hands!

MY HiGH todAY WAS:

MY LOW todAY WAS:

MY PRAYER todAY is:

DAY #2

todAY'S BiBLE VERSE:

PROVERBS 22:1B

A good name is to be chosen rather than great riches.

MY HiGH todAY WAS:

MY LOW todAY WAS:

MY PRAYER todAY is:

DAY #3

todAY'S BiBLE VERSE:

MATTHEW 5:45

(God) makes his sun rise on the evil and on the good, and sends the rain on the righteous and on the unrighteous.

MY HiGH todAY WAS:

MY LOW todAY WAS:

MY PRAYER todAY is:

1. **SHARE** HIGHS & LOWS OF THE DAY.

2. **READ** AND HIGHLIGHT THE VERSE OF THE DAY IN YOUR BIBLES.

3. **TALK** ABOUT HOW TODAY'S VERSE RELATES TO YOUR HIGHS & LOWS.

4. **PRAY** FOR YOUR HIGHS & LOWS, FOR YOUR FAMILY AND FOR THE WORLD.

5. **BLESS** ONE ANOTHER USING THIS WEEK'S BLESSING (ON THE PREVIOUS PAGE).

MY HIGH TODAY WAS:

MY LOW TODAY WAS:

MY PRAYER TODAY IS:

DAY #4

TODAY'S BIBLE VERSE:

2 Corinthians 9:8

And God is able to provide you with every blessing in abundance, so that by always having enough of everything, you may share abundantly in every good work.

MY HIGH TODAY WAS:

MY LOW TODAY WAS:

MY PRAYER TODAY IS:

DAY #5

TODAY'S BIBLE VERSE:

Matthew 6:26

Look at the birds of the air; they neither sow nor reap nor gather into barns, and yet your heavenly Father feeds them. Are you not of more value than they?

MY HIGH TODAY WAS:

MY LOW TODAY WAS:

MY PRAYER TODAY IS:

DAY #6

TODAY'S BIBLE VERSE:

Psalm 136:1

O give thanks to the Lord, for he is good, for his steadfast love endures forever.

THEME iN REVIEW

WE DiDN'T HAVE MUCH,
BUT WE SURE HAD PLENTY.

SHERRY THOMAS

DAY #7

MY FAVORITE VERSE
FROM THE THEME WAS:

....

....

....

....

....

....

LOOKiNG BACK ON THESE TWO WEEKS, MY HiGHEST HiGH WAS:

....

MY LOWEST LOW THESE PAST WEEKS WAS:

....

ONE WAY GOD ANSWERED MY PRAYERS WAS:

....

ONE WAY GOD MiGHT USE ME AS A SACRED AGENT
TO ANSWER THESE PRAYERS:

....

....

FAMiLY COVENANT

We have shared *Highs & Lows* this week, read and highlighted the verses assigned in our Bibles, talked about our lives, prayed for one another's highs and lows, and blessed one another.

.... | .... | ....
Parent's Signature | Teen's Signature | Date

THE FINKMANIA QUIZBOWL

QUESTION 1:

The Fourth Petition of the Lord's Prayer is:

(A) Give us this day all that we want,

(B) Give us this day our daily bread,

(C) Give us this day our daily lotto ticket,

(D) Give us this day our daily immunity idol

QUESTION 2:

What does "daily bread" include?:

(A) Everything we need for life,

(B) Food and clothing, home and property, work and income,

(C) A devoted family, an orderly community, good government, favorable weather, peace, health, a good name,

(D) All of the above, plus true friends and neighbors

QUESTION 3:

"One day at a time…":

(A) Is a good philosophy for someone struggling to stay sober,

(B) Is a good philosophy for someone living with a difficult medical problem,

(C) Is a good philosophy for someone with a family problem,

(D) All of the above and it's a great "daily bread" lifestyle

QUESTION 4:

God gives the gifts of "daily bread" to:

(A) Only those who deserve it,

(B) Only those who are thankful,

(C) Only the good and not the evil,

(D) Both the good and the evil

QUESTION 5:

What word best describes a Christian's attitude?:

(A) Gratitude,

(B) Gratitude,

(C) Gratitude,

(D) All of the above, plus gratitude

QUESTION 6:

What "daily bread" do you need most to stay healthy physically?:

(A) Twinkies, Mountain Dew and pizza,

(B) Xbox 360, instant messaging and a DSL line in your bedroom,

(C) A 60-inch plasma television, a remote control and Klipsch speakers,

(D) Exercise, a balanced diet and plenty of sleep

QUESTION 7:

What "daily bread" do you need most to stay healthy emotionally?:

(A) Popularity and status,

(B) Meaningful work, a loving family life and true friends,

(C) A daily dose of Dr. Phil,

(D) Prozac

QUESTION 8:

What "daily bread" do you need most to stay healthy spiritually?:

(A) A Zen Master, a séance and a spirit guide,

(B) A Thigh Master, a sail boat and a TV Guide,

(C) The true master (God), a savior (Jesus) and a life guide (The Holy Spirit),

(D) Your own cell phone

QUESTION 9:

When God provided bread in the wilderness to Israel, they called it:

(A) Manna (Literally "what is it?"),

(B) Manna (Literally "it's white and bland"),

(C) Manna (Literally "it's white and it sticks to the roof of your mouth"),

(D) Manna (Literally "yuck")

FINKMANIA FINAL QUESTION:

The Fourth Petition to the Lord's Prayer, Matthew 6:11, tells us:

(A) God is like an endless ATM who doesn't care about how we spend our money,

(B) God is like a rich old aunt who is trying to buy our love and attention by supplying us with money,

(C) God will provide our every want,

(D) God will provide our every need

 Play this online game using FINKlink

THE WEAKEST FINK

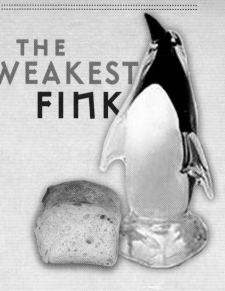

WHEN THE GODS CHOOSE TO PUNISH US, THEY MERELY ANSWER OUR PRAYERS.

OSCAR WILDE

TERMS
WRITE A DEFINITION BELOW.

DAILY BREAD

MANNA

NEED

PROVIDENCE

WANT

FORGIVE US

"The Prodigal Son" Dr. He Qi. Order prints at www.heqiarts.com

"FORGIVE US OUR DEBTS, AS WE ALSO HAVE

FORGIVEN OUR DEBTORS."

— MATTHEW 6:12

Listen to this song using FINKlink
LF16 @ www.faithink.com

You are climbing up a rocky cliff. You reach to hoist yourself up when suddenly you feel something tugging on your legs.

You look below and there, shackled to your leg, is a heavy, rusted chain with a large iron ball padlocked to the end. You have been dragging this heavy weight all along, but only noticed it now.

The wind is biting and the chain is cold around your leg. Your hands are blistered and bleeding as you wrap the chain around your neck and attempt to lift the ball. Slowly, using every ounce of strength, you manage to hoist it onto your shoulders and resume the climb. You inch up to a ledge and pause to rest. Your back is aching and your neck is tight. You stretch. You decide to keep going, so you hoist the weight onto your shoulders again and continue up toward a second ledge. Suddenly you lose balance. The ball slips, cutting further into you leg and dragging you down with it. You slide, gashing hands against sharp rocks. Down. Down. Finally, you manage to grasp a gnarled tree and hold on. The ball dangles over a steep gorge. You feel your strength fading. Your fingers are losing their grip. You close your eyes and bite your lower lip.

A moment later you become aware that you are not alone. A strong arm reaches down from above and takes hold of your wrist. You look up into the eyes of Jesus. He places a key in your hands and begins to lift, then stops. "Let go of the weight," whispers Jesus. "Unlock it. Let go. It will only pull you down."

How do you answer? What do you do? In another moment you realize this weight isn't simply an iron ball. If it were only that easy! This weight is your anger. Your grudge against someone who has wronged you. This lack of forgiveness is actually pulling you down, threatening your very life. Your health. Your ability to continue upward. Until you take Jesus' key and unlock this deadly anger, you will never be rescued. You will hang there until you fall.

Unlock the chains. Go ahead. Unlock the chains.

THE FIFTH PETITION

Have you ever held a grudge? Have you ever been so angry with someone you could hardly stand to look them in the face? A funny thing about anger: it usually hurts the angry person more than it hurts the people with whom they are angry! Living with a grudge can raise your blood pressure, give you headaches, and increase stress chemicals pumping into your stomach and throughout your body.

"I'll show you! I'm so angry I'll give myself hemorrhoids, ulcers and migraines!" How much sense does this statement make? Not much.

TO FORGIVE IS
TO SET A PRISONER FREE
AND DISCOVER THAT THE
PRISONER WAS YOU.

LEWIS SMEDES

Order this art print using FINKlink
LF16 @ www.faithink.com

IMAGES IN ART

- What do you see in today's painting by Dr. He Qi?

- Where are you in this work of art?

- How do the image and the verse apply to your life today?

So What Does This Mean?

SEVENTY TIMES SEVEN? THAT'S HOW MANY TIMES I AM TO FORGIVE? BUT BY THE TIME I GET HALF WAY THROUGH I'LL LOSE COUNT AND HAVE TO START ALL... ALL... HEY! WAIT A MINUTE.

PRAYER

DEAR LORD, YOU HAVE PLACED THE KEY TO FREEDOM AND LIFE IN MY HANDS. YOU CALL IT FORGIVENESS. TEACH ME TO LET GO OF EVERYTHING THAT CAN DRAG ME DOWN TODAY. HELP ME TO LIVE A LIFE OF GRACE AND LOVE IN ALL OF MY WORDS AND ACTIONS.

AMEN.

Anger, grudges, and unresolved hurts are rarely hidden. They lie like slivers beneath the surface and eventually surface to poison us if they aren't cleaned out. Funny thing about slivers: if you don't get them, they will ultimately get you.

In Christ's model prayer, the Fifth Petition teaches us to ask for forgiveness and to forgive as we are forgiven. The God who made us and loves us understands the deadly power of unresolved anger. Without forgiveness, life is hopeless. With forgiveness comes joy, relief, release, and abundance.

Who needs it? This misery? Put your pride aside. Humble yourself. Confess your wrongs. Forgive the wrongs of others and get on with life. You've got a mountain to climb. Don't let anything drag you down!

BIBLE TIME

Read and highlight Matthew 6:12 in your Bible, writing "Forgive" in the margin. Christ's parable of the debtors in Matthew 18: 21-35 starts with Peter's question: "How often do I have to forgive?" Jesus gives the impossible number "seventy times seven." From there, Christ launched into a story about an impossible debt and a forgiven person who was unwilling to forgive another. Read and highlight Christ's words. Also read and highlight Psalm 103:12 and Romans 6:23. How has Christ made forgiveness possible?

ROLE PLAY

1. A friend took money from a club at school and told everyone you did it. Now your classmates all think you are a thief. The friend has come to you asking for forgiveness. What do you say?

2. You have been abused by a relative. They are threatening you telling you not to go public. They say you must forgive them if you are a Christian. What do you say? What do you do?

QUESTIONS TO PONDER

1. What does forgiveness have to do with mental and physical health?

2. Why do you think Jesus added "forgive us our sins as we forgive those who sin against us" to the Lord's Prayer?

3. Make a list of two people you need to forgive and two who need to forgive you. To whom will you speak first? Why?

SMALL GROUP
SHARE, READ, TALK, PRAY, BLESS

1. **SHARE** your highs and lows of the week one-on-one with another person. Listen carefully and record your friend's thoughts in the space below. Then return to small group and share your friend's highs and lows.

   MY HIGHS + LOWS THIS WEEK WERE:

   ....

   MY FRIEND'S HIGHS + LOWS THIS WEEK WERE:

   ....

2. **READ** and highlight the theme verse in your Bibles. Circle key words, and learn the verse in song if time permits.

3. **TALK** about how today's verse relates to your highs and lows. Review the art for today, the Quiz Bowl questions, the terms, and the cartoons. Then write a sentence on each of the following:

   ONE NEW THING I LEARNED TODAY:

   ....

   ONE THING I ALREADY KNEW THAT IS WORTH REPEATING:

   ....

   ONE THING I WOULD LIKE TO KNOW MORE ABOUT:

   ....

4. **PRAY** for one another, praising and thanking God for your highs, and asking God to be with you in your lows. Include your friend's highs and lows in your prayers.

   A PRAISING PRAYER: ....

   A THANKING PRAYER: ....

   AN ASKING PRAYER: ....

5. **BLESS** one another using the blessing of the week. (right) Mark each person with the sign of the cross as you bless them.

THIS WEEK'S BLESSING
(NAME), CHILD OF GOD, MAY YOU BE AS GRACIOUS AND FORGIVING TO OTHERS AS JESUS IS TO YOU. AMEN.

THE HOME HUDDLE jOURNAL
SHARE, READ, tALK, PRAY, BLESS

Read the full devotions using FINKlink
LL06 @ www.faithink.com

DAY #1

today's bible verse:

Matthew 6:12

And forgive us our debts, as we also have forgiven our debtors.

my HIGH today was:

my LOW today was:

my PRAYER today is:

DAY #2

today's bible verse:

Matthew 18:21-22

Peter came and said to him, "Lord, if another member of the church sins against me, how often should I forgive? As many as seven times?" Jesus said to him, "Not seven times, but, I tell you, seventy-seven times."

my HIGH today was:

my LOW today was:

my PRAYER today is:

DAY #3

today's bible verse:

Romans 12:17

Do not repay anyone evil for evil, but take thought for what is noble in the sight of all.

my HIGH today was:

my LOW today was:

my PRAYER today is:

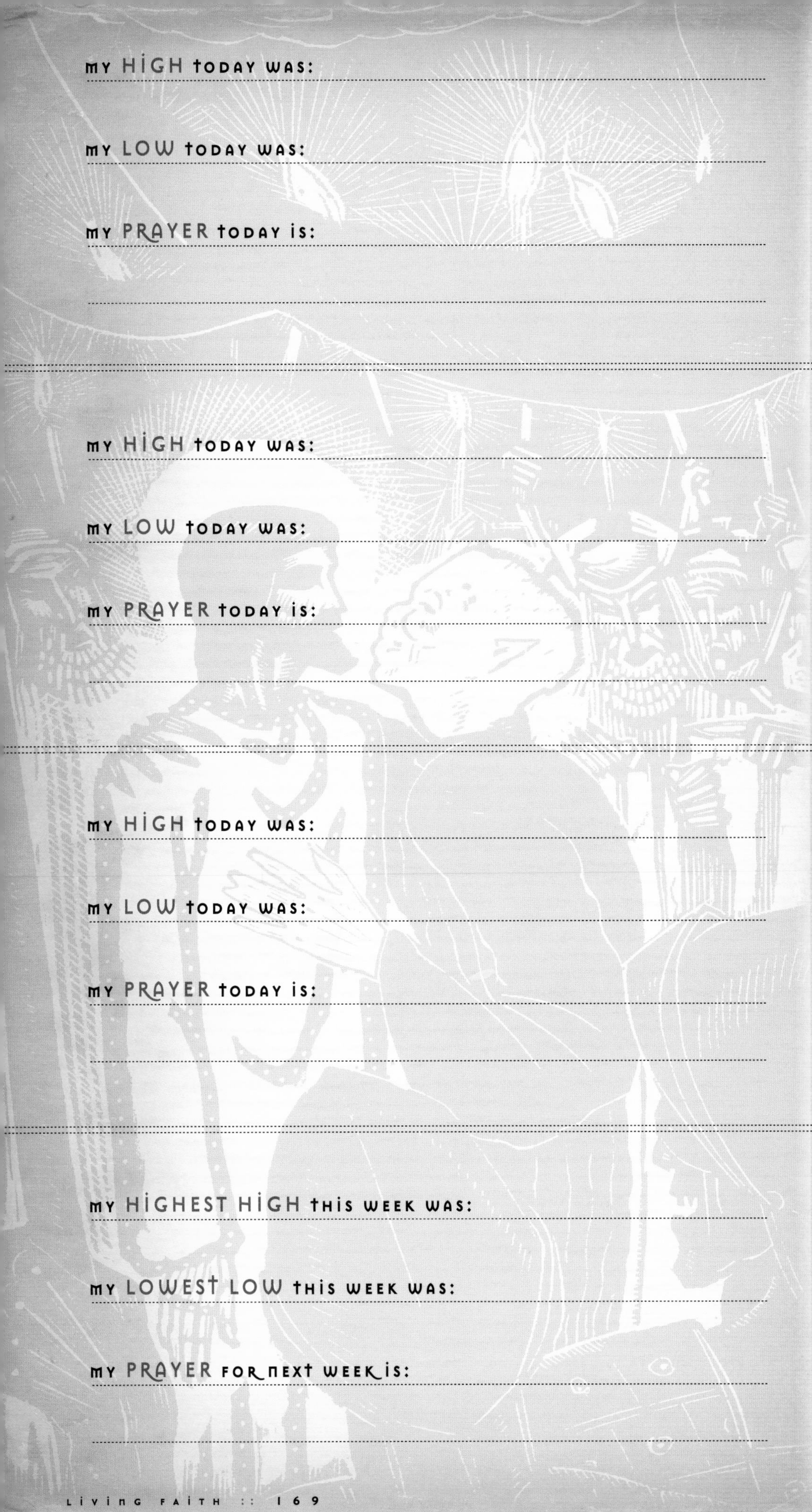

my HIGH today was: _____

my LOW today was: _____

my PRAYER today is: _____

_____

_____

TODAY'S BIBLE VERSE:

LUKE 23:34

Then Jesus said, "Father, forgive them; for they do not know what they are doing."

---

my HIGH today was: _____

my LOW today was: _____

my PRAYER today is: _____

_____

_____

DAY #5

TODAY'S BIBLE VERSE:

LUKE 6:41

Why do you see the speck in your neighbor's eye, but do not notice the log in your own eye?

---

my HIGH today was: _____

my LOW today was: _____

my PRAYER today is: _____

_____

_____

DAY #6

TODAY'S BIBLE VERSE:

MATTHEW 18:33

Should you not have had mercy on your fellow slave, as I had mercy on you?

---

my HIGHEST HIGH this week was: _____

my LOWEST LOW this week was: _____

my PRAYER for next week is: _____

_____

DAY #7

THIS WEEK'S BLESSING

(NAME), CHILD OF GOD, MAY YOU BE AS GRACIOUS AND FORGIVING TO OTHERS AS JESUS IS TO YOU. AMEN.

THE HOME HUDDLE JOURNAL
SHARE, READ, TALK, PRAY, BLESS

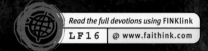

Read the full devotions using FINKlink
LF16 @ www.faithink.com

DAY #1

TODAY'S BIBLE VERSE:

Matthew 5:43-44

You have heard that it was said, "You shall love your neighbors and hate your enemy." But I say to you, Love your enemies and pray for those who persecute you..."

MY HIGH TODAY WAS:

MY LOW TODAY WAS:

MY PRAYER TODAY IS:

DAY #2

TODAY'S BIBLE VERSE:

Psalm 51:1

Have mercy on me, O God, according to your steadfast love; according to your abundant mercy blot out my transgressions.

MY HIGH TODAY WAS:

MY LOW TODAY WAS:

MY PRAYER TODAY IS:

DAY #3

TODAY'S BIBLE VERSE:

Psalm 13:1

How long, O Lord? Will you forget me forever? How long will you hide your face from me?

MY HIGH TODAY WAS:

MY LOW TODAY WAS:

MY PRAYER TODAY IS:

1. **SHARE** HIGHS & LOWS OF THE DAY.

2. **READ** AND HIGHLIGHT THE VERSE OF THE DAY IN YOUR BIBLES.

3. **TALK** ABOUT HOW TODAY'S VERSE RELATES TO YOUR HIGHS & LOWS.

4. **PRAY** FOR YOUR HIGHS & LOWS, FOR YOUR FAMILY AND FOR THE WORLD.

5. **BLESS** ONE ANOTHER USING THIS WEEK'S BLESSING (ON THE PREVIOUS PAGE).

MY HIGH TODAY WAS:

MY LOW TODAY WAS:

MY PRAYER TODAY IS:

DAY #4

TODAY'S BIBLE VERSE:

ROMANS 3:23

All have sinned and fall short of the glory of God.

MY HIGH TODAY WAS:

MY LOW TODAY WAS:

MY PRAYER TODAY IS:

DAY #5

TODAY'S BIBLE VERSE:

GENESIS 4:13

Cain said to the Lord, "My punishment is greater than I can bear!"

MY HIGH TODAY WAS:

MY LOW TODAY WAS:

MY PRAYER TODAY IS:

DAY #6

TODAY'S BIBLE VERSE:

NEHEMIAH 9:17B

You are a God ready to forgive, gracious and merciful, slow to anger and abounding in steadfast love.

THEME IN REVIEW

When I was a kid I used to pray every night for a new bicycle. Then I realized that the Lord doesn't work that way so I stole one and asked God to forgive me.

Emo Philips

DAY #7

MY FAVORITE VERSE FROM THE THEME WAS:

....

....

....

....

....

....

....

LOOKING BACK ON THESE TWO WEEKS, MY HIGHEST HIGH WAS:

....

MY LOWEST LOW THESE PAST WEEKS WAS:

....

ONE WAY GOD ANSWERED MY PRAYERS WAS:

....

ONE WAY GOD MIGHT USE ME AS A SACRED AGENT TO ANSWER THESE PRAYERS:

....

....

FAMILY COVENANT

We have shared *Highs & Lows* this week, read and highlighted the verses assigned in our Bibles, talked about our lives, prayed for one another's highs and lows, and blessed one another.

_____   _____   _____

Parent's Signature   Teen's Signature   Date

THE FINKMANIA QUIZBOWL

QUESTION 1:

The Fifth Petition is:

(A) Forgive us our debts, as we also have forgiven our debtors,

(B) Forgive us our trespasses, as we forgive those who trespass against us,

(C) Forgive us our sins as we forgive those who sin against us,

(D) All of the above, depending on the Bible translation you are using

QUESTION 2:

What does it mean to forgive as God has forgiven?:

(A) To not hold someone's sins against them,

(B) To not cut them out of relationship with you,

(C) To continue to give them a break even though they deserve nothing but punishment,

(D) All of the above and then some

QUESTION 3:

How are we to respond to God's grace and forgiveness?:

(A) We are to hardly forgive and sadly do good to those who sin against us,

(B) We are to heartily forgive and madly do good to those who sin against us,

(C) We are to heartily forgive and gladly do good to those who sin against us,

(D) I don't respond to sinners

QUESTION 4:

How is refusing to forgive like wearing a ball and chain around your neck?:

(A) Not forgiving makes you gain weight,

(B) Not forgiving weighs you down with anger, guilt and unresolved issues,

(C) Carrying an extra weight is actually good for you because it makes you stronger,

(D) None of the above

QUESTION 5:

King David was forgiven when he took another man's wife and had the man murdered, but he still:

(A) Had to suffer the consequences of his actions,

(B) Escaped the consequences of his actions,

(C) Had to earn God's love and favor by doing good,

(D) Lived a life of luxury, privilege and guilt-free pleasure

QUESTION 6:

The word "consequence" comes from two words meaning:

(A) With + what follows closely,

(B) With + punishment,

(C) With + actions,

(D) With + glittery little specks that make your ballet tutu shimmer in the Vegas stage lights

QUESTION 7:

Unforgiven sin is like:

(A) A sliver: If you don't get it, it is going to get you,

(B) Trash: If you don't take it out, it starts to stink after a while,

(C) A blister: Just leave it alone and it will heal itself,

(D) Both A & B

QUESTION 8:

Jesus taught his disciples that, when they pray, they should:

(A) Use written prayers from the hymn book with big words,

(B) Pray out loud at church and make a big deal of it,

(C) Cover their heads, especially if they are women,

(D) Pray in secret and God would reward them in secret

QUESTION 9:

God cares for us:

(A) When we are obedient,

(B) When we give lots of money to charity,

(C) When it is in God's best interest to do so,

(D) Like a parent cares for a child

FINKMANIA FINAL QUESTION:

In the Fifth Petition, Matthew 6:12, Jesus tells his followers that we should be willing to:

(A) Forgive everyone who asks for it,

(B) Forgive everyone, except our parents when they won't let us go on the Internet,

(C) Forgive everyone who deserves it,

(D) Forgive everyone if we want and expect God to forgive us

 Play this online game using FINKlink

THE WEAKEST FINK

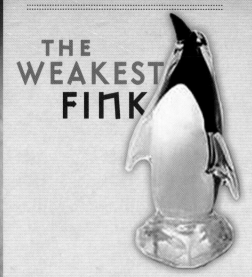

I SAY THERE ARE SPOTS THAT DON'T COME OFF... SPOTS THAT NEVER COME OFF, D'YOU KNOW WHAT I MEAN?

MAD-EYE MOODY (FROM HARRY POTTER)

TERMS
WRITE A DEFINITION BELOW.

CONSEQUENCE

DEBT

FORGIVE

GRACE

TRESPASS

TIME OF TRIAL

"Jesus Before Pilate (B)" Dr. He Qi. Order prints at www.heqiarts.com

"AND DO NOT BRING US TO THE TIME OF TRIAL..."

— MATTHEW 6:13A

Listen to this song using FINKlink
LF17 @ www.faithink.com

T he sun is baking both stone and sand in the rocky desert. Through the distant heat waves, you squint to see the figure of a gaunt man walking slowly toward you.

He is wearing a dusty tan robe and carrying a wooden staff. Suddenly, the man is not alone. A shadow crosses him, and a ghostly figure emerges from behind a rock. You move closer and hear a dark, thirsty voice: "You must be hungry. Use your power! You deserve it. If you are the Son of God, command these stones to become bread. Take care of your physical needs! It won't hurt anyone to use your power a bit. No one is watching. What good are you to anyone if you die here?"

The first man answers, "We shall not live by bread alone, but by every word that proceeds from the mouth of God." The stranger with the thirsty voice curses, then turns and smiles. He calls you by name. "You won't be as foolish as this Jesus, will you? You will give in to your physical urges. What harm can there be? After all, they are a natural part of you. Whatever it is, do it until you are satisfied." His voice trickles off, but he remains waiting for an answer. How do you respond?

Now the shadow man departs. Moments later you find yourself on the roof of a great stone temple. Crowds are milling about down below. From a ledge you see these two men again. The one with the thirsty voice whispers, "Make a show of this! Take center stage! You deserve it. Don't go the hard way—the way of the cross. Take the easy road. Jump off the building! If you are the Son of God, throw yourself down; for it is written, 'He will give his angels charge of you' and 'on their hands they will bear you up, lest you strike your foot against a stone.' " Jesus answers, "Again it is written, you shall not tempt the Lord your God." The man with the thirsty voice sneers, curses and turns his shadow down toward you. He points directly at you. "What's your problem? You're not going to chicken out on me, are you? Oh, yes. You can get away with this! Go ahead! Give in. Take the easy way. Don't fight it. It is natural. Surely God wouldn't punish you for doing something so natural." He stares, awaiting your response. How do you answer him?

In an instant you are transported to a huge mountain. There, floating like a thousand mirages about you, are the glistening kingdoms and powers of every civilization on earth. The man with the thirsty voice spreads his arms and smiles a sharp-toothed smile. "You can have it all! You deserve it! All this I will give you if you simply fall down and worship me." Jesus shouts clearly, "Be gone, Satan! For it is written, 'You shall worship the Lord your God and him only shall you serve.' " There is a blast of hot wind, and the tempter now turns to you with the same challenge: "You can have it all! You deserve it! All this I will give you if you will fall down and worship me. What do you say? It can all be yours! What will you do?" He slowly turns to vapor, leaving only the question behind:

"What will you do?"

YOU CAN'T STOP THE CROWS FROM FLYING OVER HEAD, BUT YOU CAN KEEP THEM FROM MAKING A NEST IN YOUR HAIR.

MARTIN LUTHER

Order this art print using FINKlink
LF17 @ www.faithink.com

IMAGES IN ART

- What do you see in today's painting by Dr. He Qi?

- Where are you in this work of art?

- How do the image and the verse apply to your life today?

So What Does This Mean?

When I prayed "Lead us not into temptation" this was not exactly what I had in mind.

PRAYER

DEAR GOD, PROTECT ME IN TIMES OF DANGER. SAVE ME DURING EVERY TRIAL. GUARD ME FROM THE EVIL THAT LURKS OUTSIDE, AND THE EVIL THAT LURKS WITHIN. I PRAY IN JESUS' NAME.

AMEN.

THE SIXTH PETITION

Temptation itself is not a sin. Giving in to the temptation is the sin. When we pray, "Lead us not into temptation" or "Save us from the time of trial" we aren't asking for a temptation-free life. That is not possible. We are asking for God's power to resist. Left alone, we could never fight against temptations. They would always defeat us. But we are not alone. Jesus already faced every temptation known to the human race. He knows what we are going through. Christ promises to give us the Holy Spirit's power to defeat everything the Tempter may throw against us. That's God's promise. Do you believe it?

BIBLE TIME

Read and highlight Matthew 6:13a in your Bible, writing "Temptation Insurance" in the margin. Next, read and highlight the following verses. What do each have to do with the Sixth Petition of the Lord's Prayer?

I Corinthians 10:13

I Timothy 6:9

James 1:12

ROLE PLAY

1. A classmate shows you an entire library of pirated DVDs and music CDs. They offer to make you copies of anything you want. "There's nothing wrong with copying from huge entertainment companies that charge $8 for a movie ticket and $6 for a box of popcorn! They have it coming!" What do you say?

2. A friend confides they have been spending a lot of time with internet pornography. They don't want to continue, but they think they are addicted. What do you tell them?

QUESTIONS TO PONDER

1. Why does the Bible make such a big deal about sin?

2. Martin Luther said, "You can't stop the crows from flying overhead, but you can keep them from making a nest in your hair." What do you think he meant by this?

3. Make a list of the Top Ten Temptations young people have today in your town. Which three are the easiest for you and your friends to resist? Which three are the toughest?

Small Group
SHARE, READ, TALK, PRAY, BLESS

1. **SHARE** your highs and lows of the week one-on-one with another person. Listen carefully and record your friend's thoughts in the space below. Then return to small group and share your friend's highs and lows.

   MY HIGHS + LOWS THIS WEEK WERE:

   ....

   MY FRIEND'S HIGHS + LOWS THIS WEEK WERE:

   ....

2. **READ** and highlight the theme verse in your Bibles. Circle key words, and learn the verse in song if time permits.

3. **TALK** about how today's verse relates to your highs and lows. Review the art for today, the Quiz Bowl questions, the terms, and the cartoons. Then write a sentence on each of the following:

   ONE NEW THING I LEARNED TODAY:

   ....

   ONE THING I ALREADY KNEW THAT IS WORTH REPEATING:

   ....

   ONE THING I WOULD LIKE TO KNOW MORE ABOUT:

   ....

4. **PRAY** for one another, praising and thanking God for your highs, and asking God to be with you in your lows. Include your friend's highs and lows in your prayers.

   A PRAISING PRAYER: ....

   A THANKING PRAYER: ....

   AN ASKING PRAYER: ....

5. **BLESS** one another using the blessing of the week. (right) Mark each person with the sign of the cross as you bless them.

THE FINK FIVE

THIS WEEK'S BLESSING

(NAME), CHILD OF GOD, MAY THE POWER AND PRESENCE OF GOD'S HOLY SPIRIT PROTECT YOU IN TIMES OF DANGER AND GUARD YOU FROM EVERY EVIL. IN JESUS' NAME.

THE HOME HUDDLE jOURNAL

SHARE, READ, TALK, PRAY, BLESS

Read the full devotions using FINKlink

LL06 | @ www.faithink.com

DAY #1

TODAY'S BIBLE VERSE:

MATTHEW 6:13

Save us from the time of trial.

MY HIGH TODAY WAS:

MY LOW TODAY WAS:

MY PRAYER TODAY IS:

DAY #2

TODAY'S BIBLE VERSE:

2 CORINTHIANS 4:8A

We are afflicted in every way, but not crushed; perplexed, but not driven to despair; persecuted, but not forsaken; struck down, but not destroyed...

MY HIGH TODAY WAS:

MY LOW TODAY WAS:

MY PRAYER TODAY IS:

DAY #3

TODAY'S BIBLE VERSE:

2 TIMOTHY 4:18

The Lord will rescue me from every evil attack and save me for his heavenly kingdom.

MY HIGH TODAY WAS:

MY LOW TODAY WAS:

MY PRAYER TODAY IS:

MY HIGH TODAY WAS:

MY LOW TODAY WAS:

MY PRAYER TODAY IS:

DAY #4

TODAY'S BIBLE VERSE:
1 Timothy 6:9

But those who want to be rich fall into temptation and are trapped by many sense-less and harmful desires that plunge people into ruin and destruction.

MY HIGH TODAY WAS:

MY LOW TODAY WAS:

MY PRAYER TODAY IS:

DAY #5

TODAY'S BIBLE VERSE:
Romans 8:35, 37

Who will separate us from the love of Christ? Will hardship, or distress, or per-secution, or famine, or na-kedness, or peril, or sword? No, in all these things we are more than conquerors through him who loved us.

MY HIGH TODAY WAS:

MY LOW TODAY WAS:

MY PRAYER TODAY IS:

DAY #6

TODAY'S BIBLE VERSE:
Matthew 16:23

Get behind me, Satan!

MY HIGHEST HIGH THIS WEEK WAS:

MY LOWEST LOW THIS WEEK WAS:

MY PRAYER FOR NEXT WEEK IS:

DAY #7

THIS WEEK'S BLESSING

(NAME), CHILD OF GOD, MAY THE POWER AND PRESENCE OF GOD'S HOLY SPIRIT PRO-TECT YOU IN TIMES OF DANGER AND GUARD YOU FROM EVERY EVIL. IN JESUS' NAME.

THE HOME HUDDLE JOURNAL
SHARE, READ, TALK, PRAY, BLESS

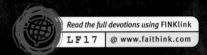

WEEK 2

Read the full devotions using FINKlink
LF17 @ www.faithink.com

DAY #1

TODAY'S BIBLE VERSE:

GENESIS 3:1

Now the serpent was more crafty than any other animal that the Lord God had made. He said to the woman, "Did God say, 'You shall not eat from any tree in the garden?'"

MY HIGH TODAY WAS:

MY LOW TODAY WAS:

MY PRAYER TODAY IS:

DAY #2

TODAY'S BIBLE VERSE:

JAMES 1:12

Blessed is anyone who endures temptation. Such a one has stood the test and will receive the crown of life that the Lord has promised to those who love him.

MY HIGH TODAY WAS:

MY LOW TODAY WAS:

MY PRAYER TODAY IS:

DAY #3

TODAY'S BIBLE VERSE:

JAMES 1:13

No one, when tempted, should say, "I am being tempted by God"; for God cannot be tempted by evil and he himself tempts no one.

MY HIGH TODAY WAS:

MY LOW TODAY WAS:

MY PRAYER TODAY IS:

1. **SHARE** HIGHS & LOWS OF THE DAY.

2. **READ** AND HIGHLIGHT THE VERSE OF THE DAY IN YOUR BIBLES.

3. **TALK** ABOUT HOW TODAY'S VERSE RELATES TO YOUR HIGHS & LOWS.

4. **PRAY** FOR YOUR HIGHS & LOWS, FOR YOUR FAMILY AND FOR THE WORLD.

5. **BLESS** ONE ANOTHER USING THIS WEEK'S BLESSING (ON THE PREVIOUS PAGE).

MY HIGH TODAY WAS:

MY LOW TODAY WAS:

MY PRAYER TODAY IS:

DAY #4

TODAY'S BIBLE VERSE:

James 1:2-3

My brothers and sisters, whenever you face trials of any kind, consider it nothing but joy, because you know that the testing of your faith produces endurance.

MY HIGH TODAY WAS:

MY LOW TODAY WAS:

MY PRAYER TODAY IS:

DAY #5

TODAY'S BIBLE VERSE:

Matthew 7:15

Beware of false prophets, who come to you in sheep's clothing but inwardly are ravenously wolves. You will know them by their fruits.

MY HIGH TODAY WAS:

MY LOW TODAY WAS:

MY PRAYER TODAY IS:

DAY #6

TODAY'S BIBLE VERSE:

Matthew 26:41

Stay awake and pray, that you may not come into the time of trial; the spirit indeed is willing, but the flesh is weak.

THEME IN REVIEW

Nothing makes it easier to resist temptation than a proper upbringing, a sound set of values and witnesses.

MARK TWAIN

DAY #7

MY FAVORITE VERSE FROM THE THEME WAS:

....

....

....

....

....

....

....

LOOKING BACK ON THESE TWO WEEKS, MY HIGHEST HIGH WAS:

....

MY LOWEST LOW THESE PAST WEEKS WAS:

....

ONE WAY GOD ANSWERED MY PRAYERS WAS:

....

ONE WAY GOD MIGHT USE ME AS A SACRED AGENT TO ANSWER THESE PRAYERS:

....

....

FAMILY COVENANT

We have shared *Highs & Lows* this week, read and highlighted the verses assigned in our Bibles, talked about our lives, prayed for one another's highs and lows, and blessed one another.

_____   _____   _____

Parent's Signature   Teen's Signature   Date

THE FINKMANIA QUIZBOWL

QUESTION 1:

Which of the following is not an accurate translation of the Sixth Petition?:

(A) "Save us from the time of trial,"

(B) "Lead us not into temptation,"

(C) "Do not bring us to the time of trial,

(D) "Save us from the consequences of our stupidity"

QUESTION 2:

What does "save us" mean?:

(A) Protect us,

(B) Watch over and keep us safe,

(C) Both A & B,

(D) Come in for us at the end of our lives and pitch the last three outs so we don't blow our lead and lose the game

QUESTION 3:

What are we asking God to save us from in the Lord's Prayer?

(A) Our parents,

(B) All trials and temptations,

(C) All trials and temptations that could lead us into false belief, despair, and other sins that would take us away from God,

(D) Mostly bad hair days and poor fashion decisions

QUESTION 4:

A temptation is:

(A) A member of a popular Motown singing group from the 60s,

(B) A short-term opportunity,

(C) A desire that lures us away from God's good and gracious will for our lives,

(D) A & C

QUESTION 5:

When the Devil tempted Jesus, he:

(A) Gave in,

(B) Resisted the temptation and focused on God's Word and his personal mission,

(C) Shot him with a pellet gun,

(D) First B, then A

QUESTION 6:

Martin Luther said, "You can't stop the crows from flying overhead, but you can...":

(A) Keep them from making a nest in your hair,

(B) Bake them into pie,

(C) Shoot them with a pellet gun,

(D) Invite them in to poop on your neighbor's carpet from time to time

QUESTION 7:

How do people set themselves up for trouble?:

(A) By hanging around people who are bad influences,

(B) By allowing dangerous thoughts to get hold of our imaginations,

(C) By engaging in risky behavior,

(D) All of the above and then some

QUESTION 8:

God tempts people to sin so that:

(A) God can catch us and punish us,

(B) God can make us better people,

(C) God can force us to change when we hit bottom,

(D) None of the above—God doesn't tempt anyone to sin

QUESTION 9:

An effective way to resist temptation is to:

(A) Go live in a monastery on top of a mountain in Tibet,

(B) Reject association with all evil people,

(C) Fill your life with prayer and God's Word, and fill your time with positive friends and influences,

(D) Beat yourself with willow branches when tempted

FINKMANIA FINAL QUESTION:

The Sixth Petition of the Lord's Prayer, Matthew 6:13, tells us to:

(A) Avoid jury duty and all trials,

(B) Ask God to keep us from facing all trials and temptations,

(C) Ask God to help us avoid sin when we face trials and temptations,

(D) Ask God to stop tempting us

 Play this online game using FINKlink
LF17 | @ www.faithink.com

THE WEAKEST FINK

I don't know! I don't know why I did it, I don't know why I enjoyed it, and I don't know why I'll do it again!

BART SIMPSON

TERMS

WRITE A DEFINITION BELOW.

SATAN

SAVE

TEST

TRIAL

TEMPTATION

 FAITH INKUBATORS

DELIVER US FROM EVIL

"Finding Moses (2005)" Dr. He Qi. Order prints at www.heqiarts.com

"BUT RESCUE US FROM THE EVIL ONE."

— MATTHEW 6:13B

Listen to this song using FINKlink
LF18 @ www.faithink.com

Stand at the ovens of Auchwitz or stare into the mountains of skulls in the killing fields of Cambodia and tell the ghosts of the murdered that evil does not exist.

Walk through endless refugee settlements in Asia and Africa. Look into the eyes of war orphans and torture victims in a hundred countries across the globe and explain to them that there is no such thing as evil. A quick read of the history of humanity will show you a lot of inhumanity. It will also show evil as a power—not simply a bad choice.

Some people don't believe in evil. They think there is no good or bad. Everything is relative. Some people don't believe in the devil or in spiritual powers. Others picture Satan as a cartoon character—some silly little guy in a red suit with a pitchfork. What do you believe?

The Bible teaches that God has a powerful adversary—a dangerous enemy who wants to destroy all that is good and drag God's children with him to hell. In Genesis, this enemy is pictured as a serpent. It tempts Adam and Eve first to doubt God ("Did God really say...") and then to disobey. In Job, Satan is the accuser, destroying a good man's life and testing him almost to the point of breaking. In the Gospels, Satan is seen as a very real spiritual being. He comes to tempt Jesus into taking the easy road to comfort, fame, and power. Even weakened by hunger, Jesus doesn't give in. He quotes scripture and keeps his eyes on God's will, not his own. In Paul's letters, Satan is described as a hungry lion, lurking about and searching for someone to devour. Satan's spiritual army torments people, but the demons are no match for Christ. A single word from Jesus can send them running. Even the name of Christ can chase them away. In the final book of the Bible, Satan is seen as a doomed cosmic general, fighting to destroy everyone he can before his army is shattered and chained.

C. S. Lewis, friend of J. R. R. Tolkein and author of *The Lion, the Witch and the Wardrobe*, wrote: "There are two equal and opposite errors into which our [culture] can fall about devils. One is to disbelieve in their existence. The other is to believe, and to feel an excessive and unhealthy interest in them."

What do you believe about evil? About Satan? About God's power to destroy the things that might destroy you? Is there a spiritual dimension to the battles going on in this world? Is there more to life than what you can see, feel, taste, and touch? Is resisting temptation simply a matter of will power? Of "won't" power? Or do you need God's Word and power to arm, equip and defend you against an unseen enemy that seeks your destruction?

Your answers to these questions are no small matter.

BART, STOP PESTERING SATAN!

MARGE SIMPSON

IMAGES in ART

- What do you see in today's painting by Dr. He Qi?

- Where are you in this work of art?

- How do the image and the verse apply to your life today?

So What Does This Mean?

HAT'S O.K. YOU DON'T HAVE TO LEAVE. SHE'S NOT BOTHERING ME.

YA? BUT YOU'RE BOTHERING HER.

PRAYER

LORD, RESCUE ME.
RESCUE ME FROM THE THINGS
I THINK I WANT THAT AREN'T
REALLY GOOD FOR ME. RESCUE
ME FROM THE POSSESSIONS I
CRAVE THAT COULD POSSESS
ME. RESCUE ME FROM THE EVIL
WITHIN, AND THE EVIL WITH-
OUT, THE EVIL OF FEAR, THE
EVIL OF DOUBT.

LORD, RESCUE ME.

AMEN.

THE SEVENTH PETITION

"Evil" or "Evil One?" Which is it? The traditional version of the Lord's Prayer that most churches use today comes from the King James Bible of 1611. It says, "Deliver us from evil." Most modern versions of the Bible—and even the New King James Version—translate the original ancient Greek manuscripts as "deliver/rescue us from the evil one." What's the difference? Does it change your understanding of the prayer to pray it one way or the other?

BIBLE TIME

Read and highlight Matthew 6:13, writing "Rescue us!" in the margin. Now turn to Matthew 4:1-11. Christ stayed focused on his mission and used God's Word as a weapon against doubt and temptation. Write "Focus!" in the margin. Finally, turn to Micah 6:8 and Matthew 28:19-20. Write "Our Commission" in the margins as reminders of what Christ calls us to be and do in this world.

ROLE PLAY

1. A classmate has been reading a lot about "wicca" (witchcraft) on the internet. She says it seems like fun. What is your response?

2. A friend says there is no such thing as evil, the devil, or spiritual powers. Everything is simply a matter of personal choice. How do you respond?

QUESTIONS TO PONDER

1. What do you think is the worst thing that can happen to a young person today? Why?

2. What do you think a conscience is? What part does a conscience play in delivering us from evil?

3. In Ephesians 6:12, St. Paul wrote: *"For our struggle is not against enemies of blood and flesh, but against the rulers, against the authorities, against the cosmic powers of this present darkness, against the spiritual forces of evil in the heavenly places."*

How can you fight against something you cannot see?

SMALL GROUP
SHARE, READ, TALK, PRAY, BLESS

1. **SHARE** your highs and lows of the week one-on-one with another person. Listen carefully and record your friend's thoughts in the space below. Then return to small group and share your friend's highs and lows.

   MY HIGHS + LOWS THIS WEEK WERE:

   ....

   MY FRIEND'S HIGHS + LOWS THIS WEEK WERE:

   ....

2. **READ** and highlight the theme verse in your Bibles. Circle key words, and learn the verse in song if time permits.

3. **TALK** about how today's verse relates to your highs and lows. Review the art for today, the Quiz Bowl questions, the terms, and the cartoons. Then write a sentence on each of the following:

   ONE NEW THING I LEARNED TODAY:

   ....

   ONE THING I ALREADY KNEW THAT IS WORTH REPEATING:

   ....

   ONE THING I WOULD LIKE TO KNOW MORE ABOUT:

   ....

4. **PRAY** for one another, praising and thanking God for your highs, and asking God to be with you in your lows. Include your friend's highs and lows in your prayers.

   A PRAISING PRAYER: ....

   A THANKING PRAYER: ....

   AN ASKING PRAYER: ....

5. **BLESS** one another using the blessing of the week. (right) Mark each person with the sign of the cross as you bless them.

THE FINK FIVE 5

THIS WEEK'S BLESSING

(NAME), CHILD OF GOD, MAY THE SPIRIT OF ALMIGHTY GOD PROTECT YOU FROM DANGER THIS DAY AND DE- LIVER YOU FROM EVERY EVIL. IN JESUS' NAME.

THE HOME HUDDLE JOURNAL
SHARE, READ, TALK, PRAY, BLESS

Read the full devotions using FINKlink
LF18 | @ www.faithink.com

DAY #1

TODAY'S BIBLE VERSE:

Matthew 6:13b

...but rescue us from the evil one.

MY HIGH TODAY WAS:

MY LOW TODAY WAS:

MY PRAYER TODAY IS:

DAY #2

TODAY'S BIBLE VERSE:

Psalm 18:3

I call upon the Lord, who is worthy to be praised, so shall I be saved from my enemies.

MY HIGH TODAY WAS:

MY LOW TODAY WAS:

MY PRAYER TODAY IS:

DAY #3

TODAY'S BIBLE VERSE:

Psalm 22:4-5

In you our ancestors trusted; they trusted, and you delivered them. To you, they cried and were saved; in you they trusted, and were not put to shame.

MY HIGH TODAY WAS:

MY LOW TODAY WAS:

MY PRAYER TODAY IS:

my HIGH today was:

my LOW today was:

my PRAYER today is:

DAY #4

TODAY'S BIBLE VERSE:

PSALM 34:19

Many are the afflictions of the righteous, but the Lord rescues them from them all.

my HIGH today was:

my LOW today was:

my PRAYER today is:

DAY #5

TODAY'S BIBLE VERSE:

PSALM 42:5-6A

Why are you cast down, O my soul, and why are you disquieted within me? Hope in God; for I shall again praise him, my help and my God.

my HIGH today was:

my LOW today was:

my PRAYER today is:

DAY #6

TODAY'S BIBLE VERSE:

PSALM 51:14

Deliver me from bloodshed, O God, O God of my salvation, and my tongue will sing aloud of your deliverance.

my HIGHEST HIGH this week was:

my LOWEST LOW this week was:

my PRAYER for next week is:

DAY #7

THIS WEEK'S BLESSING

(NAME), CHILD OF GOD, MAY THE SPIRIT OF ALMIGHTY GOD PROTECT YOU FROM DANGER THIS DAY AND DELIVER YOU FROM EVERY EVIL. IN JESUS' NAME.

THE HOME HUDDLE JOURNAL

SHARE, READ, TALK, PRAY, BLESS

WEEK 2

Read the full devotions using FINKlink LF18 @ www.faithink.com

DAY #1

TODAY'S BIBLE VERSE:

MATTHEW 8:25-26

And they went and woke him up, saying, "Lord, save us! We are perishing!" And he said to them, "Why are you afraid, you of little faith?" Then he got up and rebuked the winds and the sea; and there was a dead calm.

MY HIGH TODAY WAS:

MY LOW TODAY WAS:

MY PRAYER TODAY IS:

DAY #2

TODAY'S BIBLE VERSE:

LUKE 19:10

For the Son of Man came to seek out and to save the lost.

MY HIGH TODAY WAS:

MY LOW TODAY WAS:

MY PRAYER TODAY IS:

DAY #3

TODAY'S BIBLE VERSE:

LUKE 23:42

Jesus, remember me when you come into your kingdom.

MY HIGH TODAY WAS:

MY LOW TODAY WAS:

MY PRAYER TODAY IS:

1. SHARE HIGHS & LOWS OF THE DAY.

2. READ AND HIGHLIGHT THE VERSE OF THE DAY IN YOUR BIBLES.

3. TALK ABOUT HOW TODAY'S VERSE RELATES TO YOUR HIGHS & LOWS.

4. PRAY FOR YOUR HIGHS & LOWS, FOR YOUR FAMILY AND FOR THE WORLD.

5. BLESS ONE ANOTHER USING THIS WEEK'S BLESSING (ON THE PREVIOUS PAGE).

MY HIGH TODAY WAS:

MY LOW TODAY WAS:

MY PRAYER TODAY IS:

DAY #4

TODAY'S BIBLE VERSE:

I Corinthians 15:51

Listen, I will tell you a mystery! We will not all die, but we will all be changed...

MY HIGH TODAY WAS:

MY LOW TODAY WAS:

MY PRAYER TODAY IS:

DAY #5

TODAY'S BIBLE VERSE:

James 1:17

Every generous act of giving, with every perfect gift, is from above, coming down from the Father of lights, with whom there is no variation or shadow due to change.

MY HIGH TODAY WAS:

MY LOW TODAY WAS:

MY PRAYER TODAY IS:

DAY #6

TODAY'S BIBLE VERSE:

I Peter 5:8

Discipline yourselves, keep alert. Like a roaring lion your adversary the devil prowls around, looking for someone to devour.

THEME in REVIEW

OH THEM LIONS THEY
CAN EAT MY BODY BUT THEY
CAN'T SWALLOW MY SOUL
(NO NO NO)

THEY KEEP ON TRYING
TO CRASH MY PARTY BUT THEY
CAN'T GET CONTROL (NO NO)

NO WAY, BABY.

LOST AND FOUND
DAY #7

MY FAVORITE VERSE
FROM THE THEME WAS:

....

....

....

....

....

....

....

LOOKING BACK ON THESE TWO WEEKS, MY HIGHEST HIGH WAS:

....

MY LOWEST LOW THESE PAST WEEKS WAS:

....

ONE WAY GOD ANSWERED MY PRAYERS WAS:

....

ONE WAY GOD MIGHT USE ME AS A SACRED AGENT
TO ANSWER THESE PRAYERS:

....

....

FAMILY COVENANT

We have shared *Highs & Lows* this week, read and highlighted the verses assigned in our Bibles, talked about our lives, prayed for one another's highs and lows, and blessed one another.

....

Parent's Signature   Teen's Signature   Date

THE FINKMANIA QUIZBOWL

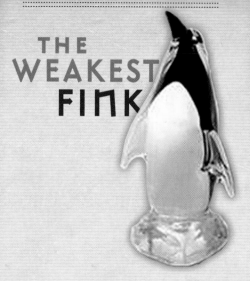

Question 1:

The Seventh Petition of the Lord's Prayer is:

(A) Deliver us from evil,

(B) Rescue us from evil,

(C) Rescue us from the evil one,

(D) All of the above, depending on which translation of the Bible you happen to be reading

Question 2:

What does "deliver us" mean?:

(A) To slap a FedEx sticker on someone,

(B) To bring us out from danger to safety,

(C) To give us a ride,

(D) To perform an emergency liverectomy

Question 3:

Which is a better definition of evil?

(A) Little brothers,

(B) Little sisters,

(C) Anything that is morally wrong, destructive, harmful and against the good and gracious will of God,

(D) Simon on *American Idol*

Question 4:

Who works to destroy everything God creates as good and holy?

(A) Little brothers,

(B) Little sisters,

(C) God's enemy, Satan,

(D) Simon on *American Idol*

Question 5:

What is the ultimate offensive weapon God gives us to fight against evil?:

(A) Polite language,

(B) Intelligence,

(C) A big stick,

(D) The Sword of the Spirit (God's Word) and the power of the Holy Spirit

Question 6:

The still, small voice of God in our minds is sometimes called:

(A) Our conscience,

(B) A headache,

(C) The Holy Spirit,

(D) Both A & C

Question 7:

God is more powerful than:

(A) Kryptonite,

(B) Any evil that could come upon you,

(C) Simon on *American Idol*,

(D) All of the above

Question 8:

What are we asking God to deliver us from in the Seventh Petition?:

(A) From every evil to our bodies,

(B) From every evil to our souls,

(C) Both A & B,

(D) Simon on *American Idol*

Question 9:

The Bible shows Satan as:

(A) A sneaky snake,

(B) A roaring lion,

(C) A tricky tempter,

(D) All of the above

FINKmania Final Question:

The Seventh Petition, Matthew 6:13b, tells us:

(A) Evil is easy to avoid,

(B) God controls every decision we make so we can blame God for the evil, pain and suffering in the world,

(C) We are to pray to God to be our ultimate defender,

(D) Absolutely nothing

Play this online game using FINKlink
LF18 @ www.faithink.com

If you meet a snake, just kill it. Don't appoint a committee on snakes.

Ross Perot

TERMS
WRITE A DEFINITION BELOW.

Deliver

Devil

Evil

Rescue

Sin

FAITH INKUBATORS

THE DOXOLOGY

"Glory to God in the Highest" Dr. He Qi. Order prints at www.heqiarts.com

"FOR THE KINGDOM, AND THE POWER, AND THE GLORY ARE

YOURS, NOW AND FOREVER. AMEN."

— THE DOXOLOGY

 Listen to this song using FINKlink
LF19 @ www.faithink.com

You are floating out into space— swirling, spinning, and dancing through the light of a billion stars out onto the edge of the universe.

You pass dazzling red novas and skid through sparkling islands of cosmic dust. You whirl past black holes from which not even light can escape and skirt a million exploding galaxies. Surrounded by a light which your eyes have never beheld, you sense the force of a radiance that exists beyond human sight. Your soul feels drawn to the light and the warmth as an amazing brilliance fills you and lifts you. The sound of thunder and rushing waters pours out from the light in joyous praise. There are no words, but the message is translated into your brain. Its pounds out a symphony of glory to the God who created it all. Strange and beautiful voices praise the Lord from the heavens. You see the entire universe in a moment! High above it all, lost in the praise, you are surrounded by glowing choirs of angel armies.

The sun and moon and stars join in praise. You spin back toward earth. Fiery volcanoes and pounding hail join the chorus. Blinding snow storms and spreading frost glorify God. A powerful wind crosses the mountains and hills. It shakes fruit trees and cedars as they sing together. Animals chatter from jungles. Cows, bugs, and birds all sing glory to the God of the morning. You glide past castles and senate buildings where rulers, courts, and peoples lift their voices in praise. You pass through stadiums bursting with young men and women, through parks filled with old people and children, all singing. All creation—by its very existence—seems to shout a piercing trumpet into your soul. "Praise the Lord! For God's name alone is exalted. Praise the Lord! God's glory is above earth and heaven. Praise the Lord! Let all that lives and breathes praise the Lord. For the kingdom and the power and the glory belong to God now and forever! Praise the Lord."

THE GLORY WORD

A beautiful word of praise was once added to the end of the Lord's Prayer. Jesus didn't pray it, but for centuries the church has used this *Doxology* (Greek for "glory word") as a fitting ending to Christ's model prayer. In your own prayer life, you might wish to add an original "glory word" every night. During family prayers this week, try adding one thing for which you are truly thankful. It could be as simple as "Thanks, God, for a good night's sleep" or "I praise you for keeping me safe during the hail storm" or "Thank you for giving me the right words for today's speech." Add these deeper prayers to your Home Huddle journal entries. Gradually your journal will become a more valuable and thoughtful record of your walk with God. Looking back, you will clearly see God's gifting presence in every circumstance, whether joyful or difficult.

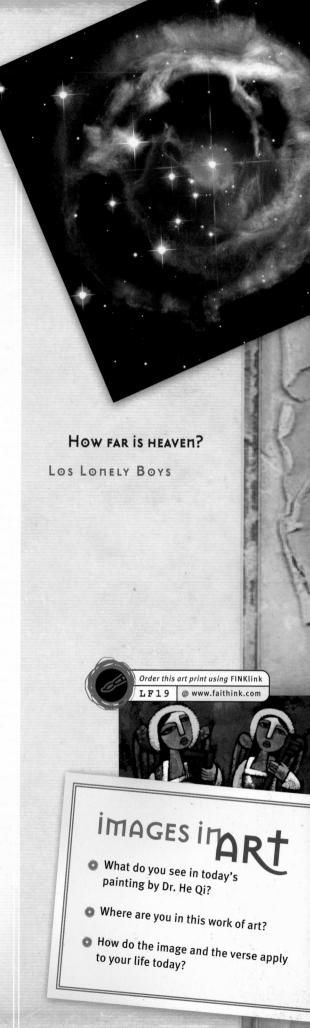

HOW FAR IS HEAVEN?

LOS LONELY BOYS

Order this art print using FINKlink
LF19 @ www.faithink.com

IMAGES IN ART

- What do you see in today's painting by Dr. He Qi?
- Where are you in this work of art?
- How do the image and the verse apply to your life today?

So What Does This Mean?

IF GOD IS SO GREAT, THEN CAN HE MAKE A ROCK SO BIG THAT NOT EVEN HE CAN MOVE IT?

YES. IT'S CALLED THE HUMAN HEART.

PRAYER

LORD GOD, YOUR GLORY FILLS THE HEAVENS. YOUR LOVE OVERFLOWS FROM THE CROSS. GIVE ME EYES TO SEE AND A MIND TO UNDERSTAND THAT YOURS IS THE KINGDOM, AND THE POWER, AND THE GLORY FOREVER AND EVER.

AMEN.

BETTER THAN BOTOX

What are you looking for? If you look for the best in people and life situations, you'll probably find it. If you look for the worst, you'll definitely find it. Some people grumble and complain a lot. After time, their attitudes can be seen in the lines of their faces. Others seem to live lives of joy. This joy, too, can be traced in wrinkles. A good wrinkle you might wish to add to your prayer life this week is praise. Why not go out of your way to look for the good in your life and thank God for it every night? Train yourself to see the best in people and situations. Then add the one thing most often missing in prayer—an attitude of gratitude. It'll change the way your face ages! (Plus, it's cheaper than Botox®.)

BIBLE TIME

Write the words to the Doxology in the margins of your Bible after Matthew 6:13, and add "Doxology: Glory Word" next to it. Next, read and highlight the following verses. What do they have to do with praise and prayer?

Psalm 68:34-35

I Chronicles 29:11-13

Revelation 22:13

ROLE PLAY

1. A friend is always grumbling and complaining. She is so negative that many people avoid or ignore her. She is negative about that, too. Talk to her about it. What do you say? What do you do?

2. A friend asks: "Why would you praise a God who lets so much suffering happen in this world?" How do you answer?

QUESTIONS TO PONDER

1. Does God need our praise? Why or why not?

2. Compose a prayer using all of these words: God, awesome, beautiful, creator, declare, excellent, fantastic, great, holy, incomprehensible, jamming, knowing, loving, magnificent, new, omniscient, powerful, quiet, regal, sensational, timeless, unbelievable, valuable, wow… and your own X, Y & Z words.

3. Take a quick tour of the book of Psalms, looking for evidence of praise. Highlight words of praise and adoration you find. Many of these psalms were written as worship songs. What can we do to add more praise to our worship?

SMALL GROUP
SHARE, READ, TALK, PRAY, BLESS

1. **SHARE** your highs and lows of the week one-on-one with another person. Listen carefully and record your friend's thoughts in the space below. Then return to small group and share your friend's highs and lows.

   MY HIGHS + LOWS THIS WEEK WERE:

   ....

   MY FRIEND'S HIGHS + LOWS THIS WEEK WERE:

   ....

2. **READ** and highlight the theme verse in your Bibles. Circle key words, and learn the verse in song if time permits.

3. **TALK** about how today's verse relates to your highs and lows. Review the art for today, the Quiz Bowl questions, the terms, and the cartoons. Then write a sentence on each of the following:

   ONE NEW THING I LEARNED TODAY:

   ....

   ONE THING I ALREADY KNEW THAT IS WORTH REPEATING:

   ....

   ONE THING I WOULD LIKE TO KNOW MORE ABOUT:

   ....

4. **PRAY** for one another, praising and thanking God for your highs, and asking God to be with you in your lows. Include your friend's highs and lows in your prayers.

   A PRAISING PRAYER: ....

   A THANKING PRAYER: ....

   AN ASKING PRAYER: ....

5. **BLESS** one another using the blessing of the week. (right) Mark each person with the sign of the cross as you bless them.

THIS WEEK'S BLESSING
(NAME), CHILD OF GOD, MAY YOU KNOW THE KINGDOM, THE POWER AND THE GLORY OF GOD IN YOUR HEART. IN JESUS' NAME.

THE HOME HUDDLE JOURNAL
SHARE, READ, TALK, PRAY, BLESS

Read the full devotions using FINKlink
LF19 | @ www.faithink.com

DAY #1

TODAY'S BIBLE VERSE:

THE DOXOLOGY

For the kingdom, the power and the glory are yours, now and forever.

MY **HIGH** TODAY WAS:

MY **LOW** TODAY WAS:

MY **PRAYER** TODAY IS:

DAY #2

TODAY'S BIBLE VERSE:

EXODUS 24:17

Now the appearance of the glory of the Lord was like a devouring fire on the top of the mountain in the sight of the people of Israel.

MY **HIGH** TODAY WAS:

MY **LOW** TODAY WAS:

MY **PRAYER** TODAY IS:

DAY #3

TODAY'S BIBLE VERSE:

ISAIAH 6:3

Holy, holy, holy is the Lord of hosts; the whole earth is full of his glory.

MY **HIGH** TODAY WAS:

MY **LOW** TODAY WAS:

MY **PRAYER** TODAY IS:

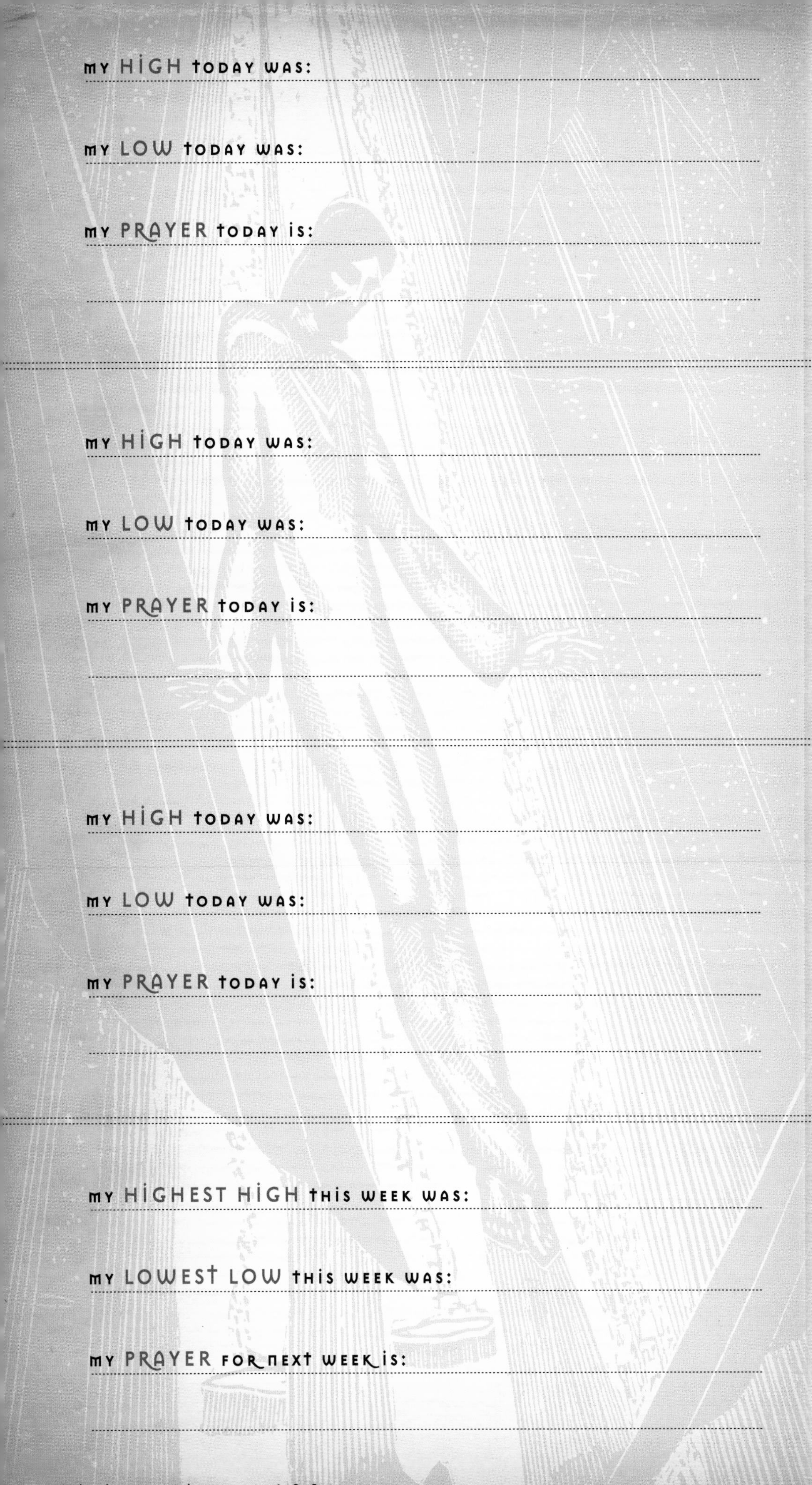

MY HIGH TODAY WAS: _____

MY LOW TODAY WAS: _____

MY PRAYER TODAY IS: _____

_____

DAY #4

TODAY'S BIBLE VERSE:

PSALM 68:34-35

Ascribe power to God, whose majesty is over Israel; and whose power is in the skies. Awesome is God in his sanctuary, the God of Israel; he gives power and strength to his people. Blessed be God!

MY HIGH TODAY WAS: _____

MY LOW TODAY WAS: _____

MY PRAYER TODAY IS: _____

_____

DAY #5

TODAY'S BIBLE VERSE:

1 JOHN 5:14

And this is the boldness we have in him, that if we ask anything according to his will, he hears us.

MY HIGH TODAY WAS: _____

MY LOW TODAY WAS: _____

MY PRAYER TODAY IS: _____

_____

DAY #6

TODAY'S BIBLE VERSE:

2 CHRONICLES 7:14

If my people who are called by my name humble themselves, pray, seek my face, and turn from their wicked ways, then I will hear from heaven, and will forgive their sin and heal their land.

MY HIGHEST HIGH THIS WEEK WAS: _____

MY LOWEST LOW THIS WEEK WAS: _____

MY PRAYER FOR NEXT WEEK IS: _____

_____

DAY #7

THIS WEEK'S BLESSING

(NAME), CHILD OF GOD, MAY YOU KNOW THE KINGDOM, THE POWER AND THE GLORY OF GOD IN YOUR HEART. IN JESUS' NAME.

THE HOME HUDDLE jOURNAL
SHARE, READ, tALK, PRAY, BLESS

Read the full devotions using FINKlink
LF19 | @ www.faithink.com

DAY #1

todAY'S BiBLE VERSE:

jOB 38:4

Where were you when I laid the foundation of the earth? Tell me, if you have understanding.

MY **HiGH** todAY WAS:

MY **LOW** todAY WAS:

MY **PRAYER** todAY iS:

DAY #2

todAY'S BiBLE VERSE:

LuKE 11:9

So I say to you, Ask, and it will be given you; search, and you will find; knock, and the door will be opened for you.

MY **HiGH** todAY WAS:

MY **LOW** todAY WAS:

MY **PRAYER** todAY iS:

DAY #3

todAY'S BiBLE VERSE:

2 PeteR 1:16

For we did not follow cleverly devised myths when we made known to you the power and coming of our Lord Jesus Christ, but we had been eyewitnesses of his majesty.

MY **HiGH** todAY WAS:

MY **LOW** todAY WAS:

MY **PRAYER** todAY iS:

1. **SHARE** HIGHS & LOWS OF THE DAY.

2. **READ** AND HIGHLIGHT THE VERSE OF THE DAY IN YOUR BIBLES.

3. **TALK** ABOUT HOW TODAY'S VERSE RELATES TO YOUR HIGHS & LOWS.

4. **PRAY** FOR YOUR HIGHS & LOWS, FOR YOUR FAMILY AND FOR THE WORLD.

5. **BLESS** ONE ANOTHER USING THIS WEEK'S BLESSING (ON THE PREVIOUS PAGE).

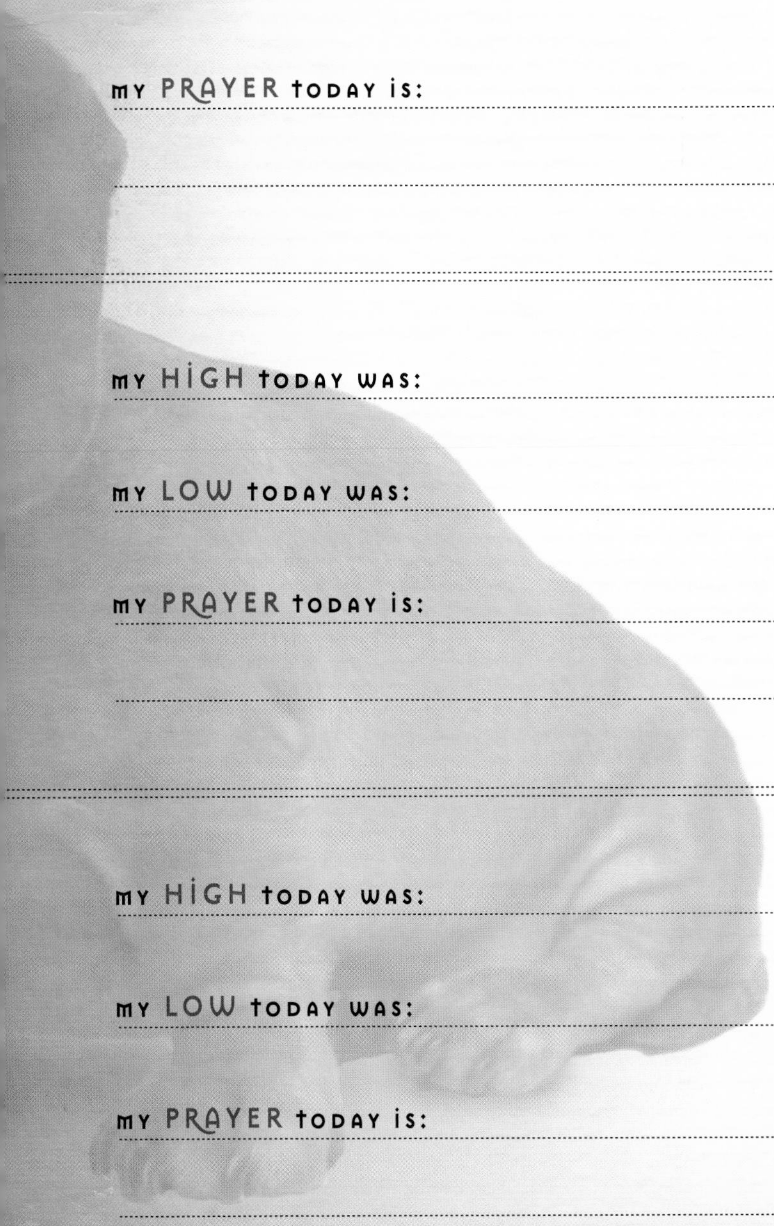

MY **HIGH** TODAY WAS:

MY **LOW** TODAY WAS:

MY **PRAYER** TODAY IS:

DAY #4

TODAY'S BIBLE VERSE:

REVELATION 11:15B

The kingdom of the world has become the kingdom of our Lord and of his Messiah, and he will reign forever and ever.

MY **HIGH** TODAY WAS:

MY **LOW** TODAY WAS:

MY **PRAYER** TODAY IS:

DAY #5

TODAY'S BIBLE VERSE:

REVELATION 22:13

I am the Alpha and the Omega, the first and the last, the beginning and the end.

MY **HIGH** TODAY WAS:

MY **LOW** TODAY WAS:

MY **PRAYER** TODAY IS:

DAY #6

TODAY'S BIBLE VERSE:

REVELATION 22:20

Amen. Come, Lord Jesus!

THEME IN REVIEW

SIM|T|WITH|F|S

> IF I AM NOT ALLOWED TO LAUGH IN HEAVEN, I DON'T WANT TO GO THERE.

Martin Luther

DAY #7

MY FAVORITE VERSE FROM THE THEME WAS:

....

....

....

....

....

....

....

....

LOOKING BACK ON THESE TWO WEEKS, MY HIGHEST **HIGH** WAS:

....

MY LOWEST **LOW** THESE PAST WEEKS WAS:

....

ONE WAY GOD ANSWERED MY **PRAYERS** WAS:

....

ONE WAY GOD MIGHT USE ME AS A **SACRED AGENT** TO ANSWER THESE PRAYERS:

....

....

FAMILY COVENANT

We have shared *Highs & Lows* this week, read and highlighted the verses assigned in our Bibles, talked about our lives, prayed for one another's highs and lows, and blessed one another.

_____ _____ _____
Parent's Signature   Teen's Signature   Date

THE FINKMANIA QUIZBOWL

Question 1:

The final line of the Lord's Prayer is called the:

(A) The End,

(B) The Great Commission,

(C) The Doxology,

(D) The Last Call

Question 2:

The Greek word "Doxology" means:

(A) Glory word,

(B) Glory log,

(C) Glory dog,

(D) Amen. It shall be so!

Question 3:

The Doxology to the Lord's Prayer says:

(A) "For the kingdom is yours now and forever,

(B) "For the kingdom and the power are yours now and forever,"

(C) "For the kingdom, the power, and the glory are yours now and forever,"

(D) "This is most certainly true!"

Question 4:

"Amen" means:

(A) "It shall be over soon,"

(B) "It shall be so,"

(C) "It shall be however I want it,"

(D) "Superhero losers who couldn't cut it as X-men"

Question 5:

The Doxology isn't found in most Bibles because:

(A) They ran out of ink,

(B) Most of the oldest and best original manuscripts of the Bible didn't include it in their text,

(C) The Council of Nicea erased it because it sounded too Gnostic,

(D) No one could spell it

Question 6:

When we say the "kingdom" belongs to God now and forever we are really saying:

(A) God reigns,

(B) God rains,

(C) God is Creator and Lord over everything on both sides of eternity,

(D) A & C

Question 7:

When we say the "power" belongs to God now and forever we mean:

(A) God is awesome,

(B) God is bigger than your biggest problem,

(C) God's good and gracious will is ultimately going to be done on earth as it is in heaven and no one can stop God,

(D) All of the above and then some

Question 8:

When we say the "glory" belongs to God now and forever we mean:

(A) God's brilliance out-shines the sun—literally and figuratively,

(B) God's wondrous majesty is mind-boggling,

(C) There is no splendor or glory on earth that even compares to God,

(D) All of the above and then some

Question 9:

If God is all powerful, why doesn't God stop wars?:

(A) God didn't create us to be puppets,

(B) God chose to share power with us and gave us free will to love or hate, to build or destroy,

(C) We live in a sin-tainted world that rebels against God's plan for love and harmony on earth,

(D) All of the above

FINKmania Final Question:

The verse of the week tells us:

(A) God's kingdom comes to us only when we pray and obey,

(B) God's power controls everything, especially how people act,

(C) God's glory is seen mostly in church,

(D) There is no "verse of the week" because the Doxology doesn't appear in most Bibles

 Play this online game using FINKlink

THE WEAKEST FINK

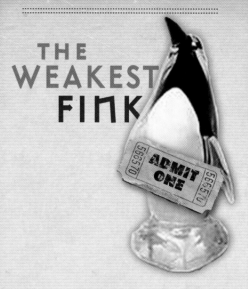

A MIRACLE OCCURS AT THE MOMENT OUR EYES CAN SEE AND OUR EARS HEAR WHAT IS THERE ABOUT US ALWAYS.

WILLA CATHER

TERMS
WRITE A DEFINITION BELOW.

AMEN

DOXOLOGY

GLORY

KINGDOM

POWER

"Praying at Gethsemane" Dr. He Qi. Order prints at www.heqiarts.com

"OUR FATHER IN HEAVEN, HALLOWED BE YOUR NAME. YOUR KING-

DOM COME. YOUR WILL BE DONE, ON EARTH AS IT IS IN HEAVEN.

GIVE US THIS DAY OUR DAILY BREAD. AND FORGIVE US OUR DEBTS,

AS WE ALSO HAVE FORGIVEN OUR DEBTORS. AND DO NOT BRING US

TO THE TIME OF TRIAL, BUT RESCUE US FROM THE EVIL ONE."

— MATTHEW 6:9B-13

Listen to this song using FINKlink
LF20 @ www.faithink.com

*O*ver the years, many people have created their own versions of the Lord's Prayer, adding thoughts and insights to make it speak to their language, culture and time.

Here are two paraphrases. Read them, then write your own:

DIVINE CONSPIRACY

BY DALLAS WILLARD

Dear Father always near us,
May your name be treasured and loved,
May your rule be completed in us—
May your will be done here on earth
In just the way it is done in heaven.
Give us today the things we need today.
And forgive us our sins and impositions
  on you
As we are forgiving all who in any way
  offend us.
Please don't put us through trials,
But deliver us from everything bad.
Because you are the one in charge,
And you have all the power,
And the glory too is all yours forever
Which is just the way we want it!

THE MESSAGE BIBLE

Our Father in heaven,
Reveal who you are.
Set the world right;
Do what's best—
  as above, so below.
Keep us alive with
  three square meals.
Keep us forgiven with you
  and forgiving others.
Keep us safe from ourselves
  and the Devil.
You're in charge!
You can do anything you want!
You're ablaze in beauty!

Yes. Yes. Yes.

WHAT IS NEEDED AT THE END OF THIS GREAT PRAYER IS A RINGING AFFIRMATION OF THE GOODNESS OF GOD AND GOD'S WORLD. TRY "WHOOPEE!" I IMAGINE GOD WILL NOT MIND.

DALLAS WILLARD

Now, you give it a try. Write your own paraphrase of the Lord's Prayer to the right of the words provided:

TRADITIONAL VERSION

MY TRANSLATION

Our Father in heaven,
hallowed be your name.
Your kingdom come.
Your will be done,
on earth as it is in heaven.
Give us this day our daily bread.
And forgive us our debts,
as we also have forgiven our debtors.
 And do not bring us to
   the time of trial,
but rescue us from
   the evil one.

Now, pray it!

Order this art print using FINKlink
LF20 @ www.faithink.com

IMAGES in ART

- What do you see in today's painting by Dr. He Qi?

- Where are you in this work of art?

- How do the image and the verse apply to your life today?

So What Does This Mean?

I UNDERSTAND YOUR SITUATION IS SERIOUS?

IF THAT'S THE CASE, YOU ARE IN EVEN WORSE SHAPE THAN YOU KNOW.

Serious! I HAVEN'T GOT A Prayer!

PRAYER

ETERNAL GOD, HELP ME TO SEEK YOU WITH ALL OF MY HEART AND SOUL.

LOVING JESUS, HELP ME TO LOVE WITH ALL OF MY MIND AND STRENGTH.

HOLY SPIRIT, LEAD ME AND GUIDE ME TO KNOW YOUR WILL THIS DAY, AND HELP ME ALWAYS WHEN I PRAY. IN JESUS' NAME.

AMEN.

LORD'S PRAYER RECAP

Although Christ's prayer is beautiful and complete, it is only a model. Use it as a framework to build your own prayer life by remembering these key insights:

OUR FATHER IN HEAVEN: Prayer is talking to the one who is both as close as a loving parent, and as great as the Creator of the universe.

HALLOWED: Prayer is not about you. It is about God! Focus on God.

KINGDOM COME: Prayer is more than wishing for God's reign. It is making yourself aware and available to help usher it into the world.

WILL BE DONE: Prayer is about "letting go" and "letting God" be God both in this world and in your life.

DAILY BREAD: Prayer is about trusting God to provide one day at a time.

FORGIVE: Prayer is about living a forgiving, forgiven lifestyle.

TIME OF TRIAL: Prayer is asking for help.

RESCUE US: Prayer is fighting the battle for good against evil.

DOXOLOGY: Prayer is praising and thanking God! Prayer is saying "Yes!"

BIBLE TIME

If you haven't done so already, read and highlight the Lord's Prayer in Matthew 6:9-13 and in Luke 11:2-4 in your Bible. Now look up the following, writing "See Matthew 6:9-13" in margins. How do these connect with the Lord's Prayer?

Matthew 7:7-8

Psalm 46:10

Hebrews 4:16

I Thessalonians 5: 16-17

ROLE PLAY

1. A friend has been diagnosed with cancer. What do you say and do?

2. A friend's mother just died. She asks, "Why did God do this?" Respond.

QUESTIONS TO PONDER

1. Who is the most powerful person you know personally? How and when do you talk to them?

2. If you could ask God one thing, what would it be?

3. Now that you've spent some time with the Lord's Prayer, which petition is the easiest for you to pray honestly? Which is the most difficult to pray? Why?

Small Group
SHARE, READ, TALK, PRAY, BLESS

1. **S H A R E** your highs and lows of the week one-on-one with another person. Listen carefully and record your friend's thoughts in the space below. Then return to small group and share your friend's highs and lows.

   ### MY HIGHS + LOWS THIS WEEK WERE:
   ....

   ### MY FRIEND'S HIGHS + LOWS THIS WEEK WERE:
   ....

2. **R E A D** and highlight the theme verse in your Bibles. Circle key words, and learn the verse in song if time permits.

3. **T A L K** about how today's verse relates to your highs and lows. Review the art for today, the Quiz Bowl questions, the terms, and the cartoons. Then write a sentence on each of the following:

   ### ONE NEW THING I LEARNED TODAY:
   ....

   ### ONE THING I ALREADY KNEW THAT IS WORTH REPEATING:
   ....

   ### ONE THING I WOULD LIKE TO KNOW MORE ABOUT:
   ....

4. **P R A Y** for one another, praising and thanking God for your highs, and asking God to be with you in your lows. Include your friend's highs and lows in your prayers.

   A PRAISING PRAYER: ....
   A THANKING PRAYER: ....
   AN ASKING PRAYER: ....

5. **B L E S S** one another using the blessing of the week. (right) Mark each person with the sign of the cross as you bless them.

THE FINK FIVE

THIS WEEK'S BLESSING

(NAME), CHILD OF GOD, MAY YOU KNOW THE JOY OF BOTH TALKING TO GOD AND LISTENING TO GOD IN PRAYER.

THE HOME HUDDLE jOURNAL

SHARE, READ, tALK, PRAY, BLESS

Read the full devotions using FINKlink
LF20 | @ www.faithink.com

DAY #1

tODAY'S BiBLE VERSE:

MAttHEW 6:9A

Pray then in this way: Our Father in heaven...

mY HiGH tODAY WAS:

mY LOW tODAY WAS:

mY PRAYER tODAY iS:

DAY #2

tODAY'S BiBLE VERSE:

MAttHEW 6:9B

Hallowed be your name...

mY HiGH tODAY WAS:

mY LOW tODAY WAS:

mY PRAYER tODAY iS:

DAY #3

tODAY'S BiBLE VERSE:

MAttHEW 6:10A

Your kingdom come.

mY HiGH tODAY WAS:

mY LOW tODAY WAS:

mY PRAYER tODAY iS:

MY HIGH TODAY WAS: ....

MY LOW TODAY WAS: ....

MY PRAYER TODAY IS: ....

....

DAY #4

TODAY'S BIBLE VERSE:

MATTHEW 6:10B

Your will be done on earth as it is in heaven.

MY HIGH TODAY WAS: ....

MY LOW TODAY WAS: ....

MY PRAYER TODAY IS: ....

....

DAY #5

TODAY'S BIBLE VERSE:

MATTHEW 6:11

Give us this day our daily bread.

MY HIGH TODAY WAS: ....

MY LOW TODAY WAS: ....

MY PRAYER TODAY IS: ....

....

DAY #6

TODAY'S BIBLE VERSE:

MATTHEW 6:12

Forgive us our debts as we also have forgiven our debtors.

MY HIGHEST HIGH THIS WEEK WAS: ....

MY LOWEST LOW THIS WEEK WAS: ....

MY PRAYER FOR NEXT WEEK IS: ....

....

DAY #7

THIS WEEK'S BLESSING

(NAME), CHILD OF GOD,

MAY YOU KNOW THE JOY

OF BOTH TALKING TO GOD

AND LISTENING TO GOD IN

PRAYER.

THE HOME HUDDLE jOURNAL
SHARE, READ, tALK, PRAY, BLESS

Read the full devotions using FINKlink
LF20 @ www.faithink.com

DAY #1

tODAY'S BiBLE VERSE:

Matthew 6:13a

And do not bring us to the time trial.

my HiGH tODAY WAS:

my LOW tODAY WAS:

my PRAYER tODAY iS:

DAY #2

tODAY'S BiBLE VERSE:

Matthew 6:13b

But rescue us from the evil one.

my HiGH tODAY WAS:

my LOW tODAY WAS:

my PRAYER tODAY iS:

DAY #3

tODAY'S BiBLE VERSE:

tHE Doxology

For the kingdom, the power, and the glory are yours, now and forever.

my HiGH tODAY WAS:

my LOW tODAY WAS:

my PRAYER tODAY iS:

1. **SHARE** HIGHS & LOWS OF THE DAY.

2. **READ** AND HIGHLIGHT THE VERSE OF THE DAY IN YOUR BIBLES.

3. **TALK** ABOUT HOW TODAY'S VERSE RELATES TO YOUR HIGHS & LOWS.

4. **PRAY** FOR YOUR HIGHS & LOWS, FOR YOUR FAMILY AND FOR THE WORLD.

5. **BLESS** ONE ANOTHER USING THIS WEEK'S BLESSING (ON THE PREVIOUS PAGE).

MY HIGH TODAY WAS:

MY LOW TODAY WAS:

MY PRAYER TODAY IS:

DAY #4

TODAY'S BIBLE VERSE:

Matthew 6:6

But whenever you pray, go into your room and shut the door and pray to your Father who is in secret; and your Father who sees in secret will reward you.

MY HIGH TODAY WAS:

MY LOW TODAY WAS:

MY PRAYER TODAY IS:

DAY #5

TODAY'S BIBLE VERSE:

I Thessalonians 5:16-18

Rejoice always, pray without ceasing, give thanks in all circumstances; for this is the will of God in Christ Jesus for you.

MY HIGH TODAY WAS:

MY LOW TODAY WAS:

MY PRAYER TODAY IS:

DAY #6

TODAY'S BIBLE VERSE:

Revelation 22:20b

Amen. Come, Lord Jesus!

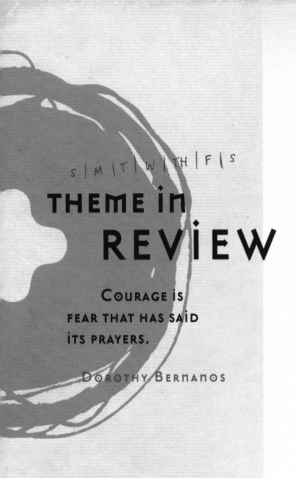

THEME in REVIEW

COURAGE is
FEAR THAT HAS SAID
iTS PRAYERS.

DOROTHY BERNANOS

DAY #7

MY FAVORITE VERSE
FROM THE THEME WAS:

....

....

....

....

....

....

....

LOOKING BACK ON THESE TWO WEEKS, MY HIGHEST HIGH WAS:

....

MY LOWEST LOW THESE PAST WEEKS WAS:

....

ONE WAY GOD ANSWERED MY PRAYERS WAS:

....

ONE WAY GOD MIGHT USE ME AS A SACRED AGENT
TO ANSWER THESE PRAYERS:

....

....

FAMILY COVENANT

We have shared *Highs & Lows* this week, read and highlighted the verses assigned in our Bibles, talked about our lives, prayed for one another's highs and lows, and blessed one another.

....

Parent's Signature   Teen's Signature   Date

THE FINKMANIA QUIZBOWL

Question 1:

The Lord's Prayer was given to the disciples when they asked Jesus:

(A) "Teach us to pray,"

(B) "Teach us to dance,"

(C) "Teach us how to get free stuff from God,"

(D) "Teach us something to pray every Sunday in church without having to think about it"

Question 2:

In the Lord's Prayer, Jesus addressed God as:

(A) Our Father in heaven,

(B) Our Mother in heaven,

(C) Your Holiness,

(D) Big Brother

Question 3:

When it comes to the Lord's Prayer, a "petition" is:

(A) A prayer of praise,

(B) A request made of God,

(C) A paper you sign and send to God with at least 10,000 signatures if you want your prayers answered,

(D) None of the above

Question 4:

The First Petition of the Lord's Prayer is:

(A) Hallowed be your name,

(B) Hollowed be your name,

(C) Harold be your name,

(D) Give me lots of stuff

Question 5:

"Your kingdom come, your will be done on earth as it is in heaven" is called:

(A) The Second Petition,

(B) The Second and Third Petitions,

(C) The Great Commission,

(D) Totally unrealistic

Question 6:

The Fourth Petition of the Lord's Prayer is:

(A) "Give us this day our daily bread,"

(B) "Give me this day my daily bread,"

(C) "Give me this day all that I want,"

(D) "Give me more than my sister"

Question 7:

The Fifth Petition of the Lord's Prayer is, "Forgive us our debts, as we..."

(A) "...rack them up,"

(B) "...prove that we are truly deserving,

(C) "...also have forgiven our debtors,"

(D) "...try to get away with them when no one is watching"

Question 8:

Two ways to pray the Sixth Petition of the Lord's Prayer are:

(A) "Lead us not into temptation" and "Save us from the time of trial,"

(B) "Lead us not into temptation" and "Deliver us from evil,"

(C) "Lead us not into temptation" and "Save us from algebra tests,"

(D) None of the above

Question 9:

Two ways to pray the Seventh Petition of the Lord's Prayer are:

(A) "Deliver us from evil" and "Rescue us from the evil one,"

(B) "Deliver us from evil" and "Rescue us from foolish pride,"

(C) "Deliver us from evil" and "Rescue us from dentists,"

(D) None of the above

FINKMANIA Final Question:

The final line of the Lord's Prayer, the "Doxology":

(A) Is "For the kingdom, the power, and the glory are yours now and forever,"

(B) Was added as a fitting end to the prayer long after it was written,

(C) Doesn't appear in most Bibles,

(D) All of the above

 Play this online game using FINKlink

THE WEAKEST FINK

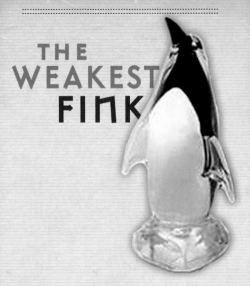

In order to be a realist you must believe in miracles.

David Ben-Gurion

TERMS
WRITE A DEFINITION BELOW.

Amen

Disciple

Petition

Prayer

The Lord's Prayer

Hot
✝opics

1. Sex and Love
2. Drugs (Your Body is a ✝emple)
3. Fast Cars and Other Risky Behavior
4. Media and Materialism
5. God and Science
6. War and Peace
7. Suicide
8. Stewardship of Time
9. Stewardship of Talents
10. Stewardship of Treasure

FAITH
INKUBATORS

SEX & LOVE

"Song of Solomon (B)" Dr. He Qi. Order prints at www.heqiarts.com

"Love is patient; love is kind; love is not envious or boastful or arrogant or rude. It does not insist on its own way; it is not irritable or resentful; it does not rejoice in wrongdoing, but rejoices in the truth. It bears all things, believes all things, hopes all things, endures all things. Love never ends. And now faith, hope, and love abide, these three; and the greatest of these is love."

— I Corinthians 13:4-8a, 13

Listen to this song using FINKlink
LF21 @ www.faithink.com

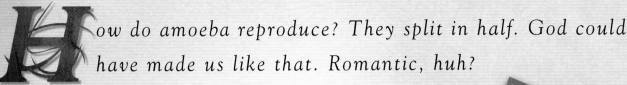

How do amoeba reproduce? They split in half. God could have made us like that. Romantic, huh?

Earthworms have both male and female parts. God could have made us like that. Some fish lay millions and millions of eggs. (And eat a few thousand for lunch.) God could have made us like that, too. But God didn't. God made us male and female, and after making us, the God said, "It was very good." The first thing to know about sex is that God invented it. The second is God blessed it. The third is God commanded it. ("Be fruitful and multiply!") Don't you just love God?

NOBEL'S NITRO

In 1866, Alfred Bernard Nobel was fooling around with nitroglycerin in his laboratory. He was trying to discover a way to hold the unstable substance in a stable state. It had great power, but he could not control it. Eventually he developed a process that allowed him to roll it up in sticks and control the explosion with a fuse. Looking through his Greek dictionary for a name for this invention, he settled on the word for power—*dunamis* and called his invention dynamite! Nobel originally harnessed this power for good, but he lived long enough to see the good invention turn bad and be used for war. Thanks in part to the explosive power of dynamite, millions were killed, maimed, and disfigured. One year before he died, Alfred set aside the huge profits from his powerful invention to create a series of awards to build the world back up. Maybe you've heard of the Nobel Prizes?

Dynamite sitting on a shelf is neither good nor bad. Good and bad can happen with it, however, depending on how people use it. Used correctly, it can speed up the process of building a tunnel. Used in the wrong way, people get burned.

HOLY DYNAMITE

Sex is dynamite. God invented it as a wonderful gift. Used in the ways God intends, it can build, bond, and make babies. It can give pleasure, joy, and comfort. But like any raw power, it can also be used to destroy. It can harm, humiliate, abuse, and tear people apart. It all depends on how you use the gift.

Some religious leaders once came to Jesus to trap him. They asked a loaded question, hoping to twist his words and get him in trouble. They asked: "Is it lawful for a man to divorce his wife for any reason?" (In those days you could divorce your wife if she burned your dinner.) Instead of giving an answer about divorce, Jesus gave them a sex lesson! He quoted the story of God making man and woman in Genesis 2. He told them the purpose of our sexual gift—the man and woman should share a complete and total intimate oneness. Jesus ended by saying whatever God joins together, no one should be allowed to tear apart.

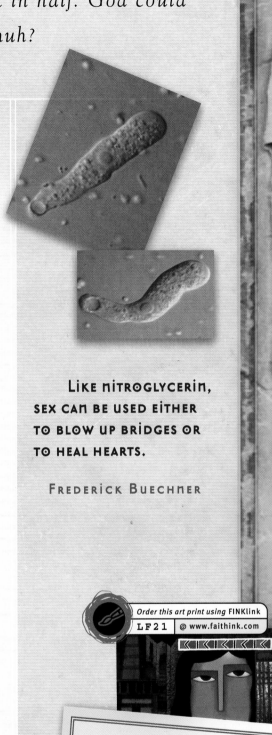

LIKE NITROGLYCERIN, SEX CAN BE USED EITHER TO BLOW UP BRIDGES OR TO HEAL HEARTS.

FREDERICK BUECHNER

Order this art print using FINKlink
LF21 @ www.faithink.com

IMAGES in ART

- What do you see in today's painting by Dr. He Qi?

- Where are you in this work of art?

- How do the image and the verse apply to your life today?

So What Does This Mean?

According to God's instruction book, the Bible, four things are clear:

1. God made sex.

2. God commanded sex. ("Be fruitful and multiply!")

3. Sex is good. (Actually, after finishing creation with man and woman, God said "it is very good!")

4. Once God joins a man and a woman together, no one is to be allowed to tear them apart.

What's Love Got to do With it? For me? Let's just say Everything!

PRAYER

Change my heart, O God. Make it ever true. Change my heart, O God. May I be like you.

Eddie Espinosa

HEBREW SEX

The Hebrew word for sex in the Bible—YADAH—means "to know." This is not a casual knowing, like you know a neighbor across the street or a classmate at school. It means to know someone completely—inside and out. We have a problem knowing and being known in our society. Look at the media's portrayal of sex. Everyone is hopping from bed to bed, from relationships to relationship, from intimacy to intimacy, as if were no bigger deal than trying on so many pairs of running shoes. These days people rarely get to know one another before they "know" one another. Is that a good idea? No. God wants more for you than that. Using the dynamite of sex in this way can get you burned. Maybe dead. Jesus said, "I came that they might have life and have it abundantly." The God who created you and loves you also knows you better than you know yourself. God doesn't want you to have anything less that the best. That means the best sex, too! But the best won't come unless you use the gift in the manner for which it was intended. (Reread the sidebar.) A love that never ends—is that what you want for yourself? A total closeness, openness and fearless love that allows you to be completely open, unashamed, and one with another person? That's the intent of the giver of the gift. That's also the kind of love that creates the best sex of all. Why would you settle for anything less?

BIBLE TIME

Highlight these glimpses into how the inventor of sex intends the gift to be used:

Genesis 1:27, 31   Genesis 2:18   Song of Solomon 8:6-7
Matthew 19:6   John 10:10b   I Corinthians 13:4-8a

ROLE PLAY

1. Your boyfriend/girlfriend is pressuring you to have sex. "If you love me, you'll do it."

2. Your best friend tells you she is being sexually abused by her cousin. What do you say?

QUESTIONS TO PONDER

1. According to what you've read above, what is God's will for the best sex?

2. Brainstorm a list of TV shows that depict sex in un-Godly and Godly ways. Which list is longer? Does the media mimic society or make it?

3. What are the consequences of using the dynamite of sex outside of God's intention of life-long commitment? Physically? Emotionally? Spiritually?

SMALL GR⊕UP
SHARE, READ, TALK, PRAY, BLESS

1. **SHARE** your highs and lows of the week one-on-one with another person. Listen carefully and record your friend's thoughts in the space below. Then return to small group and share your friend's highs and lows.

MY HIGHS + LOWS THIS WEEK WERE:

....

MY FRIEND'S HIGHS + LOWS THIS WEEK WERE:

....

2. **READ** and highlight the theme verse in your Bibles. Circle key words and learn the verse in song.

3. **TALK** about how today's verse relates to your highs and lows. Review the art for today, the Quiz Bowl questions, the terms, and the cartoons. Then write a sentence on each of the following:

ONE NEW THING I LEARNED TODAY:

....

ONE THING I ALREADY KNEW THAT IS WORTH REPEATING:

....

ONE THING I WOULD LIKE TO KNOW MORE ABOUT:

....

4. **PRAY** for one another, praising and thanking God for your highs, and asking God to be with you in your lows. Include your friend's highs and lows in your prayers.

A PRAISING PRAYER: ....

A THANKING PRAYER: ....

AN ASKING PRAYER: ....

5. **BLESS** one another using the blessing of the week. (right) Mark each person with the sign of the cross as you bless them.

THIS WEEK'S BLESSING

(NAME), CHILD OF GOD, MAY YOU BE PURE AND RIGHT AND TRUE IN EVERY- THING YOU SAY AND DO.

THE HOME HUDDLE JOURNAL

SHARE, READ, TALK, PRAY, BLESS

Read the full devotions using FINKlink
LF21 | @ www.faithink.com

DAY #1

TODAY'S BIBLE VERSE:

I Corinthians 13:4-6a

Love is patient; love is kind; love is not envious or boastful or arrogant or rude. It does not insist on its own way; it is not irritable or resentful; it does not rejoice in wrongdoing, but rejoices in the truth.

MY HIGH TODAY WAS:

MY LOW TODAY WAS:

MY PRAYER TODAY IS:

DAY #2

TODAY'S BIBLE VERSE:

I Corinthians 13:7-8a

It (love) bears all things, believes all things, hopes all things, endures all things. Love never ends.

MY HIGH TODAY WAS:

MY LOW TODAY WAS:

MY PRAYER TODAY IS:

DAY #3

TODAY'S BIBLE VERSE:

Genesis 1:27-28a

God created humankind in his image, in the image of God he created them; male and female he created them. God blessed them, and God said to them, "Be fruitful and multiply..."

MY HIGH TODAY WAS:

MY LOW TODAY WAS:

MY PRAYER TODAY IS:

MY HIGH TODAY WAS:

MY LOW TODAY WAS:

MY PRAYER TODAY IS:

MY HIGH TODAY WAS:

MY LOW TODAY WAS:

MY PRAYER TODAY IS:

MY HIGH TODAY WAS:

MY LOW TODAY WAS:

MY PRAYER TODAY IS:

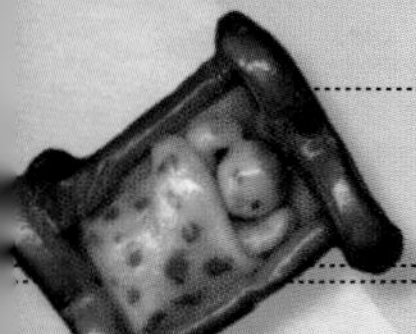

MY HIGHEST HIGH THIS WEEK WAS:

MY LOWEST LOW THIS WEEK WAS:

MY PRAYER FOR NEXT WEEK IS:

DAY #4

TODAY'S BIBLE VERSE:

Matthew 19:5-6

For this reason a man shall leave his father and mother and be joined to his wife, and the two shall become one flesh? So they are no longer two, but one flesh. Therefore what God has joined together, let no one separate.

DAY #5

TODAY'S BIBLE VERSE:

Song of Solomon 2:10

My beloved speaks and says to me: "Arise, my love, my fair one, and come away."

DAY #6

TODAY'S BIBLE VERSE:

Song of Solomon 8:6

Set me as a seal upon your heart, as a seal upon your arm; for love is strong as death, passion fierce as the grave. Its flashes are flashes of fire, a raging flame.

DAY #7

THIS WEEK'S BLESSING

(NAME), CHILD OF GOD,

MAY YOU BE PURE AND RIGHT

AND TRUE IN EVERYTHING

YOU SAY AND DO.

THE HOME HUDDLE JOURNAL
SHARE, READ, TALK, PRAY, BLESS

Read the full devotions using FINKlink
LF21 | @ www.faithink.com

DAY #1

TODAY'S BIBLE VERSE:

GENESIS 2:18

Then the Lord God said, "It is not good that the man should be alone; I will make him a helper as his partner."

MY **HIGH** TODAY WAS:

MY **LOW** TODAY WAS:

MY **PRAYER** TODAY IS:

DAY #2

TODAY'S BIBLE VERSE:

I CORINTHIANS 7:2B-3

Each man should have his own wife and each woman her own husband. The husband should give to his wife her conjugal rights, and likewise the wife to her husband.

MY **HIGH** TODAY WAS:

MY **LOW** TODAY WAS:

MY **PRAYER** TODAY IS:

DAY #3

TODAY'S BIBLE VERSE:

I CORINTHIANS 7:4

For the wife does not have authority over her own body, but the husband does; likewise the husband does not have authority over his own body, but the wife does.

MY **HIGH** TODAY WAS:

MY **LOW** TODAY WAS:

MY **PRAYER** TODAY IS:

I still
LOVE
you!

1. **SHARE** HIGHS & LOWS OF THE DAY.

2. **READ** AND HIGHLIGHT THE VERSE OF THE DAY IN YOUR BIBLES.

3. **TALK** ABOUT HOW TODAY'S VERSE RELATES TO YOUR HIGHS & LOWS.

4. **PRAY** FOR YOUR HIGHS & LOWS, FOR YOUR FAMILY AND FOR THE WORLD.

5. **BLESS** ONE ANOTHER USING THIS WEEK'S BLESSING (ON THE PREVIOUS PAGE).

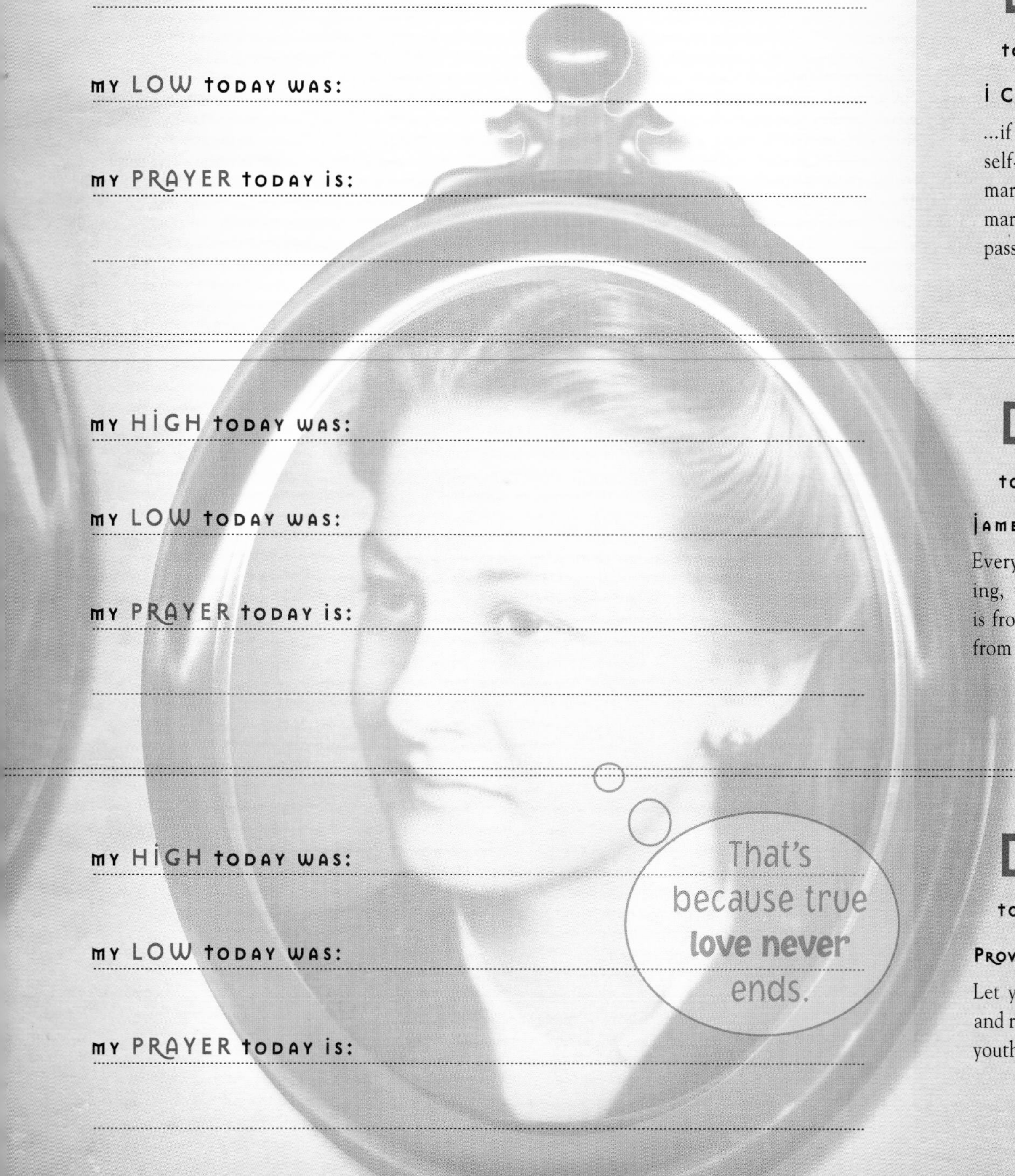

MY HIGH TODAY WAS:

MY LOW TODAY WAS:

MY PRAYER TODAY IS:

DAY #4

TODAY'S BIBLE VERSE:

i Corinthians 7:9

...if they are not practicing self-control, they should marry. For it is better to marry than to be aflame with passion.

MY HIGH TODAY WAS:

MY LOW TODAY WAS:

MY PRAYER TODAY IS:

DAY #5

TODAY'S BIBLE VERSE:

James 1:17a

Every generous act of giving, with every perfect gift, is from above, coming down from the Father of lights.

MY HIGH TODAY WAS:

MY LOW TODAY WAS:

That's because true **love never** ends.

MY PRAYER TODAY IS:

DAY #6

TODAY'S BIBLE VERSE:

Proverbs 5:18

Let your fountain be blessed, and rejoice in the wife of your youth.

S | M | T | W | TH | F | S

THEME IN REVIEW

WE ARE TO FEAR AND LOVE
GOD SO THAT IN MATTERS
OF SEX OUR WORDS AND
CONDUCT ARE PURE AND
HONORABLE.

MARTIN LUTHER

DAY #7

MY FAVORITE VERSE
FROM THE THEME WAS:

....

....

....

....

....

....

....

LOOKING BACK ON THESE TWO WEEKS, MY HIGHEST HIGH WAS:

....

MY LOWEST LOW THESE PAST WEEKS WAS:

....

ONE WAY GOD ANSWERED MY PRAYERS WAS:

....

ONE WAY GOD MIGHT USE ME AS A SACRED AGENT
TO ANSWER THESE PRAYERS:

....

....

FAMILY COVENANT

We have shared *Highs & Lows* this week, read and highlighted the verses assigned in our Bibles,
talked about our lives, prayed for one another's highs and lows, and blessed one another.

....
Parent's Signature   Teen's Signature   Date

THE FINKMANIA QUIZ BOWL

QUESTION 1:
According to Genesis 1, God's first command to the human race was:

(A) "Be fruitful and multiply,"

(B) "You shall have no other gods before me,"

(C) "Be fruitful but careful,"

(D) "Get a room!"

QUESTION 2:
According to the Bible, God gave man and woman to one another:

(A) To complete each other,

(B) To compete against each other,

(C) To nag and complain about each other,

(D) A, and also to make lots of babies

QUESTION 3:
In Hebrew, the word for sex is:

(A) Yadah,

(B) Ya don't,

(C) Yahweh,

(D) Yaba daba do

QUESTION 4:
The Hebrew word for sex —yadah—literally means:

(A) To know,

(B) To be,

(C) To be on fire,

(D) To be careful

QUESTION 5:
God intends sex to be:

(A) A physical act for pleasure,

(B) An emotional act for bonding,

(C) A spiritual act for complete intimacy and oneness,

(D) All of the above, but it's not going to happen if you hop from bed to bed trying on sex partners like so many pair of tennis shoes

QUESTION 6:
The best selling sex book in history is:

(A) Dr. Ruth's "The Sexual Being."

(B) Dr. Spock's "Human Sexuality,"

(C) Dr. Evil's "Book of Evil,"

(D) The Bible

QUESTION 7:
The Greek word "dunamis" means:

(A) Danger,

(B) Dynamite,

(C) Power,

(D) None of the above

QUESTION 8:
Sex is like dynamite because:

(A) If you don't use it carefully, you might get hurt,

(B) It can either build or destroy,

(C) It is made up of dangerous chemicals,

(D) A, B, and one could make a pretty strong argument for C

QUESTION 9:
If someone says they love you but are abusing you, hitting you, or pressuring you to have sex:

(A) They love somebody, but it isn't you,

(B) They love somebody, but it isn't you,

(C) They love somebody, but it isn't you,

(D) All of the above, and tell them to take a long walk off a short pier

FINKMANIA FINAL QUESTION:
In I Corinthian 13, Paul writes that faith, hope and love abide, but the greatest of these is:

(A) Faith,

(B) Hope,

(C) Love,

(D) Highly overrated

Will there be sex in heaven?

If God can't think of anything better.

Play this online game using FINKlink
LF21 | @ www.faithink.com

THE WEAKEST FINK

SACRED SEXPERIENCE

> LOVE IS NOT BLIND.
> IT SEES MORE, NOT LESS.
>
> RABBI JULIUS GORDON

TERMS
WRITE A DEFINITION BELOW.

AUTHOR

DUNAMIS (GREEK)

LOVE

SEX

YADAH (HEBREW)

"*Annunciation (B)*" *Dr. He Qi: Order prints at www.heqiarts.com*

DRUGS (YOUR BODY IS A TEMPLE)

"OR DO YOU NOT KNOW THAT YOUR BODY IS A TEMPLE OF THE HOLY SPIRIT WITHIN YOU, WHICH YOU HAVE FROM GOD, AND THAT YOU ARE NOT YOUR OWN? FOR YOU WERE BOUGHT WITH A PRICE; THEREFORE GLORIFY GOD IN YOUR BODY."

– I CORINTHIANS 6:19-20

Listen to this song using FINKlink
LF22 @ www.faithink.com

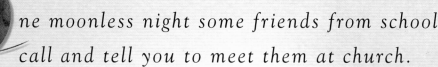

One moonless night some friends from school call and tell you to meet them at church.

Upon arrival, you find them sneaking into the sanctuary through a broken window with cans of spray paint and buckets of roofing tar. "Come on! Let's have some fun," they say. What do you do?

Most people would never think of trashing a church. Most would never even consider dumping tar on the altar or vandalizing a temple. Why? It is a holy, special, sacred space. It doesn't belong to them. It belongs to the Almighty God and is set aside for God's use.

No, most people wouldn't trash a temple, yet a lot of folks don't think twice about dumping tar on the altar of their lungs; messing up their brain cells with alcohol and pot; trashing their sacred bodies with chemicals that clog them up, fog them up, and risk destroying their future.

The Bible says your body is a temple. You belong to God. You are not your own. What do you say?

Wait a minute!

"It's my life! I can do what I want with it!" You may have heard those words before. You may have even shouted them at your parents while storming out a door recently.

"It's my life! I can do what I want with it!" It is natural to feel that way when people are bossing you around, dictating your actions, or making choices for you that you don't agree with or appreciate.

"It's my life! I can do what I want with it!"

These are natural and common words, but guess what? They are wrong.

Dead wrong. Christians know better. We know our lives are not our own. We know we are not gods. We are God's! Doubly God's. First, we belong to God because God made us. A creation is owned by its creator. Second, we belong to God because we were ransomed. Long ago, the whole human race was kidnapped by a murderous villain—God's arch enemy. Then, in an amazing act of love, the God who created us paid a huge ransom to buy us back. The price? The most precious and priceless ransom of all—the Son of God laid down his life in our place. Jesus bought us with blood. *His blood.*

You are not our own. You were bought with a price. You are doubly God's. So, what are you going to do about it? How are you going to treat God's temple?

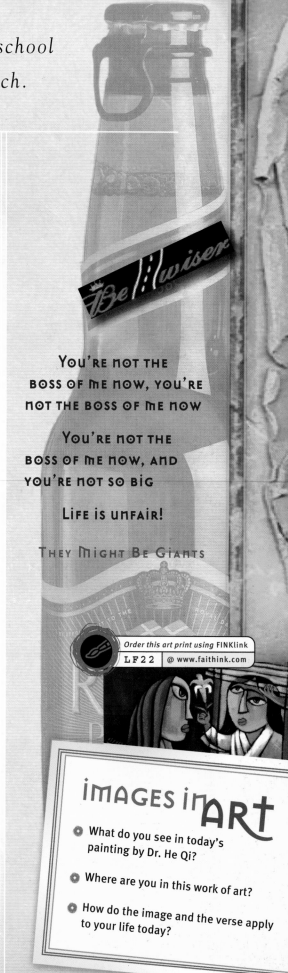

YOU'RE NOT THE BOSS OF ME NOW, YOU'RE NOT THE BOSS OF ME NOW

YOU'RE NOT THE BOSS OF ME NOW, AND YOU'RE NOT SO BIG

LIFE IS UNFAIR!

THEY MIGHT BE GIANTS

IMAGES in ART

- What do you see in today's painting by Dr. He Qi?

- Where are you in this work of art?

- How do the image and the verse apply to your life today?

So What Does This Mean?

YOUR FATHER AND I WOULD LIKE TO CONGRATULATE YOU FOR REMAINING **Drug Free** ALL THESE YEARS. HERE. HAVE A CIGAR!

PRAYER

OKAY, GOD. I HEAR YOU. I AM NOT MY OWN. I BELONG TO YOU. I AM DOUBLY YOURS. YOU MADE ME. YOU OWN ME. I WAS KIDNAPPED AND YOU TRADED YOUR SON, JESUS, FOR ME. HIS BLOOD BOUGHT MY FREEDOM. HELP ME TO BE AWARE AND THANKFUL. HELP ME TO BE SMART WHEN IT COMES TO HOW I TREAT THIS PRECIOUS TEMPLE YOU HAVE GIVEN ME—MY BODY. YOUR BODY. IN JESUS' NAME.

AMEN.

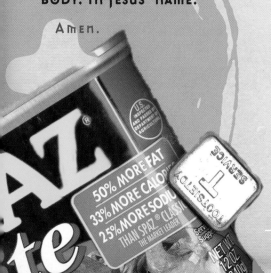

SO WHAT?

What does this have to do with how young Christians should treat alcohol, drugs, cigarettes, steroids, diet pills, or any other substance that could harm them? The Bible is clear—your body is a temple. You are not your own. You are to glorify God with your body.

Period.

BIBLE TIME

Read and highlight I Corinthians 6:19-20 in your Bible, writing "Temple" in the margin. Now read and highlight the following verses, writing "See I Corinthians 6:19-20" in the margin. What do these verses tell you about God's will for your life as it relates to alcohol, drugs, and even doing legal things dangerously?

Romans 14:21

Ephesians 5:18

I Timothy 3:8

I Timothy 5:23

ROLE PLAY

1. You believe a friend is using and abusing an illegal chemical. What do you say to them?

2. You believe a friend is abusing a legal chemical. What do you say to them?

3. You believe a friend is cutting herself. What do you say to her?

4. You believe a friend is using steroids. What do you say to him?

QUESTIONS TO PONDER

1. How do you think I Corinthians 6:19-20 relates to:

Alcohol	Smoking	Diet pills
Steroids	Violent Media	Online Porn

2. Here's a tougher set of questions. What do you think the theme verse has to say about:

Sugar	Caffeine	Fatty Fast Foods
Sleeping Pills	Driving too fast	Not getting enough sleep
Body Piercing	Abortion	Driving without a seat belt

Small Group
SHARE, READ, TALK, PRAY, BLESS

1. **SHARE** your highs and lows of the week one-on-one with another person. Listen carefully and record your friend's thoughts in the space below. Then return to small group and share your friend's highs and lows.

   MY HIGHS + LOWS THIS WEEK WERE:

   ....

   MY FRIEND'S HIGHS + LOWS THIS WEEK WERE:

   ....

2. **READ** and highlight the theme verse in your Bibles. Circle key words and learn the verse in song.

3. **TALK** about how today's verse relates to your highs and lows. Review the art for today, the Quiz Bowl questions, the terms, and the cartoons. Then write a sentence on each of the following:

   ONE NEW THING I LEARNED TODAY:

   ....

   ONE THING I ALREADY KNEW THAT IS WORTH REPEATING:

   ....

   ONE THING I WOULD LIKE TO KNOW MORE ABOUT:

   ....

4. **PRAY** for one another, praising and thanking God for your highs, and asking God to be with you in your lows. Include your friend's highs and lows in your prayers.

   A PRAISING PRAYER: ....

   A THANKING PRAYER: ....

   AN ASKING PRAYER: ....

5. **BLESS** one another using the blessing of the week. (right) Mark each person with the sign of the cross as you bless them.

THIS WEEK'S BLESSING

(NAME), CHILD OF GOD, MAY YOU TREAT YOUR BODY LIKE GOD'S HOLY TEMPLE THIS DAY.

THE HOME HUDDLE JOURNAL
SHARE, READ, TALK, PRAY, BLESS

Read the full devotions using FINKlink
LF22 @ www.faithink.com

DAY #1

TODAY'S BIBLE VERSE:

1 Corinthians 6:19-20

Or do you not know that your body is a temple of the Holy Spirit within you, which you have from God, and that you are not your own? For you were bought with a price; therefore glorify God in your body.

MY **HIGH** TODAY WAS:

MY **LOW** TODAY WAS:

MY **PRAYER** TODAY IS:

DAY #2

TODAY'S BIBLE VERSE:

1 Timothy 4:12

Let no one despise your youth, but set the believers an example in speech and conduct, in love, in faith, in purity.

MY **HIGH** TODAY WAS:

MY **LOW** TODAY WAS:

MY **PRAYER** TODAY IS:

DAY #3

TODAY'S BIBLE VERSE:

Ephesians 5:18

Do not get drunk with wine, for that is debauchery; but be filled with the Spirit.

MY **HIGH** TODAY WAS:

MY **LOW** TODAY WAS:

MY **PRAYER** TODAY IS:

my HIGH today was:

my LOW today was:

my PRAYER today is:

TODAY'S BIBLE VERSE:

Luke 21:34

Be on guard so that your hearts are not weighed down with dissipation and drunkenness and the worries of this life, and that day does not catch you unexpectedly.

---

my HIGH today was:

my LOW today was:

my PRAYER today is:

DAY #5

TODAY'S BIBLE VERSE:

Galatians 5:13

For you were called to freedom, brothers and sisters; only do not use your freedom as an opportunity for self-indulgence, but through love become slaves to one another.

---

my HIGH today was:

my LOW today was:

my PRAYER today is:

DAY #6

TODAY'S BIBLE VERSE:

1 Thessalonians 5:8

But since we belong to the day, let us be sober, and put on the breastplate of faith and love, and for a helmet the hope of salvation.

---

my HIGHEST HIGH this week was:

my LOWEST LOW this week was:

my PRAYER for next week is:

DAY #7

THIS WEEK'S BLESSING

(NAME), CHILD OF GOD, MAY YOU TREAT YOUR BODY LIKE GOD'S HOLY TEMPLE THIS DAY.

The Bible says my body is a temple.

Hey, I worship you!

THE HOME HUDDLE JOURNAL
SHARE, READ, TALK, PRAY, BLESS

WEEK 2

Read the full devotions using FINKlink
LF22 | @ www.faithink.com

DAY #1

TODAY'S BIBLE VERSE:
1 Corinthians 6:12

"All things are lawful for me," but not all things are beneficial. "All things are lawful for me," but I will not be dominated by anything.

MY **HIGH** TODAY WAS:
....

MY **LOW** TODAY WAS:
....

MY **PRAYER** TODAY IS:
....
....

DAY #2

TODAY'S BIBLE VERSE:
Romans 14:21

It is good not to eat meat or drink wine or do anything that makes your brother or sister stumble.

MY **HIGH** TODAY WAS:
....

MY **LOW** TODAY WAS:
....

MY **PRAYER** TODAY IS:
....
....

DAY #3

TODAY'S BIBLE VERSE:
Proverbs 26:11

Like a dog that returns to its vomit is a fool who reverts to his folly.

MY **HIGH** TODAY WAS:
....

MY **LOW** TODAY WAS:
....

MY **PRAYER** TODAY IS:
....
....

1. **SHARE** HIGHS & LOWS OF THE DAY.

2. **READ** AND HIGHLIGHT THE VERSE OF THE DAY IN YOUR BIBLES.

3. **TALK** ABOUT HOW TODAY'S VERSE RELATES TO YOUR HIGHS & LOWS.

4. **PRAY** FOR YOUR HIGHS & LOWS, FOR YOUR FAMILY AND FOR THE WORLD.

5. **BLESS** ONE ANOTHER USING THIS WEEK'S BLESSING (ON THE PREVIOUS PAGE).

MY HIGH TODAY WAS:

MY LOW TODAY WAS:

MY PRAYER TODAY IS:

DAY #4

TODAY'S BIBLE VERSE:

Acts 2:15

Indeed, these are not drunk, as you suppose, for it is only nine o'clock in the morning.

MY HIGH TODAY WAS:

MY LOW TODAY WAS:

MY PRAYER TODAY IS:

DAY #5

TODAY'S BIBLE VERSE:

i Timothy 3:8

Deacons likewise must be serious, not double-tongued, not indulging in much wine, not greedy for money.

MY HIGH TODAY WAS:

MY LOW TODAY WAS:

MY PRAYER TODAY IS:

DAY #6

TODAY'S BIBLE VERSE:

i Timothy 5:23

No longer drink only water, but take a little wine for the sake of your stomach and your frequent ailments.

THEME IN REVIEW

IF WE BURN OUR-
SELVES OUT WITH DRUGS
OR ALCOHOL, WE WON'T
HAVE LONG TO GO IN
THIS BUSINESS.

JOHN BELUSHI
1949–1982

DAY #7

MY FAVORITE VERSE
FROM THE THEME WAS:

....
....
....
....
....
....

LOOKING BACK ON THESE TWO WEEKS, MY HIGHEST HIGH WAS:

....

MY LOWEST LOW THESE PAST WEEKS WAS:

....

ONE WAY GOD ANSWERED MY PRAYERS WAS:

....

ONE WAY GOD MIGHT USE ME AS A SACRED AGENT
TO ANSWER THESE PRAYERS:

....

....

FAMILY COVENANT

We have shared *Highs & Lows* this week, read and highlighted the verses assigned in our Bibles, talked about our lives, prayed for one another's highs and lows, and blessed one another.

....

Parent's Signature   Teen's Signature   Date

THE FINKMANIA QUIZBOWL

Question 1:

In the creation story in Genesis, God created and called the first people to be:

(A) Stewards,
(B) Caretakers of all creation,
(C) Baby-makers,
(D) All of the above

Question 2:

In I Corinthians 6:19, St. Paul writes, "Your body is...":

(A) Made up of 90% water,
(B) A temple of the Holy Spirit,
(C) A terrible thing to waste,
(D) A lean, mean fighting machine

Question 3:

If your body is, indeed, a temple, that means you were created to:

(A) Boogie,
(B) Glorify God,
(C) Eat everything you can get your hands on,
(D) Collect dust and only be visited on Sundays between 8 and 11

Question 4:

Which of the following is not an example of mis-using your temple?:

(A) Drinking too much,
(B) Overeating,
(C) Under sleeping,
(D) None of the above

Question 5:

Taking risks with God's temple is:

(A) Fun,
(B) Dangerous,
(C) A bad way to show gratitude to your Creator,
(D) B, C, and unfortunately sometimes A

Question 6:

The price paid by God to ransom your temple from death was:

(A) Thirty pieces of silver,
(B) A 10% self-indulgence tax,
(C) The holy and precious blood of Jesus and his innocent suffering and death on your behalf,
(D) None of the above

Question 7:

Christ's blood saved us from:

(A) Sin, death, and the power of the devil,
(B) Sin, death, and homework,
(C) Sin, death, and an annoying skin condition on class picture day,
(D) Sin, death, and terminal halitosis

Question 8:

Which could happen as a result of abusing drugs or alcohol:

(A) Death,
(B) Broken relationships,
(C) Separation from God,
(D) A & B, but nothing can separate us from the love of God which is ours in Christ Jesus

Question 9:

If you have a friend abusing drugs or alcohol, you should:

(A) Tell them they are going to hell,
(B) Tell them you love them and don't want to see them hurt,
(C) Tell them God loves them and can help them,
(D) B & C, and then get them some help or you might lose them

FINKMANIA Final Question:

In I Corinthians 6:19, St. Paul says your body belongs to:

(A) Your parents,
(B) You and you alone,
(C) Whoever you happen to be dating at the time,
(D) None of the above

 Play this online game using FINKlink
LF22 @ www.faithink.com

THE WEAKEST FINK

AH, BEER. NOW THERE'S A TEMPORARY SOLUTION.

HOMER SIMPSON

TERMS
WRITE A DEFINITION BELOW.

ABUSE

GLORIFY

HOLY SPIRIT

RANSOM

TEMPLE

FAITH INKUBATORS

Fast Cars & Other Risky Business

"Mary Magdalene" Dr. He Qi: Order prints at www.heqiarts.com

"I APPEAL TO YOU THEREFORE, BROTHERS AND SISTERS,

BY THE MERCIES OF GOD, TO PRESENT YOUR BODIES AS A

LIVING SACRIFICE, HOLY AND ACCEPTABLE TO GOD, WHICH

IS YOUR SPIRITUAL WORSHIP. DO NOT BE CONFORMED TO THIS

WORLD, BUT BE TRANSFORMED BY THE RENEWING OF YOUR MINDS,

SO THAT YOU MAY DISCERN WHAT IS THE WILL OF GOD—

WHAT IS GOOD AND ACCEPTABLE AND PERFECT."

— ROMANS 12:1-2

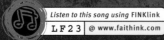

Listen to this song using FINKlink
LF23 @ www.faithink.com

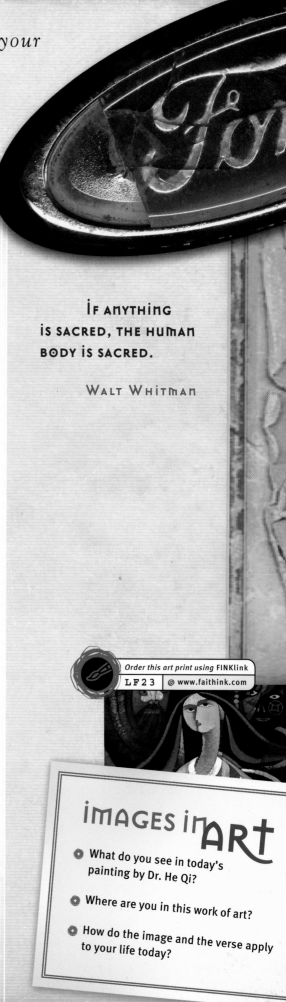

Imagine walking home from school on your 16th birthday – the day you get your driver's licence.

As you turn the corner onto your street your heart starts to pound and then skips a beat. There, in the driveway, sits a brand new baby-blue Mustang convertible, complete with a giant red birthday ribbon. Suddenly you remember your grandmother saying something about getting you a "little surprise" and spending some of her money on you while she could still watch you enjoy it! Could it be true? Is this car really yours?

You run into the kitchen and spy grannie grinning with a decaf, a donut, and her huge Denture Cream smile. She winks and rises to give you her classic vice-grip. "Happy birthday, sweetie!" She smiles, tweaking your red cheeks redder. "I thought I'd give you a little something you can enjoy before I kick off." Now she dangles the keys in front of your face and pronounces her first condition. "Condition One: You'll take really good care of this, won't you?" How do you answer?

"It's all yours, but here come conditions two, three, four and five: You'll change the oil every 3000 miles. And you'll take me for a ride once in a while when I need to go out for bingo night. And you will have to promise me not to go more than 5 or 10 over the speed limit. Never. Will you promise?" What do you say? How do you answer? Do you promise? Of course you promise! A new car would be a wonderful gift. You wouldn't take it out and risk damaging it or disregard grandma's conditions. Would you? You wouldn't abuse it, run the oil dry, drive like an idiot, or intentionally put it, yourself or your friends at risk. No way! You'd take wonderful care of such a gift. Right?

WHAT'S A BODY WORTH?

Right. So here's a question: What about your body? What about your life? According to *Wired* magazine, your body would fetch upwards of $45 million on the open market if you could extract every last ounce from every last cell and sell it to the right people. Your bone marrow alone is worth $23 million. Your DNA would fetch $9.7 million. A kidney sells for $116,400. If you are female, you could sell 32 egg cells over eight years for $224,000. Your body is worth a lot! But your life and future are worth infinitely more—certainly more than any car you could own. Life is the most marvelous and irreplaceable gift of all! Yet every day millions of people do stupid things that put the priceless gift at risk. Some people drive too fast and don't buckle their seat belts. Some pour junk into their gas tanks ruining their engines. (Drugs, excessive alcohol, cigarette smoke, a steady diet of junk food, steroids, diet pills, etc.) Others abuse their bodies, overwork their engines, and take countless other risks. Stupid!

> **IF ANYTHING IS SACRED, THE HUMAN BODY IS SACRED.**
>
> WALT WHITMAN

Order this art print using FINKlink
LF23 @ www.faithink.com

IMAGES IN ART

- What do you see in today's painting by Dr. He Qi?
- Where are you in this work of art?
- How do the image and the verse apply to your life today?

So What Does This Mean?

So What?

People with life-threatening diseases sometimes spend fortunes trying to get healthy again. They know life is worth immeasurably more than money or possessions. Parents who have lost a child and adults who have lost a loved one often say they would give everything they own for one more day, one more hour with the person they loved and lost. Standing at a grave side, people often realize, for the first time, how precious and priceless the gift of life really is.

So what? Here's what! God gave you your body. Take care of it! Don't take risks that endanger the best gift you've been given. Don't fill your lungs with smoke and tar. Don't fill your engine with junk food. Don't clutter up your brain cells with anything that could impair your judgment or land you in the emergency room. Don't risk it. Don't be thoughtless. Careless. Ungrateful. It's all a gift. It's all yours. It's all from God. And it's all good.

Bible Time

Read and highlight the verse of the week, Romans 12:1-2, in your Bible, writing "Living Sacrifice" in the margin. Next, look up the following verses. What does each say about why you need to care for your body?

Galatians 6:9   2 Thessalonians 3:13   Ephesians 4:1

Role Play

1. A friend's parent is driving carelessly and risking the lives of everyone in your car pool. You want to be respectful, but you don't want anyone to get hurt. How do you approach this person?

2. Write five types of risky behaviors that people your age regularly engage in on five separate sheets of paper. Fold the papers and choose one. Act out an intervention. One person is involved in the risky behavior. Three try to stop them.

Questions to Ponder

1. What is the best gift you ever were given? How did you thank the giver? How did you treat the gift? How does this relate to God?

2. What are the five riskiest things kids your age do on a regular basis? Why do they do them?

3. Search Institute says 47% of teens who get drunk every weekend don't like what they drink. Why would anyone do something they don't like? Is this a form of self-abuse? Why or why not?

Prayer

Dear God, you have given me one life. Help to cherish it. You have given me one body. Help me to care for it. You have given me a beautiful future. Help me to be a good and careful steward of the future you have laid out before me. In Jesus' name and in thanks to him.

Amen.

Small Group
SHARE, READ, TALK, PRAY, BLESS

1. **SHARE** your highs and lows of the week one-on-one with another person. Listen carefully and record your friend's thoughts in the space below. Then return to small group and share your friend's highs and lows.

   MY HIGHS + LOWS THIS WEEK WERE:

   ....

   MY FRIEND'S HIGHS + LOWS THIS WEEK WERE:

   ....

2. **READ** and highlight the theme verse in your Bibles. Circle key words and learn the verse in song.

3. **TALK** about how today's verse relates to your highs and lows. Review the art for today, the Quiz Bowl questions, the terms, and the cartoons. Then write a sentence on each of the following:

   ONE NEW THING I LEARNED TODAY:

   ....

   ONE THING I ALREADY KNEW THAT IS WORTH REPEATING:

   ....

   ONE THING I WOULD LIKE TO KNOW MORE ABOUT:

   ....

4. **PRAY** for one another, praising and thanking God for your highs, and asking God to be with you in your lows. Include your friend's highs and lows in your prayers.

   A PRAISING PRAYER: ....

   A THANKING PRAYER: ....

   AN ASKING PRAYER: ....

5. **BLESS** one another using the blessing of the week. (right) Mark each person with the sign of the cross as you bless them.

THIS WEEK'S BLESSING

(NAME), CHILD OF GOD, MAY GOD GIVE YOU POWER AND WISDOM TO GUARD YOUR FUTURE AS A GIFT.

THE HOME HUDDLE JOURNAL

SHARE, READ, TALK, PRAY, BLESS

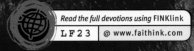

Read the full devotions using FINKlink

LF23 | @ www.faithink.com

DAY #1

TODAY'S BIBLE VERSE:

Romans 12:1

I appeal to you therefore, brothers and sisters, by the mercies of God, to present your bodies as a living sacrifice, holy and acceptable to God, which is your spiritual worship.

MY **HIGH** TODAY WAS:

MY **LOW** TODAY WAS:

MY **PRAYER** TODAY IS:

DAY #2

TODAY'S BIBLE VERSE:

Romans 12:2

Do not be conformed to this world, but be transformed by the renewing of your minds, so that you may discern what is the will of God—what is good and acceptable and perfect.

MY **HIGH** TODAY WAS:

MY **LOW** TODAY WAS:

MY **PRAYER** TODAY IS:

DAY #3

TODAY'S BIBLE VERSE:

Galatians 6:9

So let us not grow weary in doing what is right, for we will reap at harvest time, if we do not give up.

MY **HIGH** TODAY WAS:

MY **LOW** TODAY WAS:

MY **PRAYER** TODAY IS:

DAY #4

TODAY'S BIBLE VERSE:

Matthew 6:22

The eye is the lamp of the body. So, if your eye is healthy, your whole body will be full of light.

MY HIGH TODAY WAS:

MY LOW TODAY WAS:

MY PRAYER TODAY IS:

DAY #5

TODAY'S BIBLE VERSE:

Job 28:28

Truly, the fear of the Lord, that is wisdom; and to depart from evil is understanding.

MY HIGH TODAY WAS:

MY LOW TODAY WAS:

MY PRAYER TODAY IS:

DAY #6

TODAY'S BIBLE VERSE:

2 Thessalonians 3:13

Brothers and sisters, do not be weary in doing what is right.

MY HIGH TODAY WAS:

MY LOW TODAY WAS:

MY PRAYER TODAY IS:

DAY #7

THIS WEEK'S BLESSING

(NAME), CHILD OF GOD, MAY GOD GIVE YOU POWER AND WISDOM TO GUARD YOUR FUTURE AS A GIFT.

MY HIGHEST HIGH THIS WEEK WAS:

MY LOWEST LOW THIS WEEK WAS:

MY PRAYER FOR NEXT WEEK IS:

THE HOME HUDDLE JOURNAL
SHARE, READ, TALK, PRAY, BLESS

Read the full devotions using FINKlink
LF23 | @ www.faithink.com

DAY #1

today's bible verse:
EPHESIANS 4:1

I therefore, the prisoner in the Lord, beg you to lead a life worthy of the calling to which you have been called.

my HIGH today was:

my LOW today was:

my PRAYER today is:

DAY #2

today's bible verse:
EPHESIANS 4:17

Now this I affirm and insist on in the Lord: you must no longer live as the Gentiles live, in the futility of their minds.

my HIGH today was:

my LOW today was:

my PRAYER today is:

DAY #3

today's bible verse:
EPHESIANS 4:22

You were taught to put away your former way of life, your old self, corrupt and deluded by its lusts.

my HIGH today was:

my LOW today was:

my PRAYER today is:

1. SHARE HIGHS & LOWS OF THE DAY.

2. READ AND HIGHLIGHT THE VERSE OF THE DAY IN YOUR BIBLES.

3. TALK ABOUT HOW TODAY'S VERSE RELATES TO YOUR HIGHS & LOWS.

4. PRAY FOR YOUR HIGHS & LOWS, FOR YOUR FAMILY AND FOR THE WORLD.

5. BLESS ONE ANOTHER USING THIS WEEK'S BLESSING (ON THE PREVIOUS PAGE).

MY HIGH TODAY WAS:

MY LOW TODAY WAS:

MY PRAYER TODAY IS:

DAY #4

TODAY'S BIBLE VERSE:

EPHESIANS 4:23-24

And to be renewed in the spirit of your minds, and to clothe yourselves with the new self, created according to the likeness of God in true righteousness and holiness.

MY HIGH TODAY WAS:

MY LOW TODAY WAS:

MY PRAYER TODAY IS:

DAY #5

TODAY'S BIBLE VERSE:

1 CORINTHIANS 15:30

And why are we putting ourselves in danger every hour?

MY HIGH TODAY WAS:

MY LOW TODAY WAS:

MY PRAYER TODAY IS:

DAY #6

TODAY'S BIBLE VERSE:

MATTHEW 4:7B

Do not put the Lord your God to the test.

THEME IN REVIEW

THE ONLY REAL RULE YOU NEED FOR MAKING MOST OF LIFE'S DECISIONS:

DON'T BE DUMB.

MONTY LYSNE

DAY #7

MY FAVORITE VERSE FROM THE THEME WAS:

....

....

....

....

....

....

....

....

LOOKING BACK ON THESE TWO WEEKS, MY HIGHEST HIGH WAS:

....

MY LOWEST LOW THESE PAST WEEKS WAS:

....

ONE WAY GOD ANSWERED MY PRAYERS WAS:

....

ONE WAY GOD MIGHT USE ME AS A SACRED AGENT TO ANSWER THESE PRAYERS:

....

....

FAMILY COVENANT

We have shared *Highs & Lows* this week, read and highlighted the verses assigned in our Bibles, talked about our lives, prayed for one another's highs and lows, and blessed one another.

....

Parent's Signature   *Teen's Signature*   *Date*

THE FINKMANIA QUIZ BOWL

QUESTION 1:

The ancient act of killing a valuable animal from your herds or flocks and offering it to God was called a:

(A) Tithe,
(B) Bribe,
(C) Sacrifice,
(D) None of the above

QUESTION 2:

Which person in the Old Testament was ready to offer his son as a living sacrifice to God?:

(A) Abraham,
(B) Isaac,
(C) Jacob,
(D) Most of them—they all had teenagers

QUESTION 3:

Taking dangerous or unhealthy risks with your body is:

(A) Fun,
(B) Stupid,
(C) A way to show that you are not thankful,
(D) C, B and, unfortunately, sometimes A

QUESTION 4:

A risk that is worth taking is:

(A) Speaking God's truth,
(B) Resisting negative peer pressure,
(C) Being kind to the kid everyone is picking on in school,
(D) All of the above

QUESTION 5:

A word for acting in accordance with popular customs:

(A) Norm,
(B) Transform,
(C) Conform,
(D) Reform

QUESTION 6:

A word for changing the nature of something:

(A) Risk,
(B) Transform,
(C) Conform,
(D) None of the above

QUESTION 7:

This writer of the book of Romans was transformed by a blinding encounter with Jesus:

(A) Paul,
(B) Saul,
(C) Darth Maul,
(D) A & B

QUESTION 8:

According to Romans 12, transformation happens when you:

(A) Are baptized,
(B) Take communion,
(C) Confess your sins,
(D) All of the above are good answers, but in Romans 12 transformation happens when you have your mind renewed by the power of the Holy Spirit

QUESTION 9:

According to St. Paul, the will of God is:

(A) Difficult to know,
(B) Difficult to understand,
(C) Communicated during American Idol,
(D) Good, acceptable, perfect, and definitely worth seeking out

FINKMANIA FINAL QUESTION:

St. Paul urges all Christians to present their bodies as a:

(A) Science experiment,
(B) Blood donor,
(C) Living sacrifice,
(D) None of the above

 Play this online game using FINKlink
LF23 @ www.faithink.com

THE WEAKEST FINK

TRANSFORMATION LITERALLY MEANS GOING BEYOND YOUR FORM.

WAYNE DYER

TERMS
WRITE A DEFINITION BELOW.

SACRIFICE

CONFORM

TRANSFORM

WILL

RISK

 FAITH INKUBATORS

MEDIA & MATERIALISM

"Martha and Mary" Dr. He Qi. Order prints at www.heqiarts.com

"HO, EVERYONE WHO THIRSTS, COME TO THE WATERS; AND YOU THAT HAVE NO MONEY, COME, BUY AND EAT! COME, BUY WINE AND MILK WITHOUT MONEY AND WITHOUT PRICE. WHY DO YOU SPEND YOUR MONEY FOR THAT WHICH IS NOT BREAD, AND YOUR LABOR FOR THAT WHICH DOES NOT SATISFY? LISTEN CAREFULLY TO ME, AND EAT WHAT IS GOOD, AND DELIGHT YOURSELVES IN RICH FOOD. INCLINE YOUR EAR, AND COME TO ME; LISTEN, SO THAT YOU MAY LIVE."

— ISAIAH 55:1-3A

Listen to this song using FINKlink
LF24 @ www.faithink.com

By the time a child reaches sixth grade in America, she will already have spent more time with television than she will spend with her dad during the rest of his life.

What messages are we getting from all this television, advertising and other media? Here's a song by musician and pastor Bryan Sirchio on the topic of greed, media, and materialism from his *Wise As Serpents* album.

IF MY SOUL SHOULD BE REQUIRED TONIGHT

Once there was a farmer whose land produced so well
his barns could not contain the excess grain.
He built the barns up larger and then said to himself
"I've all I need for years now laid away"
But God said to him, "Fool! This night
your soul shall be required
And all this wealth of yours whose will it be?"

And if my soul should be required tonight
What would Jesus say to me?
If my soul should be required tonight
Would my treasure stay with me?
Would he find me rich in things
Or find me rich in Christ
If my soul should be required tonight?

There is always someone who's urging me to buy
Who's making luxury look like a need
Investments in convenience
In comfort and in style
With all my satisfaction guaranteed
And its bigger, better, newer, faster
Buy now pay tomorrow
Seduced with credit cards and toll free lines

And if my soul should be required tonight
What would Jesus say to me?
If my soul should be required tonight
Would my treasure stay with me?
Would he find me rich in things or find me rich in Christ
If my soul should be required tonight?

And its so easy to justify the way I live, and all these things I buy
But this world's so hungry, Lord I've seen the need
Can I truly love, and keep the piles for me?

(This album is full of conscience, beat, soul, and poetry just like this. Order a copy at www.sirchio.com and tell him your FINK Living Faith Journal sent you.)

IMAGES in ART

- What do you see in today's painting by Dr. He Qi?

- Where are you in this work of art?

- How do the image and the verse apply to your life today?

So What Does This Mean?

DID YOU KNOW THAT HALF OF THE CHILDREN OF THE WORLD GO TO BED HUNGRY EVERY NIGHT?

WOW! THAT'S ALMOST ENOUGH TO MAKE ME THINK TWICE ABOUT WASTING SO MUCH MONEY ON VIDEO GAMES AND CDs.

ALMOST? AS IN...

AS IN NOT QUITE...

PRAYER

DEAR GOD, SOMETIMES IT SEEMS LIKE I'M FULL, BUT EMPTY. MAYBE I'M NOT EATING THE RIGHT STUFF. THE WORLD CALLS OUT FOR ME TO FILL MY EGO WITH EMPTY CALORIES. PLEASE, DON'T LET THEM FOOL ME AND DON'T LET ME FOOL MYSELF. FEED ME WITH THE GOOD STUFF—THE BREAD OF LIFE. FILL ME WITH THE THINGS THAT WILL SATISFY MY HUNGRY HEART. THEN SEND ME OUT TO SHARE YOUR LIVING BREAD WITH OTHERS WHO ARE EMPTY. PLEASE, JESUS. FILL ME. I AM GETTING REALLY, REALLY HUNGRY.

AMEN.

In the darkest days of WWII during the siege of Leningrad, the town elders had a difficult decision to make. Nazis were bombing the city and had cut their supply lines. The winter was harsh and there wasn't enough grain to make bread for all of the people. It looked like they might have enough to keep 1/3 of the city alive. Rather than choosing those who would live and those who would die, they made their bread with 1/3 wheat, 1/3 saw dust, and 1/3 horse manure.

Every night that winter, tens of thousands of children went to sleep starving to death on a full stomach. They thought they were full, but what they were eating couldn't keep them alive. It filled them but gave them nothing that would satisfy. Maybe that's what we're doing in this country, today. The media bombards us with messages to "buy, buy, buy" things that won't satisfy. And we wonder how we can be so full, and yet so empty.

SO WHAT?

We live in a world of extremes. Some have everything they want, but still feel a terrific void in their existence. They have full houses and empty homes. Full schedules and empty lives. We fill our lives, garages, and attics with gadgets that soon turn to clutter. We are told to get more, do more, buy more, and we'll be more. But it doesn't happen. Sometimes the more we have the less we have. Sometimes the only thing we don't have is more. Where does it all end? Where should it all end? Will it ever end? How should a Christian live? And why should a Christian care?

BIBLE TIME

Read and highlight Isaiah 55:1-3 in your Bible, writing "What Satisfies" in the margin. Then find the following passages and relate them to this verse:

Ecclesiastes 5:10   1 John 3:17-18   James 2:15-17

ROLE PLAY

1. A friend tells you "Greed is good!" How do you respond?

2. A neighbor often brags about all the expensive toys she owns, but she won't donate when you come collecting for the local food shelf. Respond.

QUESTIONS TO PONDER

1. What are five current television ads with bad messages? What are five current ads with good messages? What makes a good one good?

2. Think about the five bad television commercials. What are they selling? No. Really. What are they selling?

3. Who are the happiest people you know? Why are they happy? How can someone with little material wealth be happy? How can one have a full house but an empty home? A full schedule but an empty life?

Small Group
SHARE, READ, TALK, PRAY, BLESS

1. **SHARE** your highs and lows of the week one-on-one with another person. Listen carefully and record your friend's thoughts in the space below. Then return to small group and share your friend's highs and lows.

   MY HIGHS + LOWS THIS WEEK WERE:

   ....

   MY FRIEND'S HIGHS + LOWS THIS WEEK WERE:

   ....

2. **READ** and highlight the theme verse in your Bibles. Circle key words and learn the verse in song.

3. **TALK** about how today's verse relates to your highs and lows. Review the art for today, the Quiz Bowl questions, the terms, and the cartoons. Then write a sentence on each of the following:

   ONE NEW THING I LEARNED TODAY:

   ....

   ONE THING I ALREADY KNEW THAT IS WORTH REPEATING:

   ....

   ONE THING I WOULD LIKE TO KNOW MORE ABOUT:

   ....

4. **PRAY** for one another, praising and thanking God for your highs, and asking God to be with you in your lows. Include your friend's highs and lows in your prayers.

   A PRAISING PRAYER: ....

   A THANKING PRAYER: ....

   AN ASKING PRAYER: ....

5. **BLESS** one another using the blessing of the week. (right) Mark each person with the sign of the cross as you bless them.

THIS WEEK'S BLESSING

(NAME), CHILD OF GOD, MAY YOU BE BLESSED WITH JUST ENOUGH TO KEEP YOU THANKFUL.

THE HOME HUDDLE JOURNAL

SHARE, READ, TALK, PRAY, BLESS

Read the full devotions using FINKlink
LF24 | @ www.faithink.com

DAY #1

TODAY'S BIBLE VERSE:

Isaiah 55:1

Ho, everyone who thirsts, come to the waters; and you that have no money, come, buy and eat! Come, buy wine and milk without money and without price.

MY **HIGH** TODAY WAS:

MY **LOW** TODAY WAS:

MY **PRAYER** TODAY IS:

DAY #2

TODAY'S BIBLE VERSE:

Isaiah 55:2

Why do you spend your money for that which is not bread, and your labor for that which does not satisfy? Listen carefully to me, and eat what is good, and delight yourself in rich food.

MY **HIGH** TODAY WAS:

MY **LOW** TODAY WAS:

MY **PRAYER** TODAY IS:

DAY #3

TODAY'S BIBLE VERSE:

Isaiah 55:3a

Incline your ear, and come to me; listen, so that you may live.

MY **HIGH** TODAY WAS:

MY **LOW** TODAY WAS:

MY **PRAYER** TODAY IS:

MY HIGH TODAY WAS:

....

MY LOW TODAY WAS:

....

MY PRAYER TODAY IS:

....

....

DAY #4

TODAY'S BIBLE VERSE:

ECCLESIASTES 5:10

The lover of money will not be satisfied with money; nor the lover of wealth, with gain. This also is vanity.

MY HIGH TODAY WAS:

....

MY LOW TODAY WAS:

....

MY PRAYER TODAY IS:

....

....

DAY #5

TODAY'S BIBLE VERSE:

MARK 10:17

As he was setting out on a journey, a man ran up and knelt before him, and asked him, "Good Teacher, what must I do to inherit eternal life?"

MY HIGH TODAY WAS:

....

MY LOW TODAY WAS:

....

MY PRAYER TODAY IS:

....

DAY #6

TODAY'S BIBLE VERSE:

MARK 10:21B-22

"You lack one thing; go, sell what you own, and give the money to the poor, and you will have treasure in heaven; then come, follow me." When he heard this, he was shocked and went away grieving, for he had many possessions.

MY HIGHEST HIGH THIS WEEK WAS:

....

MY LOWEST LOW THIS WEEK WAS:

....

MY PRAYER FOR NEXT WEEK IS:

....

....

DAY #7

THIS WEEK'S BLESSING

(NAME), CHILD OF GOD,

MAY YOU BE BLESSED WITH

JUST ENOUGH TO KEEP YOU

THANKFUL.

THE HOME HUDDLE JOURNAL
SHARE, READ, TALK, PRAY, BLESS

Read the full devotions using FINKlink
LF24 @ www.faithink.com

DAY #1

TODAY'S BIBLE VERSE:

DEUTERONOMY 6:11B-12

When you have eaten your fill, take care that you do not forget the Lord, who brought you out of the land of Egypt, out of the house of slavery.

MY HIGH TODAY WAS:

MY LOW TODAY WAS:

MY PRAYER TODAY IS:

DAY #2

TODAY'S BIBLE VERSE:

EXODUS 16:20

But they did not listen to Moses; some left part of it (the manna) until morning, and it bred worms and became foul. And Moses was angry with them.

MY HIGH TODAY WAS:

MY LOW TODAY WAS:

MY PRAYER TODAY IS:

DAY #3

TODAY'S BIBLE VERSE:

LUKE 10:41B-42

"Martha, Martha, you are worried and distracted by many things; there is need of only one thing. Mary has chosen the better part, which will not be taken away from her."

MY HIGH TODAY WAS:

MY LOW TODAY WAS:

MY PRAYER TODAY IS:

What is it?

I don't know. But it must be good. There's a line.

1. **SHARE** HIGHS & LOWS OF THE DAY.

2. **READ** AND HIGHLIGHT THE VERSE OF THE DAY IN YOUR BIBLES.

3. **TALK** ABOUT HOW TODAY'S VERSE RELATES TO YOUR HIGHS & LOWS.

4. **PRAY** FOR YOUR HIGHS & LOWS, FOR YOUR FAMILY AND FOR THE WORLD.

5. **BLESS** ONE ANOTHER USING THIS WEEK'S BLESSING (ON THE PREVIOUS PAGE).

MY **HIGH** TODAY WAS:

MY **LOW** TODAY WAS:

MY **PRAYER** TODAY IS:

DAY #4

TODAY'S BIBLE VERSE:

Matthew 6:20-21

But store up for yourselves treasures in heaven, where neither moth nor rust consumes and where thieves do not break in and steal. For where your treasure is, there your heart will be also.

MY **HIGH** TODAY WAS:

MY **LOW** TODAY WAS:

MY **PRAYER** TODAY IS:

DAY #5

TODAY'S BIBLE VERSE:

Luke 12:22-23

He said to his disciples, "Therefore I tell you, do not worry about your life, what you will eat, or about your body, what you will wear. For life is more than food, and the body more than clothing!"

MY **HIGH** TODAY WAS:

MY **LOW** TODAY WAS:

MY **PRAYER** TODAY IS:

DAY #6

TODAY'S BIBLE VERSE:

Proverbs 16:8

Better is a little with righteousness than large income with injustice.

Greetings consumers!
We, the media, would like to sell you some things you don't need to buy with money you don't have to impress people you don't like.

THEME IN
REVIEW

**THE ONLY THING
HE DOESN'T HAVE IS MORE.**

RICH MELHEIM

DAY #7

MY FAVORITE **VERSE**
FROM THE THEME WAS:

....
....
....
....
....
....

LOOKING BACK ON THESE TWO WEEKS, MY HIGHEST **HIGH** WAS:

....

MY LOWEST **LOW** THESE PAST WEEKS WAS:

....

ONE WAY GOD ANSWERED MY **PRAYERS** WAS:

....

ONE WAY GOD MIGHT USE ME AS A **SACRED AGENT**
TO ANSWER THESE PRAYERS:

....

....

FAMILY COVENANT

We have shared *Highs & Lows* this week, read and highlighted the verses assigned in our Bibles, talked about our lives, prayed for one another's highs and lows, and blessed one another.

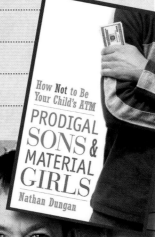

_____   _____   _____
Parent's Signature   Teen's Signature   Date

CHECKOUT WWW.SHARESAVESPEND.COM

THE FINKMANIA QUIZ BOWL

QUESTION 1:

Finish this bumper sticker: "Whoever dies with the most toys...:"

(A) Wins,
(B) Is eternally happy,
(C) Is eternally stupid,
(D) Is still dead

QUESTION 2:

Buying and consuming tons of things we don't need with borrowed money we don't have in order to impress friends we don't like is:

(A) Stupid,
(B) Sad,
(C) The American Way,
(D) All of the above

QUESTION 3:

The Bible does not say money is the root of all evil, but...:

(A) "The love of money is the root of all evil,"
(B) "The lust for money is the root of all evil,"
(C) "Dentists who do root canals are all evil,"
(D) "The love of evil is the root of all money"

QUESTION 4:

The philosophy that "worldly possessions make up the greatest good and highest value in life" is most often called:

(A) Me-ism,
(B) Materialism,
(C) Paris Hiltonism,
(D) The American Way

QUESTION 5:

Excess materialism is closely related to which commandment:

(A) You shall have no other gods before me,
(B) You shall not steal,
(C) You shall not covet,
(D) All of the above, and probably most of the rest if you think about it

QUESTION 6:

Which of the following is NOT God's will:

(A) Loving things and using people,
(B) Loving people and using things,
(C) Sharing what you have with the poor,
(D) Living a humble, thankful life, sharing with the poor and modeling a lifestyle that will help others want to live in God's will

QUESTION 7:

Giving in to all physical desires and whims to an excessive degree in order to please the body and feed the ego is called:

(A) Hedonism,
(B) Infancy,
(C) Both A & B,
(D) The American Way

QUESTION 8:

The media often bombard us with messages that are contrary to Christian principles. Which message does not conflict with the words of Jesus?:

(A) Get more,
(B) Have it your way,
(C) Greed is good,
(D) Talk to your kids about drugs

QUESTION 9:

Isaiah 55:1-3a invites us to buy wine and milk (meaning God's good stuff) without:

(A) Long lines,
(B) Preservatives,
(C) Leaving your home,
(D) Money and price—meaning the best stuff in life isn't stuff and it doesn't cost a penny

FINKMANIA FINAL QUESTION:

In Isaiah 55:1-3 we are asked to listen to God so that:

(A) We don't miss anything,
(B) We know what's on the test,
(C) We may live—really live,
(D) None of the above

Play this online game using FINKlink
LF24 @ www.faithink.com

THE WEAKEST FINK

IF ONLY GOD WOULD GIVE ME SOME CLEAR SIGN! LIKE MAKING A LARGE DEPOSIT IN MY NAME AT A SWISS BANK.

WOODY ALLEN

TERMS
WRITE A DEFINITION BELOW.

MATERIALISM

MEDIA

EXCESS

POVERTY

RICHES

FAITH INKUBATORS

GOD & SCIENCE

"Knocking at the Door" Dr. He Qi. Order prints at www.heqiarts.com

"CAN YOU FIND OUT THE DEEP THINGS OF GOD? CAN YOU FIND OUT THE LIMIT OF THE ALMIGHTY? IT IS HIGHER THAN HEAVEN - WHAT CAN YOU DO? DEEPER THAN SHEOL - WHAT CAN YOU KNOW? ITS MEASURE IS LONGER THAN THE EARTH, AND BROADER THAN THE SEA. IF HE PASSES THROUGH, AND IMPRISONS, AND ASSEMBLES FOR JUDGMENT, WHO CAN HINDER HIM? FOR HE KNOWS THOSE WHO ARE WORTHLESS; WHEN HE SEES INIQUITY, WILL HE NOT CONSIDER IT? BUT A STUPID PERSON WILL GET UNDERSTANDING, WHEN A WILD ASS IS BORN HUMAN."

Listen to this song using FINKlink
LF25 @ www.faithink.com

— JOB 11:7-12

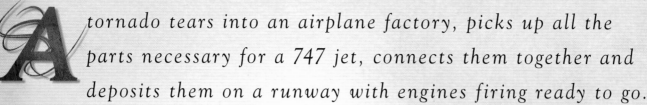

A tornado tears into an airplane factory, picks up all the parts necessary for a 747 jet, connects them together and deposits them on a runway with engines firing ready to go.

Not going to happen? Highly unlikely? Now consider this—there is no factory. In order to assemble the plane, three earlier tornados had to tear into three separate mines and pick up enough raw copper, bauxite, and magnesium to produce 171 miles of wiring and 5 miles of tubing. These mindless forces processed the raw ore and spun it into sheets of metal, wire and fasteners for six million distinct parts. At the same moment other tornados tore into other mines on another continent and pulled up enough raw ore to make 147,000 pounds of high-strength aluminum for the airplane's body. Then each of the parts flew into the same space, randomly aligned and bolts screwed themselves in place. Then lightening struck a half million times in the exact right places and the body was completely welded.

Another tornado processed synthetic rubber for 18 landing gear tires to carry the 63 foot beast. Others tore into the ground, sucked up tons of crude oil, then somehow processed 63,500 pounds of high performance jet fuel and poured it into the tanks. Others swept over beaches, pulled sand (silicon) into the air, pressed it into computer chips and circuit boards, then assembled and installed the onboard computers. A final random storm lifted a dozen cows from a field, tanned their hides, dyed them gray and sewed them into plush leather seats for first class. In all, 775,000,000 pounds of raw materials were nabbed to produce 775,000 pounds of airplane. All of this happened randomly with no intelligence behind it, bypassing 75,000 engineering drawings and the work of tens of thousands of scientists, designers and builders who normally assemble such a complex machine. All this happened by chance. Random chance. Highly unlikely?

This is what it would take to build a machine with **SIX MILLION** parts by chance. What about a living being like you? The human brain alone contains a **HUNDRED MILLION** cells. Each of these cells has a DNA strand with **THREE BILLION** chemical base pairs lined up in perfect order. The cells assemble themselves with a **QUADRILLION** connections. Each one of these cells is infinitely more complex than any machine ever conceived or built by any human designer. Oh, yeah. And they are alive.

Some say there is not God. This all happened by chance. What do you say?

SCIENCE AND FAITH

We live in a time when science and faith seem to be at odds. Some would say they don't belong together in the same discussion—certainly not in the classroom. Some would say you have to check your faith at the door when you walk into a science lab, and your brain at the door when you walk into a church. But is that how Christians should think? Is faith always blind? Is science always soulless? Does it have to be this way?

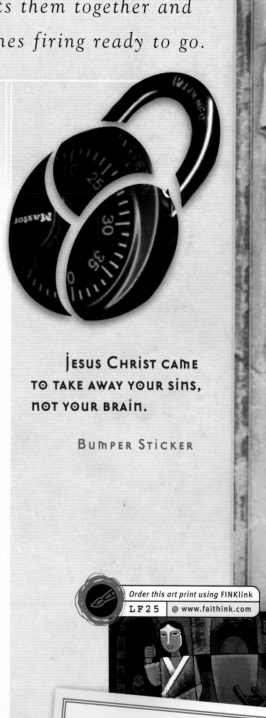

JESUS CHRIST CAME TO TAKE AWAY YOUR SINS, NOT YOUR BRAIN.

BUMPER STICKER

Order this art print using FINKlink
LF25 @ www.faithink.com

IMAGES in ART

- What do you see in today's painting by Dr. He Qi?
- Where are you in this work of art?
- How do the image and the verse apply to your life today?

So What Does This Mean?

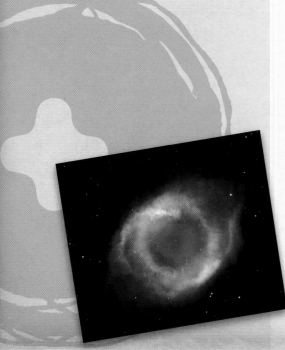

You're telling me that the moment before the **BIG BANG** there was no matter, energy time or space? Then what for the love of God **BANGED?**

Easy. The **LOVE** of God!

PRAYER

CREATOR GOD, THIS WORLD IS ONE AMAZING PLACE! YOUR HANDIWORK SHOUTS OUT YOUR LOVE TO ALL WHO ASK AND SEEK AND KNOCK. HELP ME TO HEAR YOU LOUD AND CLEAR. IN JESUS' NAME.

AMEN.

TESTING, TESTING, TESTING

The Bible says we are to love God with all of our heart, soul, *mind*, and strength. The Bible also says we are to test everything. That sounds like pretty good science! Einstein said, "I want to know God's thoughts. The rest is detail," and "I dance to the tune of an Invisible Piper. He stands behind the universe. He is God!" Einstein was no dummy.

The closer we get to understanding the fine-tuned nature of the physics of the universe, and the intricacies and complexities of even the simplest forms of life, the more we see elements of elegance, perfection, and, some would say "design" in it all. To say it is all random, purposeless and here by chance is to ignore one ultimate reality: Chance is not a rational explanation for the origin of the universe. Chance only works if it has something to work upon. Before the Big Bang, chance had nothing to work upon. No matter. No energy. No time. No space. Chance is a random coincidence. For a coincidence to occur, you need two or more incidents. And for an incident to occur, you need matter, energy, time and space. Before the Big Bang, there were none of these. Therefore, there was no chance! There must have been something that stood above and beyond the laws of physics as we know them—some First Cause—that broke (or made) all natural laws. Something that stood above nature. In Latin the word for "above nature" is supernatural. Is it rational to believe in the super-natural? At the end of science, that's all you have left.

Christians believe there was a First Cause. And that first cause came as Jesus Christ to take away our sins. Not our brains. So test! Seek. Knock. Ask. Search. Study. Question. The God who stands behind the Universe is big enough to remain God even through all of your searching.

BIBLE TIME

Read and highlight Job 11:7-12, writing "The Deep Things" in the margin.

ROLE PLAY

1. A friend says, "The universe created itself and is here by chance." Respond.

2. A teacher says, "You are either a person of science or a person of faith. You can't be both." How do you respond?

QUESTIONS TO PONDER

1. Which is more difficult to believe and why? A. There is a God Creator, B. Everything came from nothing, C. The Creator loves you, D. You will one day be more like your parents than you can ever imagine.

2. Why doesn't chance work as an explanation for the origin of the universe and the Big Bang?

3. Is it rational to believe in the supernatural? Why or why not?

Small Gr⊕up
SHARE, READ, TALK, PRAY, BLESS

1. SHARE your highs and lows of the week one-on-one with another person. Listen carefully and record your friend's thoughts in the space below. Then return to small group and share your friend's highs and lows.

> **MY HIGHS + LOWS THIS WEEK WERE:**
>
> ....
>
> **MY FRIEND'S HIGHS + LOWS THIS WEEK WERE:**
>
> ....

2. READ and highlight the theme verse in your Bibles. Circle key words and learn the verse in song.

3. TALK about how today's verse relates to your highs and lows. Review the art for today, the Quiz Bowl questions, the terms, and the cartoons. Then write a sentence on each of the following:

> **ONE NEW THING I LEARNED TODAY:**
>
> ....
>
> **ONE THING I ALREADY KNEW THAT IS WORTH REPEATING:**
>
> ....
>
> **ONE THING I WOULD LIKE TO KNOW MORE ABOUT:**
>
> ....

4. PRAY for one another, praising and thanking God for your highs, and asking God to be with you in your lows. Include your friend's highs and lows in your prayers.

> **A PRAISING PRAYER:** ....
>
> **A THANKING PRAYER:** ....
>
> **AN ASKING PRAYER:** ....

5. BLESS one another using the blessing of the week. (right) Mark each person with the sign of the cross as you bless them.

THIS WEEK'S BLESSING
(NAME), MAY YOU
CATCH A LITTLE GLIMPSE
OF THE DEEP THINGS OF
GOD TODAY.

THE HOME HUDDLE JOURNAL
SHARE, READ, TALK, PRAY, BLESS

WEEK 1

Read the full devotions using FINKlink
LF25 @ www.faithink.com

DAY #1

TODAY'S BIBLE VERSE:

JOB 11:7-9

Can you find out the deep things of God? Can you find out the limit of the Almighty? It is higher than heaven—what can you do? Deeper than Sheol—what can you know? Its measure is longer than the earth, and broader than the sea.

MY **HIGH** TODAY WAS:

MY **LOW** TODAY WAS:

MY **PRAYER** TODAY IS:

DAY #2

TODAY'S BIBLE VERSE:

Matthew 7:7

Ask, and it will be given you; search, and you will find; knock, and the door will be opened for you.

MY **HIGH** TODAY WAS:

MY **LOW** TODAY WAS:

MY **PRAYER** TODAY IS:

DAY #3

TODAY'S BIBLE VERSE:

Isaiah 40:28

Have you not known? Have you not heard? The Lord is the everlasting God, the Creator of the ends of the earth. He does not faint or grow weary; his understanding is unsearchable.

MY **HIGH** TODAY WAS:

MY **LOW** TODAY WAS:

MY **PRAYER** TODAY IS:

MY HIGH TODAY WAS: ....

MY LOW TODAY WAS: ....

MY PRAYER TODAY IS: ....

....

DAY #4

TODAY'S BIBLE VERSE:
PSALM 19:1-2
The heavens are telling the glory of God; and the firmament proclaims his handiwork. Day to day pours forth speech, and night to night declares knowledge.

MY HIGH TODAY WAS: ....

MY LOW TODAY WAS: ....

MY PRAYER TODAY IS: ....

....

DAY #5

TODAY'S BIBLE VERSE:
PSALM 19:3-4A
There is no speech, nor are there words; their voice is not heard; yet their voice goes out through all the earth, and their words to the end of the world.

MY HIGH TODAY WAS: ....

MY LOW TODAY WAS: ....

MY PRAYER TODAY IS: ....

....

DAY #6

TODAY'S BIBLE VERSE:
1 THESSALONIANS 5:21
But test everything; hold fast to what is good.

MY HIGHEST HIGH THIS WEEK WAS: ....

MY LOWEST LOW THIS WEEK WAS: ....

MY PRAYER FOR NEXT WEEK IS: ....

....

DAY #7

THIS WEEK'S BLESSING

(NAME), MAY YOU CATCH A LITTLE GLIMPSE OF THE DEEP THINGS OF GOD TODAY.

THE HOME HUDDLE JOURNAL
SHARE, READ, TALK, PRAY, BLESS

WEEK 2

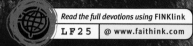
Read the full devotions using FINKlink
LF25 @ www.faithink.com

DAY #1

TODAY'S BIBLE VERSE:
Psalm 8:3-4

When I look at your heavens, the work of your fingers, the moon and the stars that you have established; what are human beings that you are mindful of them, mortals that you care for them?

MY **HIGH** TODAY WAS:

MY **LOW** TODAY WAS:

MY **PRAYER** TODAY IS:

DAY #2

TODAY'S BIBLE VERSE:
Isaiah 45:12

I made the earth, and created humankind upon it; it was my hands that stretched out the heavens, and I commanded all their host.

MY **HIGH** TODAY WAS:

MY **LOW** TODAY WAS:

MY **PRAYER** TODAY IS:

DAY #3

TODAY'S BIBLE VERSE:
Psalm 14:1a

Fools say in their hearts, "There is no God."

MY **HIGH** TODAY WAS:

MY **LOW** TODAY WAS:

MY **PRAYER** TODAY IS:

1. SHARE HIGHS & LOWS OF THE DAY.

2. READ AND HIGHLIGHT THE VERSE OF THE DAY IN YOUR BIBLES.

3. TALK ABOUT HOW TODAY'S VERSE RELATES TO YOUR HIGHS & LOWS.

4. PRAY FOR YOUR HIGHS & LOWS, FOR YOUR FAMILY AND FOR THE WORLD.

5. BLESS ONE ANOTHER USING THIS WEEK'S BLESSING (ON THE PREVIOUS PAGE).

MY HIGH TODAY WAS:

MY LOW TODAY WAS:

MY PRAYER TODAY IS:

DAY #4

TODAY'S BIBLE VERSE:

JOB 9:7-8

Who commands the sun, and it did not rise; who seals up the stars; who alone stretched out the heavens and trampled the waves of the sea.

MY HIGH TODAY WAS:

MY LOW TODAY WAS:

MY PRAYER TODAY IS:

DAY #5

TODAY'S BIBLE VERSE:

JOB 9:9-10

...who made the Bear and Orion, the Pleiades and the chambers of the south; who does great things beyond understanding, and marvelous things without number.

MY HIGH TODAY WAS:

MY LOW TODAY WAS:

MY PRAYER TODAY IS:

DAY #6

TODAY'S BIBLE VERSE:

PSALM 51:6

You desire truth in the inward being; therefore teach me wisdom in my secret heart.

S | M | T | W | TH | F | S

THEME IN REVIEW

CHANCE IS NOT A RATIONAL EXPLANATION FOR THE ORIGIN OF THE UNIVERSE. CHANCE IS A CONCEPT—NOT A THING. CHANCE IS NO THING. N-o-T-H-i-N-G. AND NOTHING COMES FROM NOTHING.

RICH MELHEIM

DAY #7

MY FAVORITE VERSE FROM THE THEME WAS:

....

....

....

....

....

....

Most people approach prayer like they were talking to their dog. They expect a lot of sympathy, but not a lot of answers.

DO YOU REALIZE THE SMALLEST SINGLE-CELLED LIFE FORM IS A BACTERIA MADE UP OF 280 PROTEINS THAT ALL HAVE TO ASSEMBLE IN EXACTLY THE PERFECT SEQUENCE AND ORDER FOR IT TO HAVE EVOLVED ON ITS OWN?

YEAH. SO?

$1\% \times 10.^{128}$

LET ME PUT THIS IN PERSPECTIVE. DO YOU THINK IT IS THEORETICALLY POSSIBLE THAT ALL OF THE ATOMS IN THIS ROOM AT 2000°F WOULD CONGEAL AROUND YOUR BODY AND YOU WOULD SPONTANEOUSLY COMBUST AND BURN TO A CRISP RIGHT WHERE YOU STAND?

I DON'T LIE AWAKE AT NIGHT WORRYING ABOUT IT. NO.

THAT'S ONE TIMES 10,000,000,000,000,000,000,000,000,000,000,000,000,000,000,000,000,000,000,000,000,000,000,000,000,000,000,000,000,000,000,000,000,000,000,000!

BUT THE ODDS OF ALL THE HOT ATOMS AND MOLECULES GATHERING AROUND YOUR BODY ARE 1×10^{32}. IN OTHER WORDS, A TRILLION TRILLION, TRILLION, TRILLION, TRILLION, TRILLION, TRILLION TIMES MORE LIKELY THAT YOU COULD SPONTANEOUSLY COMBUST ON THE SPOT THAN THOSE FOR ONE SIMPLE SINGLE CELLED LIFE FORM TO HAVE EVOLVED WITH NO DIVINE INTERVENTION. WHAT DO YOU THINK OF THAT?

LOOKING BACK ON THESE TWO WEEKS, MY HIGHEST HIGH WAS:

....

MY LOWEST LOW THESE PAST WEEKS WAS:

....

ONE WAY GOD ANSWERED MY PRAYERS WAS:

....

ONE WAY GOD MIGHT USE ME AS A SACRED AGENT TO ANSWER THESE PRAYERS:

....

....

FAMILY COVENANT

We have shared *Highs & Lows* this week, read and highlighted the verses assigned in our Bibles, talked about our lives, prayed for one another's highs and lows, and blessed one another.

_____   _____   _____
Parent's Signature   Teen's Signature   Date

THE FINKMANIA QUIZBOWL

Question 1:

The moment before the Big Bang:

(A) There was no matter or energy,

(B) There was no time or space,

(C) Both A and B,

(D) All of the above and there was no homework, either

Question 2:

Chance is not a rational explanation for the origin of the universe because:

(A) Chance can only work on existing matter,

(B) Chance can only work within the context of matter, energy, time and space,

(C) Chance is a concept, and a concept cannot create a thing

(D) All the above

Question 3:

Coincidence is not a rational explanation for the origin of the universe because:

(A) For a coincidence to occur, you need at least two incidents,

(B) For a coincidence to occur, you need existing mass, energy, time and space

(C) Both A and B

(D) The universe isn't rational

Question 4:

When it was written thousands of years ago, the Bible explained which of the following things science is revealing today?:

(A) There was a Single Creation Event,

(B) The universe was created out of nothing,

(C) The universe is expanding,

(D) All of the above

Question 5:

In order for the simplest living cell to form you need:

(A) A mommy cell and a daddy cell

(B) Between 3 and 5 protein molecules,

(C) Between 30 and 50 protein molecules,

(D) Between 300 and 500 protein molecules, and they need to line up in absolute perfect order

Question 6:

In order for the simplest protein for this simplest cell to form you need:

(A) Between 12 and 20 DNA letters lined up perfectly,

(B) Between 120 and 200 DNA letters all lined up perfectly,

(C) Between 1200 and 2000 DNA letters all lined up perfectly

(D) C, and by the way, this is statistically impossible!

Question 7:

Human DNA:

(A) Contains 20-25,000 genes,

(B) Contains 3 billion chemical base pairs lined up,

(C) Has to be wound in exact perfect order on the twisted helix ladder or humans don't form,

(D) All of the above, and the odds of this happening are also statistically and mathematically impossible

Question 8:

Jesus Christ came to take away your sins, not:

(A) Your Brain,

(B) Your Brain,

(C) Your Brain

(D) All of the above—so don't be afraid to use it!

Question 9:

The word for something that stands "above the natural" in Latin is:

(A) The Big Bang,

(B) The Big Coincidence,

(C) The Big Fluke,

(D) Super-Natural

FINKmania Final Question:

The verse of the week, Job 11:7-12 tells us:

(A) God has a deep voice,

(B) God's creation is amazing and difficult for mere humans to understand,

(C) The Bible actually contains swear words,

(D) God has a credit limit on heaven's VISA®

Play this online game using FINKlink
LF25 | @ www.faithink.com

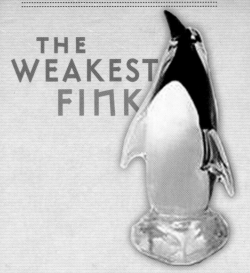

THE WEAKEST FINK

THE MORE I KNOW OF ASTRONOMY, THE MORE I BELIEVE IN GOD.

ASTRONOMER
HERBER D. CURTIS

TERMS
WRITE A DEFINITION BELOW.

BIG BANG

CHANCE

DESIGN

FIRST CAUSE

UNIVERSE

FAITH INKUBATORS

WAR & PEACE

"Freedom and Peace" Dr. He Qi. Order prints at www.heqiarts.com

"THEREFORE, JUST AS SIN CAME INTO THE WORLD THROUGH ONE

MAN, AND DEATH CAME THROUGH SIN, AND SO DEATH SPREAD TO

ALL BECAUSE ALL HAVE SINNED."

— ROMANS 5:12

Listen to this song using FINKlink
LF26 @ www.faithink.com

Dr. He Qi was riding in a taxi in Nanjing, China, on September 12, 2001. The buzz around the city—around the world—was the attack on America the day before.

Thousands of deaths had occurred on 9/11 when terrorists flew two airplanes into the World Trade Center Twin Towers and they collapsed. "It serves them right," said the taxi driver. "They got what they deserved." The artist was so shaken by these comments that he immediately stopped the taxi, stepped out, walked home, and painted the picture to the left.

On That Same Night

A world away in a small Minnesota town, a pastor knelt and kissed his babies good night. Then he sat down and wrote the following bedtime reflections:

I put my children to sleep tonight with a more somber tone than usual. Normally, if they have their teeth brushed and "jammies" on by 8 p.m., we do a little kick boxing, pillow fighting and weight training before devotions and prayers. But instead of our routine of raucous fun, this night started out differently.

We began with the story of Jesus' arrest in Matthew 26 and his "put away your sword" command. We talked about the violence done to Jesus and his unwillingness to allow Peter to pick up the sword in his defense. "Those who live by the sword will die by the sword," Jesus told his friends. Violence was not the answer to violence. Violence would only cause more violence.

We spoke of our sorrow for the unspeakable tragedy of the morning. We shared Highs & Lows for the day and had a little discussion. We prayed for the poor and powerless of the world who often pay the price for the sins of their leaders or a few fanatics in their midst. Then I found myself blessing my 12-year-old football player, Kathryn, and eight-year-old LEGO™ grandmaster, Joseph, with the strangest blessing they've ever received: "I hope this is the darkest night of your life," I whispered. "I hope and pray this is the most hateful, evil night you will ever know."

I'm not sure my not-so-little ones fully understood what their crazy dad was saying as he knelt down to kiss their foreheads and made the sign of the cross. I'm not sure I understood it, either. But deep down I fear the 911 call on 9.11.01 was only the first of many uglier nights. For when our collective national shock turns to anger — and it will — and that anger turns to rage, we may soon find our nation but a trip-wire away from the kind of blind stupidity that lashes out at innocents along with the guilty in some foreign lands half a world away. And that will only plant the seeds of hatred for many, many more nights like this.

Many more heartaches. Many more tears to come.

"I hope this is the darkest night of your life. The most hateful, evil night you will ever know."

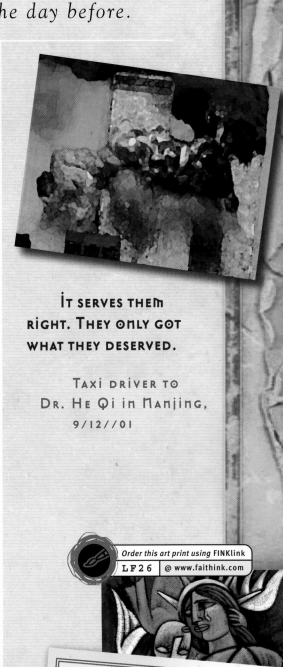

It serves them right. They only got what they deserved.

Taxi driver to Dr. He Qi in Nanjing, 9/12//01

Order this art print using FINKlink
LF26 | @ www.faithink.com

images in Art

- What do you see in today's painting by Dr. He Qi?

- Where are you in this work of art?

- How do the image and the verse apply to your life today?

So What Does This Mean?

EXACTLY WHAT KIND OF A CHURCH GROUP IS THIS?

Ez fer war, I call it
murder,—Ther you hev it
plain and flat;

    I don't want to go no
furder Than my Testyment
fer that.

    Ef you take a sword
an' dror it, An' go stick a
feller thru,

    Guv'ment aint to
answer for it, God'll send
the bill to you.

    Wut's the use of
meetin'-goin, Every Sab-
bath, wet or dry,

    Ef it's right to go a-
mowin Feller-men like oats
and rye?

    I dunno but wut it's
pooty Trainin' round in
bobtail coats,

    But it's curus Chris-
tian duty This 'ere cuttin'
o' folks' throats.

James Russel Lowell
(The Bigelow Papers)

Bible Time

Read and highlight Romans 5:12, writing "Why War?" in the margin. Then look up the following verses. What does Jesus say about war and peace?

Matthew 5:9

Matthew 26:52

Matthew 5:38-39

Matthew 5:43-45a

Luke 19:41-42

Role Play

1. A friend says, "The Bible teaches an eye for an eye and a tooth for a tooth." How do you answer?

2. A teacher you respect says, "It is impractical, unrealistic, unhealthy and impossible to love like Jesus. Whether on a personal or national basis, you will invite more abuse by not defending yourself." How do you respond?

Prayer

Holy God, we come to you in confusion, shock and sorrow at the level of hate that fills our world. The powers of evil are so close and so quick to grip us. We are helpless and hopeless without you, not knowing where to turn or what to do.

Lord Jesus, you are always faithful to us and quick to show mercy. Show mercy on both the victims and the perpetrators of war and evil, that they may know the things that make for peace.

Holy Spirit, comfort those who mourn. Forgive those who, in their anger, lash out in hateful acts. Empower and encourage us called by your name to live our lives, shape our words, and make all of our decisions following the example of the one we call our Lord, Jesus Christ. In your merciful name we pray. Amen.

Questions to Ponder

1. The book of Ecclesiastes tells us there is a time for war and a time for peace. How does a follower of Christ determine the difference?

2. Is war ever the answer? Under what conditions would you consider a war a "just war?" What would Jesus say?

3. When someone hurts you, how do you balance your physical need for security and the emotional desire for revenge with Christ's anti-violent words and example?

Small Group
SHARE, READ, TALK, PRAY, BLESS

So, what's a **"just war?"**

That's an awfully **big** question for such a little person.

1. **SHARE** your highs and lows of the week one-on-one with another person. Listen carefully and record your friend's thoughts in the space below. Then return to small group and share your friend's highs and lows.

   MY HIGHS + LOWS THIS WEEK WERE:

   ....

   MY FRIEND'S HIGHS + LOWS THIS WEEK WERE:

   ....

2. **READ** and highlight the theme verse in your Bibles. Circle key words and learn the verse in song.

3. **TALK** about how today's verse relates to your highs and lows. Review the art for today, the Quiz Bowl questions, the terms, and the cartoons. Then write a sentence on each of the following:

   ONE NEW THING I LEARNED TODAY:

   ....

   ONE THING I ALREADY KNEW THAT IS WORTH REPEATING:

   ....

   ONE THING I WOULD LIKE TO KNOW MORE ABOUT:

   ....

4. **PRAY** for one another, praising and thanking God for your highs, and asking God to be with you in your lows. Include your friend's highs and lows in your prayers.

   A PRAISING PRAYER: ....

   A THANKING PRAYER: ....

   AN ASKING PRAYER: ....

5. **BLESS** one another using the blessing of the week. (right) Mark each person with the sign of the cross as you bless them.

THIS WEEK'S BLESSING

(NAME), CHILD OF GOD, MAY YOU BE A POWERFUL FORCE FOR PEACE IN JESUS' NAME. AMEN.

THE HOME HUDDLE jOURNAL
SHARE, READ, tALK, PRAY, BLESS

Read the full devotions using FINKlink
LF26 @ www.faithink.com

DAY #1

TODAY'S BIBLE VERSE:

Romans 5:12

Therefore, just as sin came into the world through one man, and death came through sin, and so death spread to all because all have sinned.

MY HIGH TODAY WAS:

MY LOW TODAY WAS:

MY PRAYER TODAY IS:

DAY #2

TODAY'S BIBLE VERSE:

Matthew 5:9

Blessed are the peacemakers, for they will be called children of God.

MY HIGH TODAY WAS:

MY LOW TODAY WAS:

MY PRAYER TODAY IS:

DAY #3

TODAY'S BIBLE VERSE:

Matthew 5:38-39

You have heard that it was said, "An eye for an eye and a tooth for a tooth." But I say to you, Do not resist an evildoer. But if anyone strikes you on the right cheek, turn the other also.

MY HIGH TODAY WAS:

MY LOW TODAY WAS:

MY PRAYER TODAY IS:

my HIGH today was:

my LOW today was:

my PRAYER today is:

DAY #4

TODAY'S BIBLE VERSE:
Matthew 5:43-45a

You have heard that it was said, "You shall love your neighbor and hate your enemy," But I say to you, Love your enemies and pray for those who persecute you, so that you may be children of your Father in heaven.

---

my HIGH today was:

my LOW today was:

my PRAYER today is:

DAY #5

TODAY'S BIBLE VERSE:
Matthew 26:52

Then Jesus said to him, "Put your sword back into its place; for all who take the sword will perish by the sword."

---

my HIGH today was:

my LOW today was:

my PRAYER today is:

DAY #6

TODAY'S BIBLE VERSE:
Luke 19:41-42

As he came near and saw the city, he wept over it, saying, "If you, even you, had only recognized on this day the things that make for peace! But now they are hidden from your eyes."

---

my HIGHEST HIGH this week was:

my LOWEST LOW this week was:

my PRAYER for next week is:

DAY #7

THIS WEEK'S BLESSING

(NAME), CHILD OF GOD, MAY YOU BE A POWERFUL FORCE FOR PEACE IN JESUS' NAME. AMEN.

Exactly how many guns and bombs does a Christian need?

One more. Always just one more.

THE HOME HUDDLE JOURNAL

SHARE, READ, TALK, PRAY, BLESS

WEEK 2

Read the full devotions using FINKlink
LF26 | @ www.faithink.com

DAY #1

TODAY'S BIBLE VERSE:
Romans 12:19

Beloved, never avenge yourselves, but leave room for the wrath of God; for it is written, "Vengeance is mine, I will repay, says the Lord."

MY **HIGH** TODAY WAS:

MY **LOW** TODAY WAS:

MY **PRAYER** TODAY IS:

DAY #2

TODAY'S BIBLE VERSE:
Matthew 5:4-7

Blessed are those who mourn, for they will be comforted. Blessed are the meek, for they will inherit the earth. Blessed are those who hunger and thirst for righteousness, for they will be filled. Blessed are the merciful, for they will receive mercy.

MY **HIGH** TODAY WAS:

MY **LOW** TODAY WAS:

MY **PRAYER** TODAY IS:

DAY #3

TODAY'S BIBLE VERSE:
Matthew 18:21-22

Then Peter came and said to him, "Lord, if another member of the church sins against me, how often should I forgive? As many as seven times?" Jesus said to him, "Not seven times, but, I tell you, seventy-seven times."

MY **HIGH** TODAY WAS:

MY **LOW** TODAY WAS:

MY **PRAYER** TODAY IS:

1. SHARE HIGHS & LOWS OF THE DAY.

2. READ AND HIGHLIGHT THE VERSE OF THE DAY IN YOUR BIBLES.

3. TALK ABOUT HOW TODAY'S VERSE RELATES TO YOUR HIGHS & LOWS.

4. PRAY FOR YOUR HIGHS & LOWS, FOR YOUR FAMILY AND FOR THE WORLD.

5. BLESS ONE ANOTHER USING THIS WEEK'S BLESSING (ON THE PREVIOUS PAGE).

MY HIGH TODAY WAS:

MY LOW TODAY WAS:

MY PRAYER TODAY IS:

"FOR WHAT IS JUST WAR BUT THE PUNISHMENT OF EVILDOERS AND THE MAINTENANCE OF PEACE?

DAY #4

TODAY'S BIBLE VERSE:
MATTHEW 25:40

And the king will answer them, "Truly I tell you, just as you did it to one of the least of these who are members of my family, you did it to me."

MY HIGH TODAY WAS:

MY LOW TODAY WAS:

MY PRAYER TODAY IS:

DAY #5

TODAY'S BIBLE VERSE:
ROMANS 15:13

May the God of hope fill you with all joy and peace in believing, so that you may abound in hope by the power of the Holy Spirit.

MY HIGH TODAY WAS:

MY LOW TODAY WAS:

MY PRAYER TODAY IS:

DAY #6

TODAY'S BIBLE VERSE:
LUKE 23:34

Father, forgive them; for they do not know what they are doing.

THEME IN REVIEW

VOICE OR NO VOICE, THE PEOPLE CAN ALWAYS BE BROUGHT TO THE BIDDING OF THE LEADERS. THAT IS EASY. ALL YOU HAVE TO DO IS TO TELL THEM THEY ARE BEING ATTACKED, AND DENOUNCE THE PACIFISTS FOR LACK OF PATRIOTISM AND EXPOSING THE COUNTRY TO DANGER. IT WORKS THE SAME IN ANY COUNTRY.

HERMANN GOERRING

DAY #7

MY FAVORITE VERSE FROM THE THEME WAS:

....
....
....
....
....
....
....

FOR WHAT IS JUST WAR BUT THE PUNISHMENT OF EVILDOERS AND THE MAINTENANCE OF PEACE?

MARTIN LUTHER

LOOKING BACK ON THESE TWO WEEKS, MY HIGHEST HIGH WAS:

....

MY LOWEST LOW THESE PAST WEEKS WAS:

....

ONE WAY GOD ANSWERED MY PRAYERS WAS:

....

ONE WAY GOD MIGHT USE ME AS A SACRED AGENT TO ANSWER THESE PRAYERS:

....

....

FAMILY COVENANT

We have shared *Highs & Lows* this week, read and highlighted the verses assigned in our Bibles, talked about our lives, prayed for one another's highs and lows, and blessed one another.

....
Parent's Signature   Teen's Signature   Date

THE FINKMANIA QUIZBOWL

Question 1:

Jesus said, "Blessed are the peacemakers, for they shall be called...":

(A) Unpatriotic,

(B) Un-American,

(C) Un-realistic

(D) None of the above

Question 2:

Mohandas Gandhi said: "An eye for an eye makes the whole world...":

(A) Blind,

(B) Even,

(C) Stupid,

(D) See better

Question 3:

Eleanor Roosevelt said: "Either all of us are going to die together or we are going to learn to live together; and if we are to live together we have to...:"

(A) Do lunch more often,

(B) Learn how to take a joke,

(C) Let the women be in charge for a change,

(D) Talk

Question 4:

Bart Simpson said: "There are no good wars, with the following exceptions: The American Revolution, World War II, and..."

(A) The first Gulf War,

(B) The current Gulf War,

(C) The next Gulf War (once Iran gets nukes),

(D) The Star Wars Trilogy

Question 5:

Jesus said: "Put away your sword! Those who live by the sword will..."

(A) Die by the sword,

(B) Die by the sword,

(C) Die by the sword,

(D) All of the above (get the picture?)

Question 6:

WWII-era pastor Dietrich Bonhoeffer said, "If I see a madman driving a car into a group of innocent bystanders... ":

(A) I can't simply wait for the catastrophe and then comfort the wounded and bury the dead,

(B) I will hope the victims had AFLAC,

(C) I will close my eyes and pray real hard about it,

(D) I'll wait around for the TV news to show up

Question 7:

Martin Luther, the Protestant Reformer, said: "For what is a 'just war' but the punishment of evil doers and the maintenance of...":

(A) Peace,

(B) Pride,

(C) The Statue Quo,

(D) Oil at a decent price

Question 8:

Jeanette Rankin, the first woman in the US House of Representatives, said:

(A) You can no more win a war than you can win an earthquake,

(B) War. Huah! Good God, y'all, what is it good for?

(C) It's the end of the world as we know it, and I feel fine,

(D) Civilian deaths? Naw, it's just collateral damage...

Question 9:

Albert Einstein said: "I do not know with what weapons World War 3 will be fought, but World War 4 will be fought with...":

(A) Broken beer bottles and tire irons,

(B) Sticks and stones,

(C) Nuclear weapons and nerve gas,

(D) Character smears and insults

FINKmania Final Question:

In Romans 5:12, Paul says "Death came to all because..."

(A) All sinned,

(B) God is vengeful,

(C) Living forever would be boring,

(D) You gotta go sometime

Play this online game using FINKlink
LF26 @ www.faithink.com

THE WEAKEST FINK

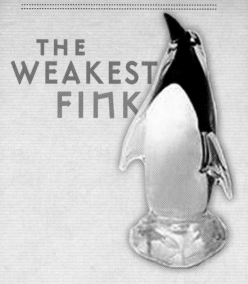

AN EYE FOR AN EYE MAKES THE WHOLE WORLD BLIND.

MOHANDAS GANDHI

TERMS
WRITE A DEFINITION BELOW.

DEATH

GENOCIDE

JUST WAR

VENGEANCE

WAR

FAITH INKUBATORS

SUICIDE

A Panel from "Creation" Dr. He Qi. Order prints at www.heqiarts.com

"AS A DEER LONGS FOR FLOWING STREAMS, SO MY SOUL LONGS

FOR YOU, O GOD. WHY ARE YOU CAST DOWN, O MY SOUL,

AND WHY ARE YOU DISQUIETED WITHIN ME? HOPE IN GOD;

FOR I SHALL AGAIN PRAISE HIM, MY HELP AND MY GOD."

— PSALM 42:1, 5-6A

Listen to this song using FINKlink
LF27 | @ www.faithink.com

*T*erry was a tall, good-looking star of most every sport at his high school. Marcus was a loner. Nobody really knew him. Dale was the most popular youth pastor in the city.

Terry was the pitcher of the baseball team, goalie of the hockey team, and first chair trumpet in the school band. Marcus was quite the opposite. He was the short quiet kid. Not a lot of people knew he had any talents, although he wrote some beautiful poetry late at night while fixing things in his dad's garage. Dale could get literally hundreds of kids out for anything he planned at church. He always drove a flashy car or new motorcycle.

Terry went away to college and didn't get the royal treatment he was used to getting at his high school. He came home for homecoming, waited out on a highway, and jumped in front of a truck. Marcus came home a few weeks after Terry's funeral and found his old girlfriend in love with someone else. He gave his mom his laundry, kissed her good night, went into his basement, put a shotgun in his mouth and pulled the trigger. Dale, the youth pastor, waited until the day when the leaders of his community were going to award him with the Outstanding Young Adult award. He walked into his garage, turned on his SUV, lay himself down on the cement and never woke up.

Three sad stories. Three true stories. The names were changed. That's it.

The star athlete's dad had a heart attack within a few months of his suicide. The quiet kid's mom died a year after burying her son. The autopsy said she died of a stroke, but her husband knew better. She died of a broken heart. And Dale's church? Some kids from his youth group lost their faith in God, left the church and never came back. True again.

Mass Murder?

Some see suicide as the ultimate sin. It is a hijacking of something precious that doesn't belong to you—God's temple—and destroying it so nothing can be done with it ever again. Some say suicide is the most selfish act one can accomplish. It is like telling everyone who loves you that you won't let them into your pain. Some see suicide as the most powerful act of idolatry and defiance against God. It is making yourself into your own little god, then telling the creator that not even the Almighty God of the Universe is big enough to fix your problems. Some see suicide in even darker terms. When you kill yourself, you don't just kill yourself. You kill a little piece of everyone who ever loved you. If that's the case, every suicide is a mass murder.

Before making any judgments about anyone's suicide, it is important to know that Jesus ordered his followers not to judge anyone. He said Christians should simply love one another and leave the judgment to God. Period.

SUICIDE IS A PERMANENT SOLUTION TO A TEMPORARY PROBLEM.

Anonymous

Order this art print using FINKlink
LF27 @ www.faithink.com

IMAGES in ART

● What do you see in today's painting by Dr. He Qi?

● Where are you in this work of art?

● How do the image and the verse apply to your life today?

So What Does This Mean?

EVERY SUICIDE IS A MASS Murder

Methun '06

PRAYER

DEAR GOD, HELP ME TO RUN TO YOU WHEN I WANT TO RUN AWAY. HELP ME TO TRUST IN YOUR LOVE WHEN I CAN'T SEE ANY POSSIBLE GOOD COMING FROM THE BAD SITUATIONS IN MY LIFE. HELP ME TO KNOW THAT I AM NEVER ALONE, AND THAT YOU ARE ALWAYS BIGGER THAN MY BIGGEST PROBLEMS.

AMEN.

Is Suicide ever Sane?

Psychologists say that the will to live is one of the strongest instincts we posses. It is normal, rational, and sane to want to live. But some people who have gone through extreme physical pain will tell you there comes a point where your will to live—even as strong as it is—simply buckles under the pain. Would you judge a hopelessly suffering person? Could you condemn someone who was in such terrible pain if they wanted to slip away to be with God? No. They wouldn't need your judgment. They would simply need your love and understanding. So much for physical pain. Now imagine being in so much emotional or spiritual pain that you couldn't think rationally. Can you imagine being in so much mental anguish that everything seems hopeless, inescapable and unbearable? A person in that situation doesn't need your judgment, either. Followers of Jesus don't judge people in pain. They try to love them.

Next time you are depressed, remember this: As long as you have life, you have hope. As long as you have breath, there's a chance things will change. As long as you have Christ, even the grave is not the end. Nothing is hopeless to our awesome God. If you wouldn't let a friend get beat up, why would you beat yourself up? If you wouldn't leave a friend alone to suffer in their depression, despair, and hopelessness, why would you let yourself suffer alone? Maybe we need to learn to love ourselves with the kind of love Jesus has for us. God will give you a new tomorrow. Will you give it to yourself?

BIBLE TIME

Read and highlight Psalm 42:1, 5-6a in your Bible, writing "Hope in God!" in the margins. King David had plenty of depression in his life. Read Psalm 22. Jesus quoted it from the cross. Write "See Matthew 27:46" in the margin and flip to the Matthew verse and write "See Psalm 22" in the margin. Now turn to the Psalms and find three other verses that show how David handled his suffering.

ROLE PLAY

1. A friend who has been very depressed for months is suddenly extremely happy. They start giving all of their favorite possessions away. Confront them.

2. After a painful break up, your best friend tells you he wants to die. Respond.

QUESTIONS TO PONDER

1. Do you think suicide is an unforgivable sin? Why or why not?

2. What are three things you can do for friends when they are depressed? Will you be enough of a friend to yourself and do these things for yourself next time your spirits are down?

Small Group
SHARE, READ, TALK, PRAY, BLESS

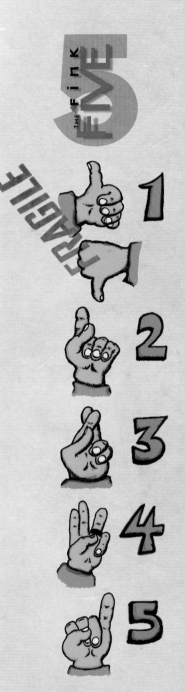

1. **S H A R E** your highs and lows of the week one-on-one with another person. Listen carefully and record your friend's thoughts in the space below. Then return to small group and share your friend's highs and lows.

   MY HIGHS + LOWS THIS WEEK WERE:

   ....

   MY FRIEND'S HIGHS + LOWS THIS WEEK WERE:

   ....

2. **R E A D** and highlight the theme verse in your Bibles. Circle key words and learn the verse in song.

3. **T A L K** about how today's verse relates to your highs and lows. Review the art for today, the Quiz Bowl questions, the terms, and the cartoons. Then write a sentence on each of the following:

   ONE NEW THING I LEARNED TODAY:

   ....

   ONE THING I ALREADY KNEW THAT IS WORTH REPEATING:

   ....

   ONE THING I WOULD LIKE TO KNOW MORE ABOUT:

   ....

4. **P R A Y** for one another, praising and thanking God for your highs, and asking God to be with you in your lows. Include your friend's highs and lows in your prayers.

   A PRAISING PRAYER: ....

   A THANKING PRAYER: ....

   AN ASKING PRAYER: ....

5. **B L E S S** one another using the blessing of the week. (right) Mark each person with the sign of the cross as you bless them.

THIS WEEK'S BLESSING

(NAME), CHILD OF GOD, MAY YOU ALWAYS KNOW THAT GOD IS BIGGER THAN YOUR BIGGEST PROBLEMS.

THE HOME HUDDLE jOURNAL
SHARE, READ, tALK, PRAY, BLESS

Read the full devotions using FINKlink
LF27 @ www.faithink.com

DAY #1

TODAY'S BIBLE VERSE:

PSALM 42:1

As a deer longs for flowing streams, so my soul longs for you, O God.

MY **HIGH** TODAY WAS:

MY **LOW** TODAY WAS:

MY **PRAYER** TODAY IS:

DAY #2

TODAY'S BIBLE VERSE:

PSALM 42:5-6A

Why are you cast down, O my soul, and why are you disquieted within me? Hope in God; for I shall again praise him, my help and my God.

MY **HIGH** TODAY WAS:

MY **LOW** TODAY WAS:

MY **PRAYER** TODAY IS:

DAY #3

TODAY'S BIBLE VERSE:

PSALM 40:1-2

I waited patiently for the Lord; he inclined to me and heard my cry. He drew me up from the desolate pit, out of the miry bog, and set my feet upon a rock, making my steps secure.

MY **HIGH** TODAY WAS:

MY **LOW** TODAY WAS:

MY **PRAYER** TODAY IS:

MY HIGH TODAY WAS:

MY LOW TODAY WAS:

MY PRAYER TODAY IS:

TODAY'S BIBLE VERSE:

PSALM 27:1

The Lord is my light and my salvation; whom shall I fear? The Lord is the stronghold of my life; of whom shall I be afraid?

MY HIGH TODAY WAS:

MY LOW TODAY WAS:

MY PRAYER TODAY IS:

DAY #5

TODAY'S BIBLE VERSE:

NAHUM 1:7-8A

The Lord is good, a stronghold in a day of trouble; he protects those who take refuge in him, even in a rushing flood.

MY HIGH TODAY WAS:

MY LOW TODAY WAS:

MY PRAYER TODAY IS:

DAY #6

TODAY'S BIBLE VERSE:

JONAH 2:7

As my life was ebbing away, I remembered the Lord; and my prayer came to you, into your holy temple.

MY HIGHEST HIGH THIS WEEK WAS:

MY LOWEST LOW THIS WEEK WAS:

MY PRAYER FOR NEXT WEEK IS:

DAY #7

THIS WEEK'S BLESSING

(NAME), CHILD OF GOD, MAY YOU ALWAYS KNOW THAT GOD IS BIGGER THAN YOUR BIGGEST PROBLEMS.

Good thing we have a **big** God.

I've got big problems!

THE HOME HUDDLE JOURNAL

SHARE, READ, TALK, PRAY, BLESS

WEEK 2

Read the full devotions using FINKlink

LF27 | @ www.faithink.com

DAY #1

TODAY'S BIBLE VERSE:

PSALM 22:1

My God, my God, why have you forsaken me? Why are you so far from helping me, from the words of my groaning?

MY **HIGH** TODAY WAS:

MY **LOW** TODAY WAS:

MY **PRAYER** TODAY IS:

DAY #2

TODAY'S BIBLE VERSE:

ROMANS 5:3B-5

Suffering produces endurance, and endurance produces character, and character produces hope, and hope does not disappoint us, because God's love has been poured into our hearts through the Holy Spirit that has been given to us.

MY **HIGH** TODAY WAS:

MY **LOW** TODAY WAS:

MY **PRAYER** TODAY IS:

DAY #3

TODAY'S BIBLE VERSE:

ROMANS 8:1

There is therefore now no condemnation for those who are in Christ Jesus.

MY **HIGH** TODAY WAS:

MY **LOW** TODAY WAS:

MY **PRAYER** TODAY IS:

1. **SHARE** HIGHS & LOWS OF THE DAY.

2. **READ** AND HIGHLIGHT THE VERSE OF THE DAY IN YOUR BIBLES.

3. **TALK** ABOUT HOW TODAY'S VERSE RELATES TO YOUR HIGHS & LOWS.

4. **PRAY** FOR YOUR HIGHS & LOWS, FOR YOUR FAMILY AND FOR THE WORLD.

5. **BLESS** ONE ANOTHER USING THIS WEEK'S BLESSING (ON THE PREVIOUS PAGE).

MY HIGH TODAY WAS:

MY LOW TODAY WAS:

MY PRAYER TODAY IS:

DAY #4

TODAY'S BIBLE VERSE:

Romans 8:26

Likewise the Spirit helps us in our weakness; for we do not know how to pray as we ought, but that very Spirit intercedes with sighs too deep for words.

MY HIGH TODAY WAS:

MY LOW TODAY WAS:

MY PRAYER TODAY IS:

DAY #5

TODAY'S BIBLE VERSE:

Romans 8:28

We know that all things work together for good for those who love God, who are called according to his purpose.

MY HIGH TODAY WAS:

MY LOW TODAY WAS:

MY PRAYER TODAY IS:

DAY #6

TODAY'S BIBLE VERSE:

Romans 15:13

May the God of hope fill you with all joy and peace in believing, so that you may abound in hope by the power of the Holy Spirit.

THEME IN REVIEW

RAZORS PAIN YOU
RIVERS ARE DAMP
ACIDS STAIN YOU
AND DRUGS CAUSE CRAMP
GUN'S AREN'T LAWFUL
NOOSES GIVE
GAS SMELLS AWFUL
YOU MIGHT AS WELL LIVE.

DOROTHY PARKER

DAY #7

MY FAVORITE VERSE
FROM THE THEME WAS:

....
....
....
....
....
....
....
....

LOOKING BACK ON THESE TWO WEEKS, MY HIGHEST HIGH WAS:

....

MY LOWEST LOW THESE PAST WEEKS WAS:

....

ONE WAY GOD ANSWERED MY PRAYERS WAS:

....

ONE WAY GOD MIGHT USE ME AS A SACRED AGENT
TO ANSWER THESE PRAYERS:

....

....

FAMILY COVENANT

We have shared *Highs & Lows* this week, read and highlighted the verses assigned in our Bibles, talked about our lives, prayed for one another's highs and lows, and blessed one another.

_____   _____   _____

Parent's Signature   *Teen's Signature*   *Date*

THE FINKMANIA QUIZ BOWL

Question 1:

God's gift of life is:

(A) One big cosmic joke, and the joke's on us

(B) A precious gift,

(C) Better than a neck tie,

(D) B and C

Question 2:

Life is God's gift to us, what we do with our lives is:

(A) Nobody's business but our own,

(B) Our gift to God,

(C) Directly proportional to how thankful and thoughtful we are,

(D) B and C (and your body is a temple that belongs to God, remember?)

Question 3:

Suicide is:

(A) A permanent solution to a temporary problem,

(B) A permanent solution to a temporary problem,

(C) A permanent solution to a temporary problem,

(D) All of the above, except that it doesn't really solve the problem

Question 4:

The statement "No one can ever just kill themselves" means:

(A) When we kill ourselves, we also kill a part of everyone who loves us,

(B) Every suicide is a mass murder,

(C) They also kill their future, and the futures of all of the people whose lives they could have touched,

(D) All of the above

Question 5:

Suicide only affects this type of person:

(A) The nerds,

(B) The Jocks,

(C) The neglected,

(D) All of the above and more

Question 6:

If a depressed friend suddenly seems cheery and starts giving all of their favorite possessions away, you should:

(A) Confront them—it's one of the warning signs that they may be close to suicide,

(B) Say nothing—it's their business

(C) Get them some help,

(D) Both A and C

Question 7:

This King wrote some beautiful, sad and gripping poem and prayers of anguish to God which were fueled by his depression:

(A) King Lear,

(B) King Kong,

(C) King David,

(D) Elvis

Question 8:

This is a gift of God that awaits you when you are in pain and despair:

(A) Dr. Phil,

(B) Oprah,

(C) The Psychic Friends Network,

(D) The Comforter (One name Jesus called the Holy Spirit)

Question 9:

If someone you know is contemplating suicide, you should:

(A) Get help immediately,

(B) Tell them to quit being so stupid,

(C) Tell them they are going to hell for even thinking about it,

(D) Leave them alone and hope for the best

FINKmania Final Question:

The gift King David talks about that can fill our longing is:

(A) Material things,

(B) Status,

(C) Hope in God,

(D) None of the above

Play this online game using FINKlink
LF27 @ www.faithink.com

THE WEAKEST FINK

FRAGILE

If we had no winter, the spring would not be so pleasant; if we did not sometimes taste of adversity, prosperity would not be so welcome.

— Anne Bradstreet

TERMS
WRITE A DEFINITION BELOW.

Depression

Despair

Hope

Hopelessness

Suicide

FAITH INKUBATORS

Stewardship of Time

"Women Arriving at the Tomb" Dr. He Qi: Order prints at www.heqiarts.com

ONE OF THE SCRIBES CAME NEAR AND HEARD THEM DISPUTING

WITH ONE ANOTHER, AND SEEING THAT HE ANSWERED THEM WELL,

HE ASKED HIM, "WHICH COMMANDMENT IS THE FIRST OF ALL?"

JESUS ANSWERED, "THE FIRST IS, 'HEAR, O ISRAEL: THE LORD

OUR GOD, THE LORD IS ONE; YOU SHALL LOVE THE LORD YOUR

GOD WITH ALL YOUR HEART, AND WITH ALL YOUR SOUL, AND

WITH ALL YOUR MIND, AND WITH ALL YOUR STRENGTH.'"

— MARK 12:28-30

Listen to this song using FINKlink
LF28 @ www.faithink.com

Riddle: You've got exactly as much of this today as Oprah, Bill Gates, and the king of Saudi Arabia. What's the answer?

Time!

Whether you're Donald Trump or the guy who shines his shoes, you've got 24 hours today. 1440 minutes. 86,400 seconds. Your heart will beat 100,000 times today, 35 million times this year and 2.5 billion times in your life. All this time and all these heartbeats will come to you whether you value them as a gift or waste them away. The time is yours whether you cherish and invest it as a precious treasure or use it to accomplish nothing at all. You've got just as much of this priceless commodity today as anyone else in the world. And you can't buy another minute of it if you were the richest person on earth.

Speaking of riches, you can always make more money. You will never make more time. You can always find another place to live if your house floods or disappears in a tornado. You can always get another backpack or skateboard or mountain bike if it is stolen. You can always find another job if you get laid off, fired, or fall asleep and burn the McDonalds down. You can replace almost every material possession. The only thing you can't replace is time. Since that's the case, time is the most valuable commodity you possess. How should a person use it? How can we make the most of it?

Don't Hold Your Breath

Hold your breath for one minute. Ready? Go! Watch a clock or count to sixty. Come on. Hold on. There. Guess what? That minute is gone. Gone forever. You will never get it back. Was holding your breath a good way to use it?

Some people live their whole lives holding their breath. They sit around accomplishing little or nothing with their time. They don't try anything that seems too difficult. They don't risk getting out of their comfort zones. They don't find it convenient to help others in need. They waste these priceless, unrenewable minutes and hours wishing they were someone else or somewhere else. They spend countless hours watching other peoples' lives on television and in the movies. They live as fantasy characters on video screens because they think their own lives aren't as interesting, powerful or meaningful, squandering the one thing they'll never get back. And then they wonder why they feel empty inside.

Maybe the biggest tragedy in life isn't to die young, but to never have really lived before you die.

Will you let that happen to you?

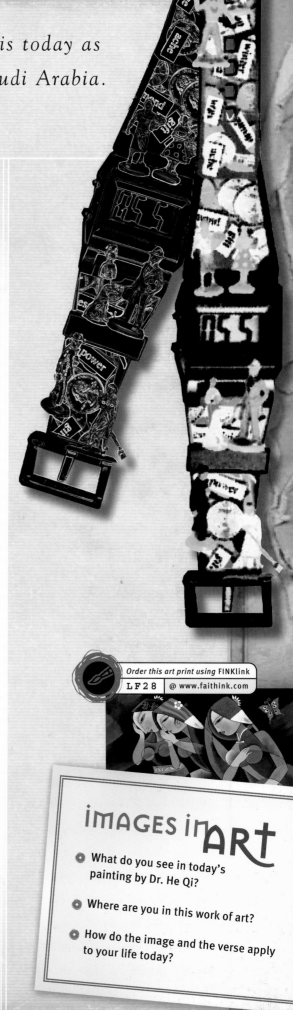

Order this art print using FINKlink
LF28 @ www.faithink.com

images in Art

- What do you see in today's painting by Dr. He Qi?

- Where are you in this work of art?

- How do the image and the verse apply to your life today?

So What Does This Mean?

WHY DO I GO ON THE PRAYER RETREAT EVERY YEAR? HECK, AS LONG AS I AM GOING TO SPEND ETERNITY WITH GOD, I FIGURE I MIGHT AS WELL GET TO KNOW HIM A BIT NOW!

+DOUBLE DARE: When finished with ROLE PLAY 2, ask your parents or pastor to give you the name of a real person who can't or doesn't leave the house much and get some friends to do a servant event by spending some time with them. Do it!

BIBLE TIME

Lou Holtz, the famous Notre Dame football coach, says, "Killing time isn't murder. It's suicide." Read and highlight Mark 12:30 writing "Life is short. Live and love!" in the margin. The Psalmist said a thousand years is nothing in God's sight. It comes and goes like the grass. We might get 70 years. (Maybe a little more if we buckle our seat belts, don't smoke, and were born with good genetics.) Then what? We're gone.

Maybe if life is so short, we ought to think about living every moment. Squeezing all of the nectar out of every second, every breath, and every heartbeat. Turn off the TV and put down the video game and do something that matters. Something that might last beyond our 70 short years. Build something great that will bless the world. Invent something marvelous that will heal the world. Invest time and money and energy in efforts that bring a little of God's kingdom to earth. Share Christ with someone who doesn't know him. Instead of pouting about what you don't have, celebrate what you do. Put aside fears and worries and inhibitions and live like every moment matters.

Try it. We dare you. We double dare you. We triple-dog dare you. Maybe then you'll finally realize you're already as rich as Oprah, Bill Gates and the king of Saudi Arabia.

ROLE PLAY

1. A friend spends all of her extra time in front of a computer screen. You ask her to go on a mission trip with you and she says she doesn't have time.

2. A classmate has a rare blood disease and must spend hours every week sitting quietly getting transfusions. You ask some other friends to spend some time with this classmate. They don't want to. What do you do? What do you say?*

PRAYER

Dear God, help me to invest the time you give me, not to simply spend it. Help me use it wisely, to do things that matter. In Jesus' name. Amen.

QUESTIONS TO PONDER

1. Look back on last week. Where did you spend most of your time? Did you spend it or invest it? (Are you seeing any dividends?)

2. What did you consider a good use of your time last week? What do you consider a personal waste of your time?

3. If you only had a limited amount of time to live—and you do—how can you make the most of tomorrow?

Small Group
SHARE, READ, TALK, PRAY, BLESS

1. **SHARE** your highs and lows of the week one-on-one with another person. Listen carefully and record your friend's thoughts in the space below. Then return to small group and share your friend's highs and lows.

   MY HIGHS + LOWS THIS WEEK WERE:

   ....

   MY FRIEND'S HIGHS + LOWS THIS WEEK WERE:

   ....

2. **READ** and highlight the theme verse in your Bibles. Circle key words and learn the verse in song.

3. **TALK** about how today's verse relates to your highs and lows. Review the art for today, the Quiz Bowl questions, the terms, and the cartoons. Then write a sentence on each of the following:

   ONE NEW THING I LEARNED TODAY:

   ....

   ONE THING I ALREADY KNEW THAT IS WORTH REPEATING:

   ....

   ONE THING I WOULD LIKE TO KNOW MORE ABOUT:

   ....

4. **PRAY** for one another, praising and thanking God for your highs, and asking God to be with you in your lows. Include your friend's highs and lows in your prayers.

   A PRAISING PRAYER: ....

   A THANKING PRAYER: ....

   AN ASKING PRAYER: ....

5. **BLESS** one another using the blessing of the week. (right) Mark each person with the sign of the cross as you bless them.

THIS WEEK'S BLESSING

(NAME), CHILD OF GOD, YOUR TIME IS A PRECIOUS GIFT FROM GOD. USE IT FOR GOD'S GLORY. AMEN.

THE HOME HUDDLE JOURNAL
SHARE, READ, TALK, PRAY, BLESS

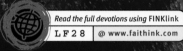
Read the full devotions using FINKlink
LF28 @ www.faithink.com

DAY #1

today's bible verse:

Deuteronomy 6:4-5

Hear, O Israel: The Lord is our God, the Lord alone. You shall love the Lord your God with all your heart, and with all your soul and with all your might.

my HIGH today was:

my LOW today was:

my PRAYER today is:

DAY #2

today's bible verse:

Deuteronomy 6:6-7

Keep these words that I am commanding you today in your heart. Recite them to your children and talk about them when you are at home and when you are away, when you lie down and when you rise.

my HIGH today was:

my LOW today was:

my PRAYER today is:

DAY #3

today's bible verse:

Ecclesiastes 3:1

For everything there is a season, and a time for every matter under heaven.

Do you have the time?

That's really the question, isn't it?

my HIGH today was:

my LOW today was:

my PRAYER today is:

my HIGH today was: _____

my LOW today was: _____

my PRAYER today is: _____

_____

DAY #4

TODAY'S BIBLE VERSE:

Psalm 90:4-5a

For a thousand years in your sight are like yesterday when it is past, or like a watch in the night. You sweep them away; they are like a dream.

---

my HIGH today was: _____

my LOW today was: _____

my PRAYER today is: _____

DAY #5

TODAY'S BIBLE VERSE:

Psalm 90:10

The days of our life are seventy years, or perhaps eighty, if we are strong; even then their span is only toil and trouble; they are soon gone, and we fly away.

---

my HIGH today was: _____

my LOW today was: _____

my PRAYER today is: _____

DAY #6

TODAY'S BIBLE VERSE:

Psalm 90:12

So teach us to count our days that we may gain a wise heart.

---

my HIGHEST HIGH this week was: _____

my LOWEST LOW this week was: _____

my PRAYER for next week is: _____

_____

DAY #7

THIS WEEK'S BLESSING

(NAME), CHILD OF GOD, YOUR TIME IS A PRECIOUS GIFT FROM GOD. USE IT FOR GOD'S GLORY. AMEN.

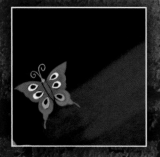

THE HOME HUDDLE JOURNAL
SHARE, READ, TALK, PRAY, BLESS

WEEK 2

Read the full devotions using FINKlink
LF28 | @ www.faithink.com

DAY #1

TODAY'S BIBLE VERSE:

COLOSSIANS 4:5-6

Conduct yourselves wisely toward outsiders, making the most of the time. Let your speech always be gracious, seasoned with salt, so that you may know how you ought to answer everyone.

MY HIGH TODAY WAS:

MY LOW TODAY WAS:

MY PRAYER TODAY IS:

DAY #2

TODAY'S BIBLE VERSE:

ESTHER 4:14B

Who knows? Perhaps you have come to royal dignity for just such a time as this.

MY HIGH TODAY WAS:

MY LOW TODAY WAS:

MY PRAYER TODAY IS:

DAY #3

TODAY'S BIBLE VERSE:

ECCLESIASTES 7:17

Do not be too wicked, and do not be a fool; why should you die before your time!

MY HIGH TODAY WAS:

MY LOW TODAY WAS:

MY PRAYER TODAY IS:

1. **SHARE** HIGHS & LOWS OF THE DAY.

2. **READ** AND HIGHLIGHT THE VERSE OF THE DAY IN YOUR BIBLES.

3. **TALK** ABOUT HOW TODAY'S VERSE RELATES TO YOUR HIGHS & LOWS.

4. **PRAY** FOR YOUR HIGHS & LOWS, FOR YOUR FAMILY AND FOR THE WORLD.

5. **BLESS** ONE ANOTHER USING THIS WEEK'S BLESSING (ON THE PREVIOUS PAGE).

MY **HIGH** TODAY WAS:

MY **LOW** TODAY WAS:

MY **PRAYER** TODAY IS:

MY **HIGH** TODAY WAS:

MY **LOW** TODAY WAS:

MY **PRAYER** TODAY IS:

MY **HIGH** TODAY WAS:

MY **LOW** TODAY WAS:

MY **PRAYER** TODAY IS:

(Handwritten timecard entries: Casey; 9:45, 1:35, 3:00, 5:15, 8:40, 2:15, 3:05, 3:30, SKIPPING AND HAVING FUN, 11 (Oops! overslept), 4:00, 8:45, 1:25, WEEK END! Yeah!)

DAY #4

TODAY'S BIBLE VERSE:

Matthew 20:26b

Whoever wishes to be great among you must be your servant.

DAY #5

TODAY'S BIBLE VERSE:

II Corinthians 6:2

For he says, "At an acceptable time I have listened to you, and on a day of salvation I have helped you." See, now is the acceptable time; see, now is the day of salvation!"

DAY #6

TODAY'S BIBLE VERSE:

Psalm 31:15a

My times are in your hand.

THEME IN REVIEW

WHAT IS LIFE? IT IS A FLASH OF A FIREFLY IN THE NIGHT. IT IS THE BREATH OF A BUFFALO IN THE WINTERTIME. IT IS THE LITTLE SHADOW WHICH RUNS ACROSS THE GRASS AND LOSES ITSELF IN THE SUNSET.

ISPWO MUKIKA CROWFOOT

DAY #7

MY FAVORITE VERSE FROM THE THEME WAS:

....
....
....
....
....
....
....

TEN MINUTES OVER ON THE SERVICE TODAY REVRUN! TEN MINUTES! YOU THINK I'VE NOTHING BETTER TO DO THAN SIT IN CHURCH ALL MORNING?

LOOK AT IT THIS WAY: IF YOU LOVE SOMEONE, HOW DIFFICULT IS IT TO FIND AN EXTRA TEN MINUTES TO SPEND WITH THEM FROM TIME TO TIME?

I'M TALKING ABOUT GOD HERE.

HRUMF

GOD I LOVE. YOU I TOLERATE.

LOOKING BACK ON THESE TWO WEEKS, MY HIGHEST HIGH WAS:

....

MY LOWEST LOW THESE PAST WEEKS WAS:

....

ONE WAY GOD ANSWERED MY PRAYERS WAS:

....

ONE WAY GOD MIGHT USE ME AS A SACRED AGENT TO ANSWER THESE PRAYERS:

....
....

FAMILY COVENANT

We have shared *Highs & Lows* this week, read and highlighted the verses assigned in our Bibles, talked about our lives, prayed for one another's highs and lows, and blessed one another.

_____   _____   _____
Parent's Signature   Teen's Signature   Date

THE FINKMANIA QUIZBOWL

QUESTION 1:

Stewardship is:

(A) Only what you do with your money,

(B) What you do with your comic book collection,

(C) What you do with your time, talents and treasure,

(D) A maritime vehicle owned and operated by someone named Stewart

QUESTION 2:

A tithe is:

(A) The Biblical principal of giving 1% of your income back to God in appreciation for all God's done for you,

(B) The Biblical principal of giving 10% of your income back to God in appreciation for all God's done for you,

(C) More than giving money, it's a way of life,

(D) Both B & C

QUESTION 3:

If one was to tithe time, how much time would one be giving to God each and every week?

(A) 1.6 hours,

(B) 2.4 hours,

(C) 4.8 hours,

(D) 16.8 hours

QUESTION 4:

Jesus told a parable about sheep and goats in which the sheep were surprised that:

(A) By helping the goats, they had helped Jesus,

(B) By helping the poor, they had helped Jesus,

(C) By helping themselves, they had helped Jesus,

(D) Goats could talk

QUESTION 5:

What percentage of our time should bring honor to God?

(A) 1%,

(B) 10%,

(C) 25%,

(D) All of it because it all belongs to God in the first place

QUESTION 6:

"First things first" means:

(A) We should get our priorities straight,

(B) We should put what matters most at the top of our schedules,

(C) We shouldn't let things that don't matter crowd out those that do,

(D) All of the above and then some

QUESTION 7:

If you are too busy for God...

(A) You are too busy,

(B) You are too busy,

(C) You are too busy,

(D) All of the above and you are too busy

QUESTION 8:

Proper stewardship of time impacts:

(A) How we spend our time,

(B) How we invest our time,

(C) Who we spend our time with,

(D) All of the above

QUESTION 9:

Nielsen Research tells us that the average person watches television:

(A) 4 hours and 32 minutes each day,

(B) Over 31 hours per week,

(C) Way too much,

(D) All of the above, and apart from zoning out and relaxing, you gotta ask yourself "was all of that really a good use of my time?"

FINKMANIA Final Question:

Mark 12:30, the verse of the week, tells us:

(A) We are to love God with our whole heart and soul,

(B) We are to love God with our whole heart, soul and mind

(C) We are to love God with our whole heart, soul, mind and strength

(D) All of the above, and that impacts our time!

Play this online game using FINKlink

LF28 @ www.faithink.com

THE WEAKEST FINK

> YOU MAY DELAY,
> BUT TIME WILL NOT.
>
> — BENJAMIN FRANKLIN

TERMS
WRITE A DEFINITION BELOW.

GENEROSITY

PRIORITIES

STEWARDSHIP

TIME

TITHE

✚ FAITH INKUBATORS

STEWARDSHIP OF TALENTS

"Song of Angels" Dr. He Qi. Order prints at www.heqiarts.com

"YOU ARE THE SALT OF THE EARTH; YOU ARE THE LIGHT OF THE

WORLD. A CITY BUILT ON A HILL CANNOT BE HID. IN THE SAME

WAY, LET YOUR LIGHT SHINE BEFORE OTHERS, SO THAT THEY MAY

SEE YOUR GOOD WORKS AND GIVE GLORY TO YOUR

FATHER IN HEAVEN."

— MATTHEW 5:13A, 14, 16

Listen to this song using FINKlink
LF29 | @ www.faithink.com

 **he "Donald" opens the back of an armored car and hands you a black suitcase. In it you find $1,875,000 staring you in the face.**

Trump has a new reality series where you and two other contestants are each given a pile of cash to see who can make the most of it. So what do you do with the money? Invest in Yu Gi Oh trading cards? Buy a race horse? Head to Vegas and try your luck at Black Jack? Or do you drive to your house, put it in a hockey bag and bury it in the back yard for safe keeping?

Jesus once told a parable about a rich man handing over five talents, two talents, and one talent to three of his servants. A talent in Bible times was a weight of metal, usually silver, worth more than 15 years' wages for a common laborer. If a day laborer today made roughly $25,000 a year, how much would that be in today's money? Do the math: $25,000 x 15 years x 5 talents =

The first servant took the five talents and made five more. (A 100% return!) He was rewarded. The second took the two and doubled it. He also was rewarded. What did the third servant do? Read Matthew 25:18 for the surprising answer.

TALENT ON LOAN FROM GOD

Talk show host Rush Limbaugh brags he has talent on loan from God. Maybe it's obvious, but so do you! Everything you have, are, and will be is on loan from God. Your talents, gifts, and abilities are all placed in your care by your loving creator. What does God expect you to do with these tremendous gifts? You are blessed to be a blessing. You are gifted in order that you may gift the world. Jesus said you are the salt of the earth. Salt doesn't do much good in the container. It must be spread around. (It's the same with manure, but saying "you are the manure of the earth" didn't have the same ring.) When spread around, salt adds flavor to everything it encounters. Do your friends think of you that way? Are you their salt? Do you add flavor, taste and zest to everything and everyone who happens to come around you?

Jesus also said you are the light of the world. A light is meant to be shared. It adds brightness, warmth, and safety to every dark corner. Do people think of you as a light? Are you the one who makes life better, brighter and safer for everyone? If you have gifts—and you do—you have them for a reason. To leave them unexplored, untested and unused is terrible stewardship. Maybe you can sing. Maybe you are good in sports. Maybe you can take things apart, put them back together or figure them out. Maybe you're a computer geek who can help the technically challenged survive in this hyper-tech world. Maybe you've got a huge heart and know how to care for people or animals. Whatever your talents and gifts, Jesus doesn't want you to bury them in the ground! Christ calls you to invest them wisely and share them with the world. You are the light. So shine! You are the salt. So add some flavor! Oh yeah. And give all the glory to God while you're at it.

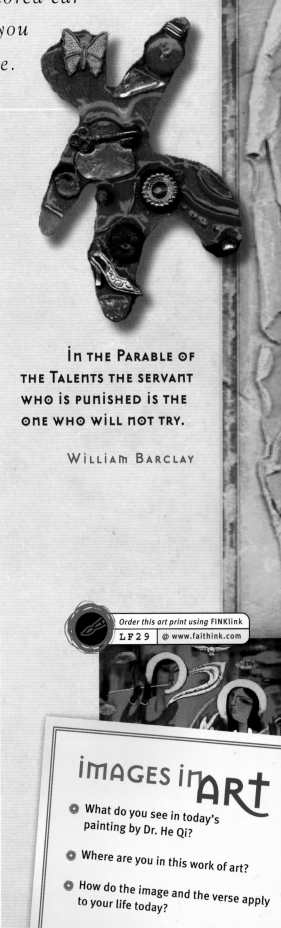

IN THE PARABLE OF THE TALENTS THE SERVANT WHO IS PUNISHED IS THE ONE WHO WILL NOT TRY.

WILLIAM BARCLAY

Order this art print using FINKlink
LF29 @ www.faithink.com

IMAGES in ART

- What do you see in today's painting by Dr. He Qi?

- Where are you in this work of art?

- How do the image and the verse apply to your life today?

So What Does This Mean?

EVERY BODY HAS SOME GIFTS.

NONSENSE! IF NOTHING ELSE YOU CAN SERVE AS AN EXCELLENT BAD EXAMPLE.

I DON'T.

PRAYER

DEAR GOD, I HEAR CHRIST'S CALL TO BE THE SALT AND THE LIGHT. HELP ME TO ADD FLAVOR AND ZEST TO MY WORLD! HELP ME TO BRING WARMTH AND SAFETY TO ALL WHO SIT IN DARKNESS. LET ME BE A REFLECTION OF YOU IN ALL I SAY AND DO. IN YOUR SALTY AND BRIGHT NAME I PRAY.

AMEN.

TALENT REPORT CARD

Grade yourself from 1 - 10 on how well you have shared your talents and gifts this week. (10 = high, 1 = low). Use the report card below based on Romans 12.

TALENTS/GIFTS	MY GRADE THIS WEEK	WHERE I WANT TO BE BY NEXT WEEK
Helpfulness	_____	_____
Encouragement	_____	_____
Leadership	_____	_____
Cheerfulness	_____	_____
Love	_____	_____
Respect	_____	_____
Patience	_____	_____
Prayerfulness	_____	_____
Kindness	_____	_____
Hospitality	_____	_____
Peacefulness	_____	_____
Tolerance	_____	_____
Humility	_____	_____

BIBLE TIME

Read and highlight Matthew 5:3-16 in your Bible, writing "The Beatitudes" in the margin. Circle key words that describe how Christ wants you to live. Write five of them here:

ROLE PLAY

1. A neighbor child is sitting on their steps looking sad. You approach and ask what's wrong. "I'm no good at anything!" they answer. What do you say?

2. A friend brags all the time about how good they are at skateboarding, computer games, and playing the drums. They aren't all that good. You suspect the reason for their bragging is really insecurity. How do you help them?

QUESTIONS TO PONDER

1. What were your highest three areas on the Talent Report Card?

2. What were your three lowest areas on the Talent Report Card?

3. What three areas will you concentrate on this week?

SMALL GROUP
SHARE, READ, TALK, PRAY, BLESS

1. S H A R E your highs and lows of the week one-on-one with another person. Listen carefully and record your friend's thoughts in the space below. Then return to small group and share your friend's highs and lows.

MY HIGHS + LOWS THIS WEEK WERE:

....

MY FRIEND'S HIGHS + LOWS THIS WEEK WERE:

....

2. R E A D and highlight the theme verse in your Bibles. Circle key words and learn the verse in song.

3. T A L K about how today's verse relates to your highs and lows. Review the art for today, the Quiz Bowl questions, the terms, and the cartoons. Then write a sentence on each of the following:

ONE NEW THING I LEARNED TODAY:

....

ONE THING I ALREADY KNEW THAT IS WORTH REPEATING:

....

ONE THING I WOULD LIKE TO KNOW MORE ABOUT:

....

4. P R A Y for one another, praising and thanking God for your highs, and asking God to be with you in your lows. Include your friend's highs and lows in your prayers.

A PRAISING PRAYER: ....

A THANKING PRAYER: ....

AN ASKING PRAYER: ....

5. B L E S S one another using the blessing of the week. (right) Mark each person with the sign of the cross as you bless them.

THIS WEEK'S BLESSING

(NAME), CHILD OF GOD,

MAY YOU BE THE SALT OF

THE EARTH TODAY. AMEN.

THE HOME HUDDLE jOURNAL

SHARE, READ, TALK, PRAY, BLESS

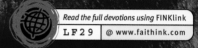

Read the full devotions using FINKlink
LF29 @ www.faithink.com

DAY #1

TODAY'S BIBLE VERSE:

Matthew 5:13a, 14, 16

You are the salt of the earth; you are the light of the world. A city built on a hill cannot be hid. In the same way, let your light shine before others, so that they may see your good works and give glory to your Father in heaven.

my HIGH today was:

my LOW today was:

my PRAYER today is:

DAY #2

TODAY'S BIBLE VERSE:

Matthew 25:14-15

For it is as if a man, going on a journey, summoned his slaves and entrusted his property to them; to one he gave five talents, to another two, to another one, to each according to his ability. Then he went away.

my HIGH today was:

my LOW today was:

my PRAYER today is:

DAY #3

TODAY'S BIBLE VERSE:

Matthew 25:16-17

The one who had received the five talents went off at once and traded with them, and made five more talents. In the same way, the one who had the two talents made two more talents.

my HIGH today was:

my LOW today was:

my PRAYER today is:

my HIGH today was:

my LOW today was:

my PRAYER today is:

DAY #4

TODAY'S BIBLE VERSE:

Matthew 25:18-19

But the one who had received the one talent went off and dug a hole in the ground and hid his master's money. After a long time the master of those slaves came and settled accounts with them.

my HIGH today was:

my LOW today was:

my PRAYER today is:

DAY #5

TODAY'S BIBLE VERSE:

Matthew 25:20

Then the one who had received the five talents came forward, bringing five more talents, saying, "Master, you handed over to me five talents; see, I have made five more talents."

my HIGH today was:

my LOW today was:

my PRAYER today is:

DAY #6

TODAY'S BIBLE VERSE:

Matthew 25:21

His master said to him, "Well done, good and trustworthy slave; you have been trustworthy in a few things, I will put you in charge of many things; enter into the joy of your master."

my HIGHEST HIGH this week was:

my LOWEST LOW this week was:

my PRAYER for next week is:

DAY #7

THIS WEEK'S BLESSING

(NAME), CHILD OF GOD, MAY YOU BE THE SALT OF THE EARTH TODAY. AMEN.

THE HOME HUDDLE JOURNAL
SHARE, READ, TALK, PRAY, BLESS

WEEK 2

Read the full devotions using FINKlink
LF29 | @ www.faithink.com

DAY #1

TODAY'S BIBLE VERSE:
Romans 12:6-8

We have gifts that differ according to the grace given to us; prophecy, in proportion to faith; ministry, in ministering; the teacher, in teaching; the exhorter, in exhortation; the giver, in generosity; the leader, in diligence...

MY HIGH TODAY WAS:

MY LOW TODAY WAS:

MY PRAYER TODAY IS:

DAY #2

TODAY'S BIBLE VERSE:
Romans 12:9-10

Let love be genuine; hate what is evil, hold fast to what is good; love one another with mutual affection; outdo one another in showing honor.

MY HIGH TODAY WAS:

MY LOW TODAY WAS:

MY PRAYER TODAY IS:

DAY #3

TODAY'S BIBLE VERSE:
Romans 12:11-13

Do not lag in zeal, be ardent in Spirit, serve the Lord. Rejoice in hope, be patient in suffering, persevere in prayer. Contribute to the needs of the saints; extend hospitality to strangers.

MY HIGH TODAY WAS:

MY LOW TODAY WAS:

MY PRAYER TODAY IS:

1. SHARE HIGHS & LOWS OF THE DAY.

2. READ AND HIGHLIGHT THE VERSE OF THE DAY IN YOUR BIBLES.

3. TALK ABOUT HOW TODAY'S VERSE RELATES TO YOUR HIGHS & LOWS.

4. PRAY FOR YOUR HIGHS & LOWS, FOR YOUR FAMILY AND FOR THE WORLD.

5. BLESS ONE ANOTHER USING THIS WEEK'S BLESSING (ON THE PREVIOUS PAGE).

MY HIGH TODAY WAS:

MY LOW TODAY WAS:

MY PRAYER TODAY IS:

DAY #4

TODAY'S BIBLE VERSE:

Romans 12:14-15

Bless those who persecute you; bless and do not curse them. Rejoice with those who rejoice, weep with those who weep.

MY HIGH TODAY WAS:

MY LOW TODAY WAS:

MY PRAYER TODAY IS:

DAY #5

TODAY'S BIBLE VERSE:

Romans 12:17-18

Do not repay anyone evil for evil, but take thought for what is noble in the sight of all. If it is possible, so far as it depends on you, live peaceably with all.

MY HIGH TODAY WAS:

MY LOW TODAY WAS:

MY PRAYER TODAY IS:

DAY #6

TODAY'S BIBLE VERSE:

Romans 12:16

Live in harmony with one another; do not be haughty, but associate with the lowly; do not claim to be wiser than you are.

Talent is like manure.

It don't do ya much good until you spread it around.

THEME IN REVIEW

THE REAL FEAR
IS NOT DEATH—IT IS FEAR
OF WASTING LIFE.

ANONYMOUS

DAY #7

MY FAVORITE VERSE
FROM THE THEME WAS:

....
....
....
....
....
....
....
....

LOOKING BACK ON THESE TWO WEEKS, MY HIGHEST HIGH WAS:

....

MY LOWEST LOW THESE PAST WEEKS WAS:

....

ONE WAY GOD ANSWERED MY PRAYERS WAS:

....

ONE WAY GOD MIGHT USE ME AS A SACRED AGENT
TO ANSWER THESE PRAYERS:

....

....

FAMILY COVENANT

We have shared *Highs & Lows* this week, read and highlighted the verses assigned in our Bibles, talked about our lives, prayed for one another's highs and lows, and blessed one another.

....

Parent's Signature   Teen's Signature   Date

THE FINKMANIA QUIZBOWL

QUESTION 1:

"Use it or lose it" is a slogan that refers to:

(A) Time,
(B) Talents,
(C) Treasure,
(D) All of the above

QUESTION 2:

In Jesus' parable of the talents, the master gave three servants:

(A) One talent, two talents and five talents to invest while he was away,
(B) One goat, two goats and five goats to milk while he was away,
(C) One vineyard, two vineyards and five to tend while he was away,
(D) Keys to the wine cellar

QUESTION 3:

In Jesus' day, a talent was:

(A) A weight of precious metal,
(B) 110 lbs. of gold,
(C) The equivalent of more than 15 years of work from a common day laborer's job,
(D) All of the above and worth about $375,000 in today's market

QUESTION 4:

In the parable of the talents, the first two servants invested their talents, but the third:

(A) Put it all in junk bonds,
(B) Spent it all on wine, women and song,
(C) Buried it in the ground,
(D) Went to the track and bet it all on a horse named Desire

QUESTION 5:

The servant with one talent was punished because:

(A) He was greedy,
(B) He risked it all and lost,
(C) He risked it all and made a lot of money—which is evil and capitalistic,
(D) He didn't even try

QUESTION 6:

In this parable, the reward for work well-done and talents well-used is:

(A) More work and responsibility, plus a party in the master's house,
(B) Less work and responsibility, plus a party in the master's house,
(C) More work and responsibility, but no party,
(D) A pink slip at the company Christmas party

QUESTION 7:

If God gives you talents:

(A) Bury them in the ground,
(B) Use them to make lots of money for yourself and the IRS,
(C) Use them for God's glory,
(D) Get an agent

QUESTION 8:

It doesn't matter how many talents you have. What matters is:

(A) Recognition,
(B) Publicity,
(C) Marketing,
(D) How you use what you've got

QUESTION 9:

Talents are:

(A) Gifts from God,
(B) Things a person does well,
(C) Things a person might do well with a little more practice and hard work,
(D) All of the above

FINKMANIA FINAL QUESTION:

Matthew 5:13-14, the verse of the week, tells us:

(A) Salty roads save lives,
(B) We are the salt of the earth and the light of the world,
(C) To pass the pepper mill,
(D) A & C

Play this online game using FINKlink
LF29 @ www.faithink.com

THE WEAKEST FINK

SOME PEOPLE GIVE TIME, SOME MONEY, SOME THEIR SKILLS AND CONNECTIONS, SOME LITERALLY GIVE THEIR LIFE'S BLOOD... BUT EVERYONE HAS SOMETHING TO GIVE.

BARBARA BUSH

TERMS
WRITE A DEFINITION BELOW.

TALENTS

STEWARDSHIP

SALT OF THE EARTH

LIGHT OF THE WORLD

GOOD WORKS

FAITH INKUBATORS

"The Adoration of the Magi" Dr. He Qi. Order prints at www.heqiarts.com

STEWARDSHIP OF TREASURE

"BRING THE FULL TITHE INTO THE STOREHOUSE, SO THAT THERE

MAY BE FOOD IN MY HOUSE, AND THUS PUT ME TO THE TEST,

SAYS THE LORD OF HOSTS; SEE IF I WILL NOT OPEN THE WIN-

DOWS OF HEAVEN FOR YOU AND POUR DOWN FOR YOU

AN OVERFLOWING BLESSING."

— MALACHI 3:10

Listen to this song using FINKlink
LF30 @ www.faithink.com

*T*he ghost of Jacob Marley slid through the heavy wooden doors into Scrooge's bed chamber, rattling chains and staring at the old skinflint with death-cold eyes.

Old Marley was dead as a doornail. There was no doubt about it. Yet there he was, hovering above Ebenezer's bed, weighed down by yards of chains and all the possessions that had possessed him in life. He came on Christmas Eve to warn his stingy friend. His message? A similar fate awaited old Scrooge if he continued to hoard his wealth at the expense of the poor and keep money as the center of his life. Did he succeed? If you remember Charles Dickens' classic A *Christmas Carol,* it took three more ghosts and staring death in the face while reading his own tombstone before Scrooge changed into the generous man who promised to keep Christmas in his heart.

THE RICH AND THE POOR

What does it take to make rich people see the needs of the poor? How can people who think mostly of themselves suddenly decide to change and decide to share, to give, and to help? In a world where every child could be fed, millions are still starving. In a country of so much wealth, there are still hungry among us. If you had the opportunity to speak to an extremely wealthy person about sharing some of their wealth with the poor, what would you say?

FACE IT—WE'RE WEALTHY

Before getting too self-righteous about the rich not helping the poor, consider some of these facts from *www.globalrichlist.com:*

- If you earn minimum wage in the USA —at the time of this writing, $5.15 per hour or about $10,712 yearly—you are in the top 13.1% richest people in the world. There are about 5,213,000,000 people poorer than you.

- If you earn $25,000/year, you are in the top 10% of the richest people in the world. There are about 5,398,000,000 people poorer than you.

- If you make $50,000/year, you are in the top 0.899% of richest people in the world. There are about 5,946,000,000 people poorer than you.

- If you make $200,000/year, you are in the top 0.001% richest people in the world. There are about 5,999,892,000 people poorer than you.

- Currently there are about 2.5 million U.S. households estimated to be worth U.S. $1 million or more, excluding real estate holdings. As of 2001, there were about 315,000 Canadian households worth at least Ca. $1 million. This number is expected to rise to 915,000 by 2010.

So, who is rich? Who should be sharing?

CHRISTMAS? HUMBUG! ANYONE CAUGHT WITH THE WORDS "MERRY CHRISTMAS" ON THEIR LIPS SHOULD BE BOILED IN THEIR OWN PUDDING AND BURIED WITH A STAKE OF HOLLY THROUGH THEIR HEART!

EBENEZER SCROOGE

Order this art print using FINKlink
LF30 @ www.faithink.com

IMAGES inART

- What do you see in today's painting by Dr. He Qi?

- Where are you in this work of art?

- How do the image and the verse apply to your life today?

So What Does This Mean?

MY TITHE THIS YEAR? OK, LET'S FIGURE THIS OUT. I MAKE 50 GRAND. SUBTRACT 18K FOR THE HOUSE, 7 FOR THE BOAT, 5 FOR THE SNOW-MOBILES AND MOTORCYCLE, 5 FOR FOOD, 5 FOR ENTER-TAINMENT, 3 FOR CLOTHES, 2 FOR MEDICAL AND 7 FOR TAXES. THAT MAKES...

HUH. WADDAYA KNOW... IT APPEARS GOD OWES ME TWO GRAND...

PRAYER

DEAR GOD,

JOLT ME. MAKE ME.

USE ME. TAKE ME.

HELP ME. HOLD ME.

SHAPE ME. MOLD ME.

SAVE ME FROM POSSESSIONS THAT POSSESS ME.

WAKE ME TO THE NEEDS OF THOSE AROUND ME.

SHAKE ME WHEN I FORGET THAT ALL I HAVE IS YOURS. NOT MINE.

LET MY LIVING AND MY GIVING

MY SHARING AND MY CARING

BE AN ABSOLUTELY DARING HYMN OF JOYFUL ROCKING PRAISE

TO YOU. TO YOU.

IN ALL MY MOMENTS, ALL MY DAYS

ALL MY ACTIONS, ALL MY WAYS

TO YOU. TO YOU. TO YOU.

AMEN.

THE JESUS WAY TO LIVE

In the "real world" money equals success. Everybody wants to be a millionaire. Everyone wants to win the lottery. The object for many people is to get as much money as they can. The more they have, the happier they should be. That's the line we've been told and sold since we were in diapers. But if this is the case, why is it that the wealthiest countries in the world have the highest rates of suicide, alcohol abuse, drug abuse and depression? It doesn't make sense. Maybe the line is a lie. Maybe possessions can too easily possess the possessor. Maybe there's a better way to happiness?

Jesus said you can gain the whole world but lose your soul. Now that would be depressing! When it comes right down to it, you can't take it with you. You will never see an armored car following a hearse. Don't be a Scrooge. Invest your time, talents and treasures in things that last. Share the things that don't last as much as you can and as fast as you can while you still have the time. That's the joyful Jesus way to live. It makes for a better world, a healthier attitude, and a happier you. And it's a lot more fun than listening to chains rattle.

BIBLE TIME

God doesn't need your money. Everything already belongs to God. But how does God expect us to live? What does God want from us? Check these out:

- Put God First . . . . Exodus 20:2
- Give God Love . . . . Hosea 6:6
- Test God by Tithing . . . . Malachi 3:10
- Store Treasures in Heaven . . . . . . Matthew 6:19-21
- Don't Worry About Money . . . . . . Matthew 6:25-30
- Give Yourself First . . . . II Corinthians 8:1-6
- Give Cheerfully . . . . II Corinthians 9:6-8

ROLE PLAY

1. A friend spends all their money on themselves. What do you say?

2. A friend gives to charity, but not to church. What do you say?

QUESTIONS TO PONDER

1. Why do you think the richest countries in the world have the highest rates of suicide, alcoholism, and depression among teens?

2. What do you think Jesus means when he says, "You can gain the whole world but lose or forfeit your soul?"

Small Group
SHARE, READ, TALK, PRAY, BLESS

1. SHARE your highs and lows of the week one-on-one with another person. Listen carefully and record your friend's thoughts in the space below. Then return to small group and share your friend's highs and lows.

MY HIGHS + LOWS THIS WEEK WERE:

....

MY FRIEND'S HIGHS + LOWS THIS WEEK WERE:

....

2. READ and highlight the theme verse in your Bibles. Circle key words and learn the verse in song.

3. TALK about how today's verse relates to your highs and lows. Review the art for today, the Quiz Bowl questions, the terms, and the cartoons. Then write a sentence on each of the following:

ONE NEW THING I LEARNED TODAY:

....

ONE THING I ALREADY KNEW THAT IS WORTH REPEATING:

....

ONE THING I WOULD LIKE TO KNOW MORE ABOUT:

....

4. PRAY for one another, praising and thanking God for your highs, and asking God to be with you in your lows. Include your friend's highs and lows in your prayers.

A PRAISING PRAYER: ....

A THANKING PRAYER: ....

AN ASKING PRAYER: ....

5. BLESS one another using the blessing of the week. (right) Mark each person with the sign of the cross as you bless them.

THIS WEEK'S BLESSING

(NAME), CHILD OF GOD, MAY YOUR TIME, TALENT, AND TREASURE BE USED FOR GOD'S GLORY TODAY. AMEN.

THE HOME HUDDLE JOURNAL
SHARE, READ, TALK, PRAY, BLESS

Read the full devotions using FINKlink
LF30 @ www.faithink.com

DAY #1

TODAY'S BIBLE VERSE:

Malachi 3:10

Bring the full tithe into the storehouse, so that there may be food in my house, and thus put me to the test, says the Lord of hosts; see if I will not open the windows of heaven for you and pour down for you an overflowing blessing.

MY HIGH TODAY WAS:

MY LOW TODAY WAS:

MY PRAYER TODAY IS:

DAY #2

TODAY'S BIBLE VERSE:

II Corinthians 9:7

Each of you must give as you have made up your mind, not reluctantly or under compulsion, for God loves a cheerful giver.

MY HIGH TODAY WAS:

MY LOW TODAY WAS:

MY PRAYER TODAY IS:

DAY #3

TODAY'S BIBLE VERSE:

Luke 6:38

Give, and it will be given to you. A good measure, pressed down, shaken together, running over, will be put in your lap; for the measure you give will be the measure you get back.

MY HIGH TODAY WAS:

MY LOW TODAY WAS:

MY PRAYER TODAY IS:

MY HIGH TODAY WAS:

MY LOW TODAY WAS:

MY PRAYER TODAY IS:

DAY #4

TODAY'S BIBLE VERSE:

Acts 4:32

Now the whole group of those who believed were of one heart and soul, and no one claimed private owner-ship of any possessions, but everything they owned was held in common.

MY HIGH TODAY WAS:

MY LOW TODAY WAS:

MY PRAYER TODAY IS:

DAY #5

TODAY'S BIBLE VERSE:

Malachi 3:8

Will anyone rob God? Yet you are robbing me! But you say, "How are we robbing you?" In your tithes and of-ferings!

MY HIGH TODAY WAS:

MY LOW TODAY WAS:

MY PRAYER TODAY IS:

DAY #6

TODAY'S BIBLE VERSE:

Luke 12:20

But God said to him [the rich farmer], "You fool! This very night your life is being demanded of you, and the things you have prepared, whose will they be?"

MY HIGHEST HIGH THIS WEEK WAS:

MY LOWEST LOW THIS WEEK WAS:

MY PRAYER FOR NEXT WEEK IS:

DAY #7

THIS WEEK'S BLESSING

(NAME), CHILD OF GOD,

MAY YOUR TIME, TALENT,

AND TREASURE BE USED FOR

GOD'S GLORY. AMEN.

THE HOME HUDDLE JOURN
SHARE, READ, TALK, PRAY, BLES

WEEK 2

Read the full devotions using FINKlink
LF30 @ www.faithink.com

DAY #1

TODAY'S BIBLE VERSE:

LUKE 21:1-4

He looked up and saw rich people putting their gifts into the treasury; he also saw a poor widow put in two small copper coins. He said, "Truly I tell you, this poor widow has put in more than all of them; for all of them contributed out of their abundance, but she out of her poverty has put in all she had to live on."

MY HIGH TODAY WAS:

MY LOW TODAY WAS:

MY PRAYER TODAY IS:

DAY #2

TODAY'S BIBLE VERSE:

MATTHEW 6:3-4

But when you give alms, do not let your left hand know what your right hand is doing, so that your alms may be done in secret; and your Father who sees in secret will reward you.

MY HIGH TODAY WAS:

MY LOW TODAY WAS:

MY PRAYER TODAY IS:

DAY #3

TODAY'S BIBLE VERSE:

I CHRONICLES 29:14

But who am I, and what is my people, that we should be able to make this freewill offering? For all things come from you, and of your own have we given you.

MY HIGH TODAY WAS:

MY LOW TODAY WAS:

MY PRAYER TODAY IS:

1. SHARE HIGHS & LOWS OF THE DAY.

2. READ AND HIGHLIGHT THE VERSE OF THE DAY IN YOUR BIBLES.

3. TALK ABOUT HOW TODAY'S VERSE RELATES TO YOUR HIGHS & LOWS.

4. PRAY FOR YOUR HIGHS & LOWS, FOR YOUR FAMILY AND FOR THE WORLD.

5. BLESS ONE ANOTHER USING THIS WEEK'S BLESSING (ON THE PREVIOUS PAGE).

MY HIGH TODAY WAS:

MY LOW TODAY WAS:

MY PRAYER TODAY IS:

DAY #4

TODAY'S BIBLE VERSE:

Matthew 6:19-20

Do not store up for yourself treasures on earth, where moth and rust consume and where thieves break in and steal, but store up for yourselves treasures in heaven...

MY HIGH TODAY WAS:

MY LOW TODAY WAS:

MY PRAYER TODAY IS:

DAY #5

TODAY'S BIBLE VERSE:

Matthew 25:35-36

For I was hungry and you gave me food, I was thirsty and you gave me something to drink, I was a stranger and you welcomed me, I was naked and you gave me clothing...

MY HIGH TODAY WAS:

MY LOW TODAY WAS:

MY PRAYER TODAY IS:

DAY #6

TODAY'S BIBLE VERSE:

Matthew 25:40

Truly I tell you, just as you did it to one of the least of these who are members of my family, you did it to me.

THEME iN REVIEW

To be clever enough to get all that money one must be stupid enough to want it.

C. K. Chesterton

DAY #7

MY FAVORITE VERSE FROM THE THEME WAS:

....

....

....

....

....

....

LOOKING BACK ON THESE TWO WEEKS, MY HIGHEST **HIGH** WAS:

....

MY LOWEST **LOW** THESE PAST WEEKS WAS:

....

ONE WAY GOD ANSWERED MY **PRAYERS** WAS:

....

ONE WAY GOD MIGHT USE ME AS A **SACRED AGENT** TO ANSWER THESE PRAYERS:

....

....

FAMILY COVENANT

We have shared *Highs & Lows* this week, read and highlighted the verses assigned in our Bibles, talked about our lives, prayed for one another's highs and lows, and blessed one another.

_____   _____   _____
Parent's Signature   Teen's Signature   Date

THE FINKMANIA QUIZBOWL

QUESTION 1:
The source of all true treasure is:
(A) The ATM,
(B) The mall,
(C) Deal or No Deal,
(D) God

QUESTION 2:
Our treasures include:
(A) Life,
(B) Money,
(C) Possessions,
(D) All of the above, plus the Star Wars Trilogy

QUESTION 3:
We should give to God because:
(A) Everything we have is God's in the first place,
(B) Giving shows God we are aware that everything is God's and that we are thankful,
(C) It is what God wants us to do, expects us to do, and asks us to do,
(D) All of the above

QUESTION 4:
A tithe is:
(A) A seldom-used tool in the wood shop,
(B) 1% of our adjusted gross income, minus expenses
(C) 10% of our adjusted gross income, minus expenses
(D) 10% of all we have (including time, talents and treasures)

QUESTION 5:
Tithing is good:
(A) In helping one trust God,
(B) For showing people you are insane,
(C) For supporting those in need,
(D) A & C

QUESTION 6:
A, person who makes $30,000 a year and tithes each year gives away:
(A) $3,
(B) $30,
(C) $300,
(D) $3,000

QUESTION 7:
When we tithe, God promises to:
(A) Pour out an overflowing blessing upon us,
(B) Ignore us,
(C) Get us great seats to the next World Series,
(D) Take our money and go to the Bahamas

QUESTION 8:
When we die:
(A) We take all of our possessions with us,
(B) We leave everything behind and face God,
(C) We become eligible for Social Security,
(D) What are you talking about? Homer Simpson says only bad people die!

QUESTION 9:
The greatest treasure any of us can have is:
(A) A bright red Ferrari,
(B) Our pastor's natural good looks,
(C) The grace of Christ,
(D) The Sports Illustrated Swim Suit Edition

FINKMANIA FINAL QUESTION:
The verse of the week, Malachi 3:10, tells us:
(A) We should give 10% of what we have and earn to God,
(B) We should trust that God will care for us,
(C) Heaven has double-hung windows,
(D) A and B, but we don't really know about C

Play this online game using FINKlink
LF30 @ www.faithink.com

THE WEAKEST FINK

> **MONEY IS BETTER THAN POVERTY, IF ONLY FOR FINANCIAL REASONS.**
>
> WOODY ALLEN

TERMS
WRITE A DEFINITION BELOW.

BLESSING
....
....

FAITHFULNESS
....
....

GIFT
....
....

TREASURE
....
....

TITHE
....
....

FAITH INKUBATORS

Take a moment to look back on the year and see how you and your friends have changed and grown.

PASTE

End of Year

PHOTO OF YOU

HERE

(my how you've grown)

This is Me

PASTE

PHOTO OF YOUR

PASTOR

HERE

(Good Looking, huh?)

(and my Pastor)

FAITH
INKUBATORS

PASTE FINAL
SMALL
GROUP
PHOTO
HERE

This is My Small Group

AUTOGRAPH
PHOTOGRAPHS
& PETROGRAPHS

S,

ALL YOU REALLY NEED FOR AN
ASYLUM IS A BIG ROOM AND THE
RIGHT KIND OF PEOPLE!

OPERATION
SPYGLASS

SACRED AGENTS GET READY... IT'S TIME TO EXPLORE YOUR YEARBOOK. FIND EACH OF THE 75 ITEMS BELOW:

- [ ] 30 PIECES OF SILVER
- [ ] ADMIT ONE TICKET
- [ ] BABY IN WOMB (DA VINCI SKETCH)
- [ ] BALL AND CHAINS OF GOLD
- [ ] BAMBOO SHOOT
- [ ] BASEBALL
- [ ] BASEBALL GLOVE
- [ ] BEER BOTTLE
- [ ] BENJAMIN FRANKLIN ON $100 BILL
- [ ] BOMBS
- [ ] BRASS MONKEYS (3)
- [ ] BREAD
- [ ] CALCULATOR
- [ ] CANADIAN FLAG
- [ ] CELL PHONE
- [ ] CHAOS (IN MANDARIN)
- [ ] CLAY MAY CALENDAR
- [ ] COFFEE STAIN
- [ ] CIRCUIT BOARD (GREEN)
- [ ] COOKIES
- [ ] CROWN
- [ ] DACHSHUND
- [ ] DECORATED GINGERBREAD GIRL COOKIE
- [ ] DIRT
- [ ] DOOR KNOB
- [ ] EYES
- [ ] EYE GLASSES
- [ ] "EYE OF GOD" HELIX NEBULA (NASA PHOTO)
- [ ] EXPLODING RED STAR
- [ ] FAITH INKUBATORS LOGO
- [ ] FAMILY (IN MANDARIN)
- [ ] FIRST CLASS (STAMPED)
- [ ] FORD EMBLEM (BROKEN)
- [ ] FRAGILE (STAMPED)
- [ ] GAVEL
- [ ] GOD (IN MANDARIN)
- [ ] HE QI (OUR AMAZING FEATURED ARTIST)
- [ ] JAN HUS BURNING AT THE STAKE

- [ ] JOLLY ROGER (PIRATE FLAG)
- [ ] KEY
- [ ] KISS
- [ ] LEAF
- [ ] LIFE JACKET
- [ ] LOVE (IN MANDARIN)
- [ ] MALAGASY WARRIOR
- [ ] MAN EATING BURGER
- [ ] MOSES
- [ ] NAVY KEY CHAIN
- [ ] OLD PEOPLE CROSSING SIGN
- [ ] PADDLE LOCK
- [ ] PAINTBALL GUN
- [ ] PARTY INVITATION & PSYCHEDELIC TIE
- [ ] PEACE PROTEST SIGN
- [ ] PHONE HOME POST-IT NOTE
- [ ] POCKET WATCH (ANTIQUE)
- [ ] PRAYING HANDS (BY ALBRECT DÜRER)
- [ ] PRODIGAL SONS & MATERIAL GIRLS BOOK
- [ ] RACE CAR TOY
- [ ] RAY & KATE MELHEIM (THE AUTHOR'S FOLKS)
- [ ] ROSES & BANDAGES
- [ ] SCALE
- [ ] SCROOGE & THE GHOST OF JACOB MARLEY
- [ ] SNAKE
- [ ] SPEAR
- [ ] STARS (10 GOLDEN)
- [ ] STRAW FAMILY
- [ ] TIME CARD (FOR RECORDING WORK HOURS)
- [ ] TOILET PAPER
- [ ] WALLET WITH $40
- [ ] WATCHES
- [ ] WATER BUCKET
- [ ] WORLD TRADE CENTER EXPLODING
- [ ] WRECK CREATION
- [ ] POST-IT
- [ ] YELLOW ROSE
- [ ] YOUR NAME